The Quran With Tafsir Ibn Kathir
Part 11 of 30: At Tauba 093 To 10: Hud 005

The Quran With
Tafsir Ibn Kathir
Part11 of 30:
At Tauba 093 To
0: Hud 005

With
Arabic Script, Transliteration of Arabic, Meaning in English
and Ibn Kathir's Abridged Tafsir (Explanation)

Muhammad Saed Abdul-Rahman
BSc, DipHE

© Muhammad Saed Abdul-Rahman,2012
ISBN 978-1-86179-858-9

All Rights reserved

British Library Cataloguing in Publication Data. A Catalogue record for this book is available from the British Library

Designed, Typeset and produced by:
MSA Publication Limited, 4 Bello Close, Herne Hill,
London SE24 9BW
United Kingdom

Cover design: Houriyah Abdul-Rahman

TABLE OF CONTENTS

TABLE OF CONTENTS V

PRELUDE XIII
    OPENING SERMAN XIII
    OUR MISSION XIV
    BIOGRAPHY OF HAFIZ IBN KATHIR (701 H - 774 H) XIV
        Ibn Kathir's Teachers xiv
        Ibn Kathir's Students xv
        Ibn Kathir's Books xv
        Ibn Kathir's Death xvi

PREFACE XVII
    ABOUT THIS BOOK XVII
    PERFORMING PROSTRATION WHILE READING THE QUR'AN XVII

PART 11 FULL ARABIC TEXT 1

CHAPTER (SURAH) 9: AT-TAWBA (REPENTANCE), VERSES 093 - 129 13
    Surah: 9 Ayah: 91, Ayah: 92 (end of Part 10) & Ayah: 93 (start of Part 11) 13
        Tafsir Ibn Kathir 14
            Legitimate Excuses for staying away from Jihad 14
    Surah: 9 Ayah: 94, Ayah: 95 & Ayah: 96 15
        Tafsir Ibn Kathir 16
            Exposing the Deceitful Ways of Hypocrites 16
    Surah: 9 Ayah: 97, Ayah: 98 & Ayah: 99 16
        Tafsir Ibn Kathir 17
            The Bedouins are the Worst in Disbelief and Hypocrisy 17
    Surah: 9 Ayah: 100 18
        Tafsir Ibn Kathir 19
            Virtues of the Muhajirin, Ansar and Those Who followed Them in Faith 19
    Surah: 9 Ayah: 101 19
        Tafsir Ibn Kathir 20
            Hypocrites among the Bedouins and Residents of Al-Madinah 20
    Surah: 9 Ayah: 102 21
        Tafsir Ibn Kathir 21
            Some Believers stayed away from Battle because They were Lazy 21
    Surah: 9 Ayah: 103 & 104 22
        Tafsir Ibn Kathir 23
            The Command to collect the Zakah and Its Benefits 23
    Surah: 9 Ayah: 105 24
        Tafsir Ibn Kathir 24
            Warning the Disobedient 24
    Surah: 9 Ayah: 106 25

Tafsir Ibn Kathir	26
Delaying the Decision about the Three Companions Who stayed away from the Battle of Tabuk	26
Surah: 9 Ayah: 107 & Ayah: 108	*26*
Tafsir Ibn Kathir	27
Masjid Ad-Dirar and Masjid At-Taqwa	27
Virtues of Masjid Quba	28
Surah: 9 Ayah: 109 & Ayah: 110	*30*
Tafsir Ibn Kathir	30
The Difference between Masjid At-Taqwa and Masjid Ad-Dirar	30
Surah: 9 Ayah: 111	*31*
Tafsir Ibn Kathir	31
Allah has purchased the Souls and Wealth of the Mujahidin in Return for Paradise	31
Surah: 9 Ayah: 112	*32*
Tafsir Ibn Kathir	33
This is the description of the believers from whom Allah has purchased their souls and wealth, who have these beautiful and honorable qualities,	33
Surah: 9 Ayah: 113 & Ayah: 114	*33*
Tafsir Ibn Kathir	34
The Prohibition of supplicating for Polytheists	34
Surah: 9 Ayah: 115 & Ayah: 116	*36*
Tafsir Ibn Kathir	36
Recompense comes after Proof is established	36
Surah: 9 Ayah: 117	*37*
Tafsir Ibn Kathir	37
Battle of Tabuk	37
Surah: 9 Ayah: 118 & Ayah: 119	*38*
Tafsir Ibn Kathir	39
The Three, Whose Decision was deferred by the Messenger of Allah	39
The Order to speak the Truth	44
Surah: 9 Ayah: 120	*45*
Tafsir Ibn Kathir	45
Rewards of Jihad	45
Surah: 9 Ayah: 121	*46*
Tafsir Ibn Kathir	46
Surah: 9 Ayah: 122	*47*
Tafsir Ibn Kathir	47
Allah the Exalted here explains His order to Muslims to march forth with the Messenger of Allah for the battle of Tabuk.	47
Surah: 9 Ayah: 123	*49*
Tafsir Ibn Kathir	49
The Order for Jihad against the Disbelievers, the Closest, then the Farthest Areas	49
Surah: 9 Ayah: 124 & Ayah: 125	*51*
Tafsir Ibn Kathir	51

Table of Contents

Faith of the Believers increases, while Hypocrites increase in Doubts and Suspicion 51
Surah: 9 Ayah: 126 & Ayah: 127 52
  Tafsir Ibn Kathir 52
    Hypocrites suffer Afflictions 52
Surah: 9 Ayah: 128 & Ayah: 129 53
  Tafsir Ibn Kathir 54

CHAPTER (SURAH) 10: YUNUS (JONAH), VERSES 001-109 55

Surah: 10 Ayah: 1 & Ayah: 2 55
  Tafsir Ibn Kathir 56
    The Messenger cannot be but a Human Being 56
Surah: 10 Ayah: 3 57
  Tafsir Ibn Kathir 57
    Allah is the Creator Who arranges the Affairs of the Universe 57
Surah: 10 Ayah: 4 58
  Tafsir Ibn Kathir 59
    The Return of Everything is to Allah 59
Surah: 10 Ayah: 5 & Ayah: 6 59
  Tafsir Ibn Kathir 60
    Everything is a Witness to the Power of Allah. 60
Surah: 10 Ayah: 7 & Ayah: 8 61
  Tafsir Ibn Kathir 61
    The Abode of Those Who deny the Hour is Hell-Fire 61
Surah: 10 Ayah: 9 & Ayah: 10 62
  Tafsir Ibn Kathir 62
    The Good Reward is for the People of Faith and Good Deeds 62
Surah: 10 Ayah: 11 63
  Tafsir Ibn Kathir 64
    Allah does not respond to the Requests for Evil like He does with the Requests for Good
    64
Surah: 10 Ayah: 12 65
  Tafsir Ibn Kathir 65
    Man remembers Allah at Times of Adversity and forgets Him at Times of Prosperity 65
Surah: 10 Ayah: 13 & Ayah: 14 66
  Tafsir Ibn Kathir 66
    The Admonition held in the Destruction of the Previous Generations 66
Surah: 10 Ayah: 15 & Ayah: 16 67
  Tafsir Ibn Kathir 68
    Obstinance of the Chiefs of the Quraysh 68
    The Evidence of the Truthfulness of the Qur'an. Muhammad then argued with supporting evidence to the truthfulness of what he had brought them: 68
Surah: 10 Ayah: 17 69
  Tafsir Ibn Kathir 69

Allah says that no one is more wrong, unjust and arrogant than he who invented a lie against Allah, forged claims about Allah, or claimed that Allah has sent a message to him but his claim was not true. 69
Surah: 10 Ayah: 18 & Ayah: 19 70
    Tafsir Ibn Kathir 71
        What do the Idolators believe about Their Gods 71
        Shirk is New 71
Surah: 10 Ayah: 20 72
    Tafsir Ibn Kathir 72
        The Idolators requested a Miracle 72
Surah: 10 Ayah: 21, Ayah: 22 & Ayah: 23 73
    Tafsir Ibn Kathir 74
        Man changes when He receives Mercy after Times of Distress 74
Surah: 10 Ayah: 24 & Ayah: 25 77
    Tafsir Ibn Kathir 77
        The Parable of this Life 77
        Invitation to the Everlasting Gifts that do not vanish 78
Surah: 10 Ayah: 26 80
    Tafsir Ibn Kathir 80
        The Reward of the Good-Doers 80
Surah: 10 Ayah: 27 81
    Tafsir Ibn Kathir 82
        The Reward of the Wicked Criminals 82
Surah: 10 Ayah: 28, Ayah: 29 & Ayah: 30 82
    Tafsir Ibn Kathir 83
        The gods of the Idolators will claim Innocence from them on the Day of Resurrection ... 83
Surah: 10 Ayah: 31, Ayah: 32 & Ayah: 33 85
    Tafsir Ibn Kathir 86
        The Idolators recognize Allah's Tawhid in Lordship and the Evidence is established against Them through this Recognition. 86
Surah: 10 Ayah: 34, Ayah: 35 & Ayah: 36 87
    Tafsir Ibn Kathir 88
        This invalidates and falsifies their claims for committing Shirk with Allah and worshipping different idols and rivals. 88
Surah: 10 Ayah: 37, Ayah: 38, Ayah: 39 & Ayah: 40 89
    Tafsir Ibn Kathir 90
        The Qur'an is the True, Inimitable Word of Allah and It is a Miracle 90
Surah: 10 Ayah: 41, Ayah: 42, Ayah: 43 & Ayah: 44 92
    Tafsir Ibn Kathir 92
        The Command to be Free and Clear from the Idolators 92
Surah: 10 Ayah: 45 93
    Tafsir Ibn Kathir 94
        The Feeling of Brevity toward the Worldly Life at the Gathering on the Day of Resurrection 94

Table of Contents

Surah: 10 Ayah: 46 & Ayah: 47 95
   Tafsir Ibn Kathir 95
      The Criminals will certainly be avenged -- whether in This World or in the Hereafter 95

Surah: 10 Ayah: 48, Ayah: 49, Ayah: 50, Ayah: 51 & Ayah: 52 96
   Tafsir Ibn Kathir 97
      The Deniers of the Day of Resurrection wish to hasten its Coming and their Response 97

Surah: 10 Ayah: 53 & Ayah: 54 98
   Tafsir Ibn Kathir 98
      The Resurrection is Real 98

Surah: 10 Ayah: 55 & Ayah: 56 99
   Tafsir Ibn Kathir 99

Surah: 10 Ayah: 57 & Ayah: 58 100
   Tafsir Ibn Kathir 100
      The Qur'an is an Admonition, Cure, Mercy and Guidance 100

Surah: 10 Ayah: 59 & Ayah: 60 101
   Tafsir Ibn Kathir 101
      None can make Anything Lawful or Unlawful except Allah or Those Whom Allah has allowed to do so 101

Surah: 10 Ayah: 61 103
   Tafsir Ibn Kathir 103
      Everything Small or Large is within the Knowledge of Allah 103

Surah: 10 Ayah: 62, Ayah: 63 & Ayah: 64 104
   Tafsir Ibn Kathir 105
      Identifying the Awliya' of Allah 105
      The True Dream is a Form of Good News 105

Surah: 10 Ayah: 65, Ayah: 66 & Ayah: 67 107
   Tafsir Ibn Kathir 108
      All Might and Honor is for Allah - He Alone has Full Authority within the Universe 108

Surah: 10 Ayah: 68, Ayah: 69 & Ayah: 70 108
   Tafsir Ibn Kathir 109
      Allah is Far Above taking a Wife or having Children 109

Surah: 10 Ayah: 71, Ayah: 72 & Ayah: 73 110
   Tafsir Ibn Kathir 111
      The Story of Nuh and His People 111
      Islam is the Religion of all of the Prophets 111
      The Evil Goal and End of Criminals 112

Surah: 10 Ayah: 74 113
   Tafsir Ibn Kathir 113
      Meaning; Then after Nuh We sent Messengers to their people. 113

Surah: 10 Ayah: 75, Ayah: 76, Ayah: 77 & Ayah: 78 114
   Tafsir Ibn Kathir 115
      The Story of Musa and Fira`wn 115

Surah: 10 Ayah: 79, Ayah: 80, Ayah: 81 & Ayah: 82 115
   Tafsir Ibn Kathir 116

- Between Musa and the Magicians 116
- Surah: 10 Ayah: 83 117
  - Tafsir Ibn Kathir 117
    - Only a Few Youth from Fir`awn's People believed in Musa 117
- Surah: 10 Ayah: 84, Ayah: 85 & Ayah: 86.. 118
  - Tafsir Ibn Kathir 118
    - Musa encouraged His People to put Their Trust in Allah 118
- Surah: 10 Ayah: 87 119
  - Tafsir Ibn Kathir 119
    - They were commanded to pray inside Their Homes 119
- Surah: 10 Ayah: 88 & Ayah: 89.. 120
  - Tafsir Ibn Kathir 120
    - Musa supplicated against Fir`awn and His Chiefs 120
- Surah: 10 Ayah: 90, Ayah: 91 & Ayah: 92.. 121
  - Tafsir Ibn Kathir 122
    - The Children of Israel were saved and Fir`awn's People drowned 122
- Surah: 10 Ayah: 93 124
  - Tafsir Ibn Kathir 125
    - The Establishment of the Children of Israel in the Land and Their Provision from the Good Things 125
- Surah: 10 Ayah: 94, Ayah: 95, Ayah: 96 & Ayah: 97.. 126
  - Tafsir Ibn Kathir 126
    - Previous books Attest to the Truth of the Qur'an 126
- Surah: 10 Ayah: 98 127
  - Tafsir Ibn Kathir 127
    - Belief at the Time of Punishment did not help except with the People of Yunus 127
- Surah: 10 Ayah: 99 & Ayah: 100.. 128
  - Tafsir Ibn Kathir 129
    - It is not Part of Allah's Decree to compel Belief 129
- Surah: 10 Ayah: 101, Ayah: 102 & Ayah: 103 130
  - Tafsir Ibn Kathir 130
    - The Command to reflect upon the Creation of the Heavens and the Earth 130
- Surah: 10 Ayah: 104, Ayah: 105, Ayah: 106 & Ayah: 107 131
  - Tafsir Ibn Kathir 132
    - The Command to worship Allah Alone and rely upon Him................................... 132
- Surah: 10 Ayah: 108 & Ayah: 109.. 133
  - Tafsir Ibn Kathir 133

INTRODUCTION TO CHAPTER (SURAH) 11: HUD 134

- IBN KATHIR'S INTRODUCTION 134
  - Surah Hud made the Prophet's Hair turn Gray.. 134

CHAPTER (SURAH) 11: HUD, VERSES 001-005 134

- Surah: 11 Ayah: 1, Ayah: 2, Ayah: 3 & Ayah: 4... 134

Table of Contents

    Tafsir Ibn Kathir 135
        The Qur'an and its Call to (worship) Allah Alone 135
Surah: 11 Ayah: 5 .... *137*
    Tafsir Ibn Kathir 137
        Allah is Aware of All Things 137

PRELUDE

Opening Serman

Indeed, all praise is due to Allah. We praise Him and seek His help and forgiveness. We seek refuge with Allah from our soul's evil and our wrong doings. He whom Allah guides, no one can misguide; and he whom He misguides, no one can guide

I bear witness that there is no (true) god except Allah – alone without a partner, and I bear witness that Muhammad (peace and blessings of Allah be upon him) is His 'abd (servant) and messenger.

يَٰٓأَيُّهَا ٱلَّذِينَ ءَامَنُوا۟ ٱتَّقُوا۟ ٱللَّهَ حَقَّ تُقَاتِهِۦ وَلَا تَمُوتُنَّ إِلَّا وَأَنتُم مُّسْلِمُونَ ﴿١٠٢﴾

O you who believe! Fear Allâh (by doing all that He has ordered and by abstaining from all that He has forbidden) as He should be feared. (Obey Him, be thankful to Him, and remember Him always), and die not except in a state of Islâm (as Muslims (with complete submission to Allâh)).

يَٰٓأَيُّهَا ٱلنَّاسُ ٱتَّقُوا۟ رَبَّكُمُ ٱلَّذِى خَلَقَكُم مِّن نَّفْسٍ وَٰحِدَةٍ وَخَلَقَ مِنْهَا زَوْجَهَا وَبَثَّ مِنْهُمَا رِجَالًا كَثِيرًا وَنِسَآءً ۚ وَٱتَّقُوا۟ ٱللَّهَ ٱلَّذِى تَسَآءَلُونَ بِهِۦ وَٱلْأَرْحَامَ ۚ إِنَّ ٱللَّهَ كَانَ عَلَيْكُمْ رَقِيبًا ﴿١﴾

O mankind! Be dutiful to your Lord, Who created you from a single person (Adam), and from him (Adam) He created his wife (Hawwâ (Eve)) and from them both He created many men and women; and fear Allâh through Whom you demand (your mutual rights), and (do not cut the relations of) the wombs (kinship). Surely, Allâh is Ever an All-Watcher over you.

يُصْلِحْ لَكُمْ أَعْمَٰلَكُمْ وَيَغْفِرْ لَكُمْ ذُنُوبَكُمْ ۗ وَمَن يُطِعِ ٱللَّهَ وَرَسُولَهُۥ فَقَدْ فَازَ فَوْزًا عَظِيمًا ﴿٧١﴾

He will direct you to do righteous good deeds and will forgive you your sins. And whosoever obeys Allâh and His Messenger (peace be upon him), he has indeed achieved a great achievement (i.e. he will be saved from the Hell-fire and will be admitted to Paradise).

Indeed, the best speech is Allah's Book and the best guidance is Muhammad's () guidance. The worst affairs (of religion) are those innovated (by people), for every such innovation is an act of misguidance leading to the Fire

Our Mission

Our mission is to gather in one place, for the English-speaking public, all relevant information needed to make the Qur'an more understandable and easier to study. This book tries to do this by providing the following:

1. The Arabic Text for those who are able to read Arabic
2. Transliteration of the Arabic text for those who are unable to read the Arabic script. This will give them a sample of the sound of the Qur'an, which they could not otherwise comprehend from reading the English meaning.
3. The meaning of the qur'an (translated by Dr. Muhammad Taqi-ud-Din Al-Hilali, Ph.D. and Dr. Muhammad Muhsin Khan)
4. Explanation (abridged Tafsir) by Ibn Kathir (translated by Safi-ur-Rahman al-Mubarakpuri)

We hope that by doing this an ordinary English-speaker will be able to pick up a copy of this book and study and comprehend The Glorious Qur'an in a way that is acceptable to the understanding of the Rightly-guided Muslim Ummah (Community).

Biography of Hafiz Ibn Kathir (701 H - 774 H)

By the Honored Shaykh `Abdul-Qadir Al-Arna'ut, may Allah protect him.

He is the respected Imam, Abu Al-Fida', `Imad Ad-Din Isma il bin 'Umar bin Kathir Al-Qurashi Al-Busrawi - Busraian in origin; Dimashqi in training, learning and residence.

Ibn Kathir was born in the city of Busra in 701 H. His father was the Friday speaker of the village, but he died while Ibn Kathir was only four years old. Ibn Kathir's brother, Shaykh Abdul-Wahhab, reared him and taught him until he moved to Damascus in 706 H., when he was five years old.

Ibn Kathir's Teachers

Ibn Kathir studied Fiqh - Islamic jurisprudence - with Burhan Ad-Din, Ibrahim bin `Abdur-Rahman Al-Fizari, known as Ibn Al-Firkah (who died in 729 H). Ibn Kathir heard Hadiths from `Isa bin Al-Mutim, Ahmad bin Abi Talib, (Ibn Ash-Shahnah) (who died in 730 H), Ibn Al-Hajjar, (who died in 730 H), and the Hadith narrator of Ash-Sham (modern day Syria and surrounding areas); Baha Ad-Din Al-Qasim bin Muzaffar bin `Asakir (who died in 723 H), and Ibn Ash-Shirdzi, Ishaq bin Yahya Al-Ammuddi, also known as `Afif Ad-Din, the Zahiriyyah Shaykh who died in 725 H, and Muhammad bin Zarrad. He remained with Jamal Ad-Din, Yusuf bin Az-Zaki AlMizzi who died in 724 H, he benefited from his knowledge and also married his daughter. He also read with Shaykh Al-Islam, Taqi Ad-Din Ahmad bin `Abdul-Halim bin `Abdus-Salam bin Taymiyyah who died in 728 H. He also read with the Imam Hafiz and historian Shams Ad-Din, Muhammad bin Ahmad bin Uthman bin Qaymaz Adh-Dhahabi, who died in 748 H. Also, Abu Musa Al-Qarafai, Abu Al-Fath Ad-Dabbusi and

'Ali bin `Umar As-Suwani and others who gave him permission to transmit the knowledge he learned with them in Egypt.

In his book, Al-Mu jam Al-Mukhtas, Al-Hafiz Adh-Dhaliabi wrote that Ibn Kathir was, "The Imam, scholar of jurisprudence, skillful scholar of Hadith, renowned Faqih and scholar of Tafsir who wrote several beneficial books."

Further, in Ad-Durar Al-Kdminah, Al-Hafiz Ibn Hajar AlAsqalani said, "Ibn Kathir worked on the subject of the Hadith in the areas of texts and chains of narrators. He had a good memory, his books became popular during his lifetime, and people benefited from them after his death."

Also, the renowned historian Abu Al-Mahasin, Jamal Ad-Din Yusuf bin Sayf Ad-Din (Ibn Taghri Bardi), said in his book, AlManhal As-Safi, "He is the Shaykh, the Imam, the great scholar `Imad Ad-Din Abu Al-Fida'. He learned extensively and was very active in collecting knowledge and writing. He was excellent in the areas of Fiqh, Tafsfr and Hadith. He collected knowledge, authored (books), taught, narrated Hadith and wrote. He had immense knowledge in the fields of Hadith, Tafsir, Fiqh, the Arabic language, and so forth. He gave Fatawa (religious verdicts) and taught until he died, may Allah grant him mercy. He was known for his precision and vast knowledge, and as a scholar of history, Hadith and Tafsir."

Ibn Kathir's Students

Ibn Hajji was one of Ibn Kathir's students, and he described Ibn Kathir: "He had the best memory of the Hadith texts. He also had the most knowledge concerning the narrators and authenticity, his contemporaries and teachers admitted to these qualities. Every time I met him I gained some benefit from him."

Also, Ibn Al-`Imad Al-Hanbali said in his book, Shadhardt Adh-Dhahab, "He is the renowned Hafiz `Imad Ad-Din, whose memory was excellent, whose forgetfulness was miniscule, whose understanding was adequate, and who had good knowledge in the Arabic language." Also, Ibn Habib said about Ibn Kathir, "He heard knowledge and collected it and wrote various books. He brought comfort to the ears with his Fatwas and narrated Hadith and brought benefit to other people. The papers that contained his Fatwas were transmitted to the various (Islamic) provinces. Further, he was known for his precision and encompassing knowledge."

Ibn Kathir's Books

1 - One of the greatest books that Ibn Kathir wrote was his Tafsir of the Noble Qur'an, which is one of the best Tafsir that rely on narrations [of Ahadith, the Tafsir of the Companions, etc.]. The Tafsir by Ibn Kathir was printed many times and several scholars have summarized it.

2- The History Collection known as Al-Biddyah, which was printed in 14 volumes under the name Al-Bidayah wanNihdyah, and contained the stories of the Prophets and previous nations, the Prophet's Seerah (life story) and Islamic history until his time. He also added a book Al-Fitan, about the Signs of the Last Hour.

3- At-Takmil ft Ma`rifat Ath-Thiqat wa Ad-Du'afa wal Majdhil which Ibn Kathir collected from the books of his two Shaykhs Al-Mizzi and Adh-Dhahabi; Al-Kdmal and Mizan Al-Ftiddl. He added several benefits regarding the subject of Al-Jarh and AtT'adil.

4- Al-Hadi was-Sunan ft Ahadith Al-Masdnfd was-Sunan which is also known by, Jami` Al-Masdnfd. In this book, Ibn Kathir collected the narrations of Imams Ahmad bin Hanbal, Al-Bazzar, Abu Ya`la Al-Mawsili, Ibn Abi Shaybah and from the six collections of Hadith: the Two Sahihs [Al-Bukhari and Muslim] and the Four Sunan [Abu Dawud, At-Tirmidhi, AnNasa and Ibn Majah]. Ibn Kathir divided this book according to areas of Fiqh.

5-Tabaqat Ash-Shaf iyah which also contains the virtues of Imam Ash-Shafi.

6- Ibn Kathir wrote references for the Ahadith of Adillat AtTanbfh, from the Shafi school of Fiqh.

7- Ibn Kathir began an explanation of Sahih Al-Bukhari, but he did not finish it.

8- He started writing a large volume on the Ahkam (Laws), but finished only up to the Hajj rituals.

9- He summarized Al-Bayhaqi's 'Al-Madkhal. Many of these books were not printed.

10- He summarized `Ulum Al-Hadith, by Abu `Amr bin AsSalah and called it Mukhtasar `Ulum Al-Hadith. Shaykh Ahmad Shakir, the Egyptian Muhaddith, printed this book along with his commentary on it and called it Al-Ba'th Al-Hathfth fi Sharh Mukhtasar `Ulum Al-Hadith.

11- As-Sfrah An-Nabawiyyah, which is contained in his book Al-Biddyah, and both of these books are in print.

12- A research on Jihad called Al-Ijtihad ft Talabi Al-Jihad, which was printed several times.

Ibn Kathir's Death

Al-Hafiz Ibn Hajar Al-Asgalani said, "Ibn Kathir lost his sight just before his life ended. He died in Damascus in 774 H." May Allah grant mercy upon Ibn Kathir and make him among the residents of His Paradise.

PREFACE

In the name of Allah, Most Gracious, Most Merciful.

About this book

The previous publication of this book included some background information to the chapters of the Qur'an by an Islamic scholar known as Abul Ala Maududi. This information was used to shed more light on the chapters by giving a summery of why each chapter was given its name, It's period of revelation and the circumstances surrounding its revelatiom. However, some Muslims objected to the inclusion of the contributions of Maududi.

In this new publication of Tafsir Ibn Kathir, we have removed all traces of the contribution of Abul Ala Maududi. Personally, I do not know the reasons for the objections to Maududi, but this work concerns only the tafsir of Ibn Kathir, so we have not included anything from Maududi in it. We have also corrected all the typing and formatting errors found in the previous publication. We have not alter the structure of the book. The reader is still able to read the full Arabic Text of the thirty Parts of the Qur'an and follow its meanings in the English language. The transliteration of the Arabic text should also give the reader a taste of the sound of the original Arabic.

May Almighty Allah accept this effort from us, and make it a source of blessings for us in this world and in the next. I bear witness that there is none worthy of worship but Allah and I bear witness that Muhammad (may the peace and blessings of Allah be upon him) is the slave and messenger of Allah.

Performing Prostration While Reading the Qur'an

Question:

Could you please give a list of the Qur'anic verses when a prostration is recommended? What happens if we read these verses and not perform a prostration?

A. Jalil

Answer:

There are 15 verses in the Qur'an that mention prostration before God Almighty as a good action by God-fearing believers. Therefore, it is strongly recommended to perform such a prostration when we read or listen to any of these verses, whether during prayer or in any situation.

Some scholars are of the view that even if one has not performed ablution, one should prostrate oneself. These verses are given here, starting with the Arabic title of the surah which is followed by two numbers, the first indicating the surah, and the second indicating the verse,: Al-Araf 7: 206; Al-Raad 13: 15; Al-Nahl 16: 50; Al-Isra 17: 109; Maryam 19: 58; Al-Hajj 22: 18 & 22: 77; Al-Furqan 25: 60; Al-Naml 27: 26;

Al-Sajdah 32: 15; Saad 38: 25; Fussilat 41: 38; Al-Najm 53: 62; Al-Inshiqaq 84: 21 and Al-Alaq 96: 19.

If you do not perform a prostration when you read or listen to any of these verses, you have done badly because you miss out on the reward of performing a prostration for God. You incur no sin and violate no divine order.

Reference:
http://archive.arabnews.com/?page=5&section=0&article=97811&d=1&m=7&y=2007

The Glorious Qur'an Juz' 11 (Part 11):
Chapter (Surah) 9: Al-Bara'at (The Immunity)
Or At-Tawba (Repentance, Dispensation) 093
To Chapter (Surah) 11: Hud 005

PART 11 FULL ARABIC TEXT

Chapter (Surah) 9: At-Tauba 093-129

۞ إِنَّمَا ٱلسَّبِيلُ عَلَى ٱلَّذِينَ يَسْتَـْٔذِنُونَكَ وَهُمْ أَغْنِيَآءُ ۚ رَضُوا۟ بِأَن يَكُونُوا۟ مَعَ ٱلْخَوَالِفِ وَطَبَعَ ٱللَّهُ عَلَىٰ قُلُوبِهِمْ فَهُمْ لَا يَعْلَمُونَ ۝ يَعْتَذِرُونَ إِلَيْكُمْ إِذَا رَجَعْتُمْ إِلَيْهِمْ ۚ قُل لَّا تَعْتَذِرُوا۟ لَن نُّؤْمِنَ لَكُمْ قَدْ نَبَّأَنَا ٱللَّهُ مِنْ أَخْبَارِكُمْ ۚ وَسَيَرَى ٱللَّهُ عَمَلَكُمْ وَرَسُولُهُۥ ثُمَّ تُرَدُّونَ إِلَىٰ عَـٰلِمِ ٱلْغَيْبِ وَٱلشَّهَـٰدَةِ فَيُنَبِّئُكُم بِمَا كُنتُمْ تَعْمَلُونَ ۝ سَيَحْلِفُونَ بِٱللَّهِ لَكُمْ إِذَا ٱنقَلَبْتُمْ إِلَيْهِمْ لِتُعْرِضُوا۟ عَنْهُمْ ۖ فَأَعْرِضُوا۟ عَنْهُمْ ۖ إِنَّهُمْ رِجْسٌ ۖ وَمَأْوَىٰهُمْ جَهَنَّمُ جَزَآءًۢ بِمَا كَانُوا۟ يَكْسِبُونَ ۝ يَحْلِفُونَ لَكُمْ لِتَرْضَوْا۟ عَنْهُمْ ۖ فَإِن تَرْضَوْا۟ عَنْهُمْ فَإِنَّ ٱللَّهَ لَا يَرْضَىٰ عَنِ ٱلْقَوْمِ ٱلْفَـٰسِقِينَ ۝ ٱلْأَعْرَابُ أَشَدُّ كُفْرًا وَنِفَاقًا وَأَجْدَرُ أَلَّا يَعْلَمُوا۟ حُدُودَ مَآ أَنزَلَ ٱللَّهُ عَلَىٰ رَسُولِهِۦ ۗ وَٱللَّهُ عَلِيمٌ حَكِيمٌ ۝ وَمِنَ ٱلْأَعْرَابِ مَن يَتَّخِذُ مَا يُنفِقُ مَغْرَمًا وَيَتَرَبَّصُ بِكُمُ ٱلدَّوَآئِرَ ۚ عَلَيْهِمْ دَآئِرَةُ ٱلسَّوْءِ ۗ وَٱللَّهُ سَمِيعٌ عَلِيمٌ ۝ وَمِنَ ٱلْأَعْرَابِ مَن يُؤْمِنُ بِٱللَّهِ وَٱلْيَوْمِ ٱلْـَٔاخِرِ وَيَتَّخِذُ مَا يُنفِقُ قُرُبَـٰتٍ عِندَ ٱللَّهِ وَصَلَوَٰتِ ٱلرَّسُولِ ۚ أَلَآ إِنَّهَا قُرْبَةٌ لَّهُمْ ۚ سَيُدْخِلُهُمُ ٱللَّهُ فِى رَحْمَتِهِۦٓ ۗ إِنَّ ٱللَّهَ غَفُورٌ رَّحِيمٌ ۝ وَٱلسَّـٰبِقُونَ ٱلْأَوَّلُونَ مِنَ ٱلْمُهَـٰجِرِينَ وَٱلْأَنصَارِ وَٱلَّذِينَ ٱتَّبَعُوهُم بِإِحْسَـٰنٍ رَّضِىَ ٱللَّهُ عَنْهُمْ وَرَضُوا۟ عَنْهُ وَأَعَدَّ لَهُمْ جَنَّـٰتٍ تَجْرِى

تَحْتَهَا ٱلْأَنْهَـٰرُ خَـٰلِدِينَ فِيهَآ أَبَدًا ۚ ذَٰلِكَ ٱلْفَوْزُ ٱلْعَظِيمُ ۝ وَمِمَّنْ حَوْلَكُم مِّنَ ٱلْأَعْرَابِ مُنَـٰفِقُونَ ۖ وَمِنْ أَهْلِ ٱلْمَدِينَةِ ۖ مَرَدُوا۟ عَلَى ٱلنِّفَاقِ لَا تَعْلَمُهُمْ ۖ نَحْنُ نَعْلَمُهُمْ ۚ سَنُعَذِّبُهُم مَّرَّتَيْنِ ثُمَّ يُرَدُّونَ إِلَىٰ عَذَابٍ عَظِيمٍ ۝ وَءَاخَرُونَ ٱعْتَرَفُوا۟ بِذُنُوبِهِمْ خَلَطُوا۟ عَمَلًا صَـٰلِحًا وَءَاخَرَ سَيِّئًا عَسَى ٱللَّهُ أَن يَتُوبَ عَلَيْهِمْ ۚ إِنَّ ٱللَّهَ غَفُورٌ رَّحِيمٌ ۝ خُذْ مِنْ أَمْوَٰلِهِمْ صَدَقَةً تُطَهِّرُهُمْ وَتُزَكِّيهِم بِهَا وَصَلِّ عَلَيْهِمْ ۖ إِنَّ صَلَوٰتَكَ سَكَنٌ لَّهُمْ ۗ وَٱللَّهُ سَمِيعٌ عَلِيمٌ ۝ أَلَمْ يَعْلَمُوٓا۟ أَنَّ ٱللَّهَ هُوَ يَقْبَلُ ٱلتَّوْبَةَ عَنْ عِبَادِهِۦ وَيَأْخُذُ ٱلصَّدَقَـٰتِ وَأَنَّ ٱللَّهَ هُوَ ٱلتَّوَّابُ ٱلرَّحِيمُ ۝ وَقُلِ ٱعْمَلُوا۟ فَسَيَرَى ٱللَّهُ عَمَلَكُمْ وَرَسُولُهُۥ وَٱلْمُؤْمِنُونَ ۖ وَسَتُرَدُّونَ إِلَىٰ عَـٰلِمِ ٱلْغَيْبِ وَٱلشَّهَـٰدَةِ فَيُنَبِّئُكُم بِمَا كُنتُمْ تَعْمَلُونَ ۝ وَءَاخَرُونَ مُرْجَوْنَ لِأَمْرِ ٱللَّهِ إِمَّا يُعَذِّبُهُمْ وَإِمَّا يَتُوبُ عَلَيْهِمْ ۗ وَٱللَّهُ عَلِيمٌ حَكِيمٌ ۝ وَٱلَّذِينَ ٱتَّخَذُوا۟ مَسْجِدًا ضِرَارًا وَكُفْرًا وَتَفْرِيقًۢا بَيْنَ ٱلْمُؤْمِنِينَ وَإِرْصَادًا لِّمَنْ حَارَبَ ٱللَّهَ وَرَسُولَهُۥ مِن قَبْلُ ۚ وَلَيَحْلِفُنَّ إِنْ أَرَدْنَآ إِلَّا ٱلْحُسْنَىٰ ۖ وَٱللَّهُ يَشْهَدُ إِنَّهُمْ لَكَـٰذِبُونَ ۝ لَا تَقُمْ فِيهِ أَبَدًا ۚ لَّمَسْجِدٌ أُسِّسَ عَلَى ٱلتَّقْوَىٰ مِنْ أَوَّلِ يَوْمٍ أَحَقُّ أَن تَقُومَ فِيهِ ۚ فِيهِ رِجَالٌ يُحِبُّونَ أَن يَتَطَهَّرُوا۟ ۚ وَٱللَّهُ يُحِبُّ ٱلْمُطَّهِّرِينَ ۝ أَفَمَنْ أَسَّسَ بُنْيَـٰنَهُۥ عَلَىٰ تَقْوَىٰ مِنَ ٱللَّهِ وَرِضْوَٰنٍ خَيْرٌ أَم مَّنْ أَسَّسَ بُنْيَـٰنَهُۥ عَلَىٰ شَفَا جُرُفٍ هَارٍ فَٱنْهَارَ بِهِۦ فِى نَارِ جَهَنَّمَ ۗ وَٱللَّهُ لَا يَهْدِى ٱلْقَوْمَ ٱلظَّـٰلِمِينَ ۝ لَا يَزَالُ بُنْيَـٰنُهُمُ ٱلَّذِى بَنَوْا۟ رِيبَةً فِى قُلُوبِهِمْ إِلَّآ أَن تَقَطَّعَ قُلُوبُهُمْ ۗ وَٱللَّهُ عَلِيمٌ حَكِيمٌ ۝ ۞ إِنَّ ٱللَّهَ ٱشْتَرَىٰ مِنَ ٱلْمُؤْمِنِينَ أَنفُسَهُمْ وَأَمْوَٰلَهُم بِأَنَّ لَهُمُ ٱلْجَنَّةَ ۚ يُقَـٰتِلُونَ فِى سَبِيلِ ٱللَّهِ فَيَقْتُلُونَ وَيُقْتَلُونَ ۖ وَعْدًا عَلَيْهِ حَقًّا فِى ٱلتَّوْرَىٰةِ وَٱلْإِنجِيلِ وَٱلْقُرْءَانِ ۚ وَمَنْ أَوْفَىٰ بِعَهْدِهِۦ مِنَ ٱللَّهِ ۚ فَٱسْتَبْشِرُوا۟

بِبَيْعِكُمُ ٱلَّذِى بَايَعْتُم بِهِۦ ۚ وَذَٰلِكَ هُوَ ٱلْفَوْزُ ٱلْعَظِيمُ ۝ ٱلتَّٰٓئِبُونَ ٱلْعَٰبِدُونَ ٱلْحَٰمِدُونَ ٱلسَّٰٓئِحُونَ ٱلرَّٰكِعُونَ ٱلسَّٰجِدُونَ ٱلْءَامِرُونَ بِٱلْمَعْرُوفِ وَٱلنَّاهُونَ عَنِ ٱلْمُنكَرِ وَٱلْحَٰفِظُونَ لِحُدُودِ ٱللَّهِ ۗ وَبَشِّرِ ٱلْمُؤْمِنِينَ ۝ مَا كَانَ لِلنَّبِىِّ وَٱلَّذِينَ ءَامَنُوٓا۟ أَن يَسْتَغْفِرُوا۟ لِلْمُشْرِكِينَ وَلَوْ كَانُوٓا۟ أُو۟لِى قُرْبَىٰ مِنۢ بَعْدِ مَا تَبَيَّنَ لَهُمْ أَنَّهُمْ أَصْحَٰبُ ٱلْجَحِيمِ ۝ وَمَا كَانَ ٱسْتِغْفَارُ إِبْرَٰهِيمَ لِأَبِيهِ إِلَّا عَن مَّوْعِدَةٍ وَعَدَهَآ إِيَّاهُ فَلَمَّا تَبَيَّنَ لَهُۥٓ أَنَّهُۥ عَدُوٌّ لِّلَّهِ تَبَرَّأَ مِنْهُ ۚ إِنَّ إِبْرَٰهِيمَ لَأَوَّٰهٌ حَلِيمٌ ۝ وَمَا كَانَ ٱللَّهُ لِيُضِلَّ قَوْمًۢا بَعْدَ إِذْ هَدَىٰهُمْ حَتَّىٰ يُبَيِّنَ لَهُم مَّا يَتَّقُونَ ۚ إِنَّ ٱللَّهَ بِكُلِّ شَىْءٍ عَلِيمٌ ۝ إِنَّ ٱللَّهَ لَهُۥ مُلْكُ ٱلسَّمَٰوَٰتِ وَٱلْأَرْضِ ۖ يُحْىِۦ وَيُمِيتُ ۚ وَمَا لَكُم مِّن دُونِ ٱللَّهِ مِن وَلِىٍّ وَلَا نَصِيرٍ ۝ لَّقَد تَّابَ ٱللَّهُ عَلَى ٱلنَّبِىِّ وَٱلْمُهَٰجِرِينَ وَٱلْأَنصَارِ ٱلَّذِينَ ٱتَّبَعُوهُ فِى سَاعَةِ ٱلْعُسْرَةِ مِنۢ بَعْدِ مَا كَادَ يَزِيغُ قُلُوبُ فَرِيقٍ مِّنْهُمْ ثُمَّ تَابَ عَلَيْهِمْ ۚ إِنَّهُۥ بِهِمْ رَءُوفٌ رَّحِيمٌ ۝ وَعَلَى ٱلثَّلَٰثَةِ ٱلَّذِينَ خُلِّفُوا۟ حَتَّىٰٓ إِذَا ضَاقَتْ عَلَيْهِمُ ٱلْأَرْضُ بِمَا رَحُبَتْ وَضَاقَتْ عَلَيْهِمْ أَنفُسُهُمْ وَظَنُّوٓا۟ أَن لَّا مَلْجَأَ مِنَ ٱللَّهِ إِلَّآ إِلَيْهِ ثُمَّ تَابَ عَلَيْهِمْ لِيَتُوبُوٓا۟ ۚ إِنَّ ٱللَّهَ هُوَ ٱلتَّوَّابُ ٱلرَّحِيمُ ۝ يَٰٓأَيُّهَا ٱلَّذِينَ ءَامَنُوا۟ ٱتَّقُوا۟ ٱللَّهَ وَكُونُوا۟ مَعَ ٱلصَّٰدِقِينَ ۝ مَا كَانَ لِأَهْلِ ٱلْمَدِينَةِ وَمَنْ حَوْلَهُم مِّنَ ٱلْأَعْرَابِ أَن يَتَخَلَّفُوا۟ عَن رَّسُولِ ٱللَّهِ وَلَا يَرْغَبُوا۟ بِأَنفُسِهِمْ عَن نَّفْسِهِۦ ۚ ذَٰلِكَ بِأَنَّهُمْ لَا يُصِيبُهُمْ ظَمَأٌ وَلَا نَصَبٌ وَلَا مَخْمَصَةٌ فِى سَبِيلِ ٱللَّهِ وَلَا يَطَـُٔونَ مَوْطِئًا يَغِيظُ ٱلْكُفَّارَ وَلَا يَنَالُونَ مِنْ عَدُوٍّ نَّيْلًا إِلَّا كُتِبَ لَهُم بِهِۦ عَمَلٌ صَٰلِحٌ ۚ إِنَّ ٱللَّهَ لَا يُضِيعُ أَجْرَ ٱلْمُحْسِنِينَ ۝ وَلَا يُنفِقُونَ نَفَقَةً صَغِيرَةً وَلَا كَبِيرَةً وَلَا يَقْطَعُونَ وَادِيًا إِلَّا كُتِبَ لَهُمْ

لِيَجْزِيَهُمُ ٱللَّهُ أَحْسَنَ مَا كَانُوا۟ يَعْمَلُونَ ۝ وَمَا كَانَ ٱلْمُؤْمِنُونَ لِيَنفِرُوا۟ كَآفَّةً ۚ فَلَوْلَا نَفَرَ مِن كُلِّ فِرْقَةٍ مِّنْهُمْ طَآئِفَةٌ لِّيَتَفَقَّهُوا۟ فِى ٱلدِّينِ وَلِيُنذِرُوا۟ قَوْمَهُمْ إِذَا رَجَعُوٓا۟ إِلَيْهِمْ لَعَلَّهُمْ يَحْذَرُونَ ۝ يَٰٓأَيُّهَا ٱلَّذِينَ ءَامَنُوا۟ قَٰتِلُوا۟ ٱلَّذِينَ يَلُونَكُم مِّنَ ٱلْكُفَّارِ وَلْيَجِدُوا۟ فِيكُمْ غِلْظَةً ۚ وَٱعْلَمُوٓا۟ أَنَّ ٱللَّهَ مَعَ ٱلْمُتَّقِينَ ۝ وَإِذَا مَآ أُنزِلَتْ سُورَةٌ فَمِنْهُم مَّن يَقُولُ أَيُّكُمْ زَادَتْهُ هَٰذِهِۦٓ إِيمَٰنًا ۚ فَأَمَّا ٱلَّذِينَ ءَامَنُوا۟ فَزَادَتْهُمْ إِيمَٰنًا وَهُمْ يَسْتَبْشِرُونَ ۝ وَأَمَّا ٱلَّذِينَ فِى قُلُوبِهِم مَّرَضٌ فَزَادَتْهُمْ رِجْسًا إِلَىٰ رِجْسِهِمْ وَمَاتُوا۟ وَهُمْ كَٰفِرُونَ ۝ أَوَلَا يَرَوْنَ أَنَّهُمْ يُفْتَنُونَ فِى كُلِّ عَامٍ مَّرَّةً أَوْ مَرَّتَيْنِ ثُمَّ لَا يَتُوبُونَ وَلَا هُمْ يَذَّكَّرُونَ ۝ وَإِذَا مَآ أُنزِلَتْ سُورَةٌ نَّظَرَ بَعْضُهُمْ إِلَىٰ بَعْضٍ هَلْ يَرَىٰكُم مِّنْ أَحَدٍ ثُمَّ ٱنصَرَفُوا۟ ۚ صَرَفَ ٱللَّهُ قُلُوبَهُم بِأَنَّهُمْ قَوْمٌ لَّا يَفْقَهُونَ ۝ لَقَدْ جَآءَكُمْ رَسُولٌ مِّنْ أَنفُسِكُمْ عَزِيزٌ عَلَيْهِ مَا عَنِتُّمْ حَرِيصٌ عَلَيْكُم بِٱلْمُؤْمِنِينَ رَءُوفٌ رَّحِيمٌ ۝ فَإِن تَوَلَّوْا۟ فَقُلْ حَسْبِىَ ٱللَّهُ لَآ إِلَٰهَ إِلَّا هُوَ ۖ عَلَيْهِ تَوَكَّلْتُ ۖ وَهُوَ رَبُّ ٱلْعَرْشِ ٱلْعَظِيمِ ۝

(At-Tauba 093-129)

Chapter (Surah) 10: Yunus 001-109

بِسْمِ ٱللَّهِ ٱلرَّحْمَٰنِ ٱلرَّحِيمِ

الٓر ۚ تِلْكَ ءَايَٰتُ ٱلْكِتَٰبِ ٱلْحَكِيمِ ۝ أَكَانَ لِلنَّاسِ عَجَبًا أَنْ أَوْحَيْنَآ إِلَىٰ رَجُلٍ مِّنْهُمْ أَنْ أَنذِرِ ٱلنَّاسَ وَبَشِّرِ ٱلَّذِينَ ءَامَنُوٓا۟ أَنَّ لَهُمْ قَدَمَ صِدْقٍ عِندَ رَبِّهِمْ ۗ قَالَ ٱلْكَٰفِرُونَ إِنَّ هَٰذَا لَسَٰحِرٌ مُّبِينٌ ۝ إِنَّ رَبَّكُمُ ٱللَّهُ ٱلَّذِى خَلَقَ ٱلسَّمَٰوَٰتِ وَٱلْأَرْضَ فِى سِتَّةِ أَيَّامٍ ثُمَّ ٱسْتَوَىٰ عَلَى ٱلْعَرْشِ ۖ يُدَبِّرُ ٱلْأَمْرَ ۖ مَا مِن شَفِيعٍ إِلَّا مِنۢ بَعْدِ إِذْنِهِۦ ۚ ذَٰلِكُمُ ٱللَّهُ رَبُّكُمْ فَٱعْبُدُوهُ ۚ أَفَلَا تَذَكَّرُونَ ۝

إِلَيْهِ مَرْجِعُكُمْ جَمِيعًا ۖ وَعْدَ ٱللَّهِ حَقًّا ۚ إِنَّهُۥ يَبْدَؤُا۟ ٱلْخَلْقَ ثُمَّ يُعِيدُهُۥ لِيَجْزِىَ ٱلَّذِينَ ءَامَنُوا۟ وَعَمِلُوا۟ ٱلصَّٰلِحَٰتِ بِٱلْقِسْطِ ۚ وَٱلَّذِينَ كَفَرُوا۟ لَهُمْ شَرَابٌ مِّنْ حَمِيمٍ وَعَذَابٌ أَلِيمٌۢ بِمَا كَانُوا۟ يَكْفُرُونَ ۝ هُوَ ٱلَّذِى جَعَلَ ٱلشَّمْسَ ضِيَآءً وَٱلْقَمَرَ نُورًا وَقَدَّرَهُۥ مَنَازِلَ لِتَعْلَمُوا۟ عَدَدَ ٱلسِّنِينَ وَٱلْحِسَابَ ۚ مَا خَلَقَ ٱللَّهُ ذَٰلِكَ إِلَّا بِٱلْحَقِّ ۚ يُفَصِّلُ ٱلْـَٔايَٰتِ لِقَوْمٍ يَعْلَمُونَ ۝ إِنَّ فِى ٱخْتِلَٰفِ ٱلَّيْلِ وَٱلنَّهَارِ وَمَا خَلَقَ ٱللَّهُ فِى ٱلسَّمَٰوَٰتِ وَٱلْأَرْضِ لَـَٔايَٰتٍ لِّقَوْمٍ يَتَّقُونَ ۝ إِنَّ ٱلَّذِينَ لَا يَرْجُونَ لِقَآءَنَا وَرَضُوا۟ بِٱلْحَيَوٰةِ ٱلدُّنْيَا وَٱطْمَأَنُّوا۟ بِهَا وَٱلَّذِينَ هُمْ عَنْ ءَايَٰتِنَا غَٰفِلُونَ ۝ أُو۟لَٰٓئِكَ مَأْوَىٰهُمُ ٱلنَّارُ بِمَا كَانُوا۟ يَكْسِبُونَ ۝ إِنَّ ٱلَّذِينَ ءَامَنُوا۟ وَعَمِلُوا۟ ٱلصَّٰلِحَٰتِ يَهْدِيهِمْ رَبُّهُم بِإِيمَٰنِهِمْ ۖ تَجْرِى مِن تَحْتِهِمُ ٱلْأَنْهَٰرُ فِى جَنَّٰتِ ٱلنَّعِيمِ ۝ دَعْوَىٰهُمْ فِيهَا سُبْحَٰنَكَ ٱللَّهُمَّ وَتَحِيَّتُهُمْ فِيهَا سَلَٰمٌ ۚ وَءَاخِرُ دَعْوَىٰهُمْ أَنِ ٱلْحَمْدُ لِلَّهِ رَبِّ ٱلْعَٰلَمِينَ ۝ ۞ وَلَوْ يُعَجِّلُ ٱللَّهُ لِلنَّاسِ ٱلشَّرَّ ٱسْتِعْجَالَهُم بِٱلْخَيْرِ لَقُضِىَ إِلَيْهِمْ أَجَلُهُمْ ۖ فَنَذَرُ ٱلَّذِينَ لَا يَرْجُونَ لِقَآءَنَا فِى طُغْيَٰنِهِمْ يَعْمَهُونَ ۝ وَإِذَا مَسَّ ٱلْإِنسَٰنَ ٱلضُّرُّ دَعَانَا لِجَنۢبِهِۦٓ أَوْ قَاعِدًا أَوْ قَآئِمًا فَلَمَّا كَشَفْنَا عَنْهُ ضُرَّهُۥ مَرَّ كَأَن لَّمْ يَدْعُنَآ إِلَىٰ ضُرٍّ مَّسَّهُۥ ۚ كَذَٰلِكَ زُيِّنَ لِلْمُسْرِفِينَ مَا كَانُوا۟ يَعْمَلُونَ ۝ وَلَقَدْ أَهْلَكْنَا ٱلْقُرُونَ مِن قَبْلِكُمْ لَمَّا ظَلَمُوا۟ ۙ وَجَآءَتْهُمْ رُسُلُهُم بِٱلْبَيِّنَٰتِ وَمَا كَانُوا۟ لِيُؤْمِنُوا۟ ۚ كَذَٰلِكَ نَجْزِى ٱلْقَوْمَ ٱلْمُجْرِمِينَ ۝ ثُمَّ جَعَلْنَٰكُمْ خَلَٰٓئِفَ فِى ٱلْأَرْضِ مِنۢ بَعْدِهِمْ لِنَنظُرَ كَيْفَ تَعْمَلُونَ ۝ وَإِذَا تُتْلَىٰ عَلَيْهِمْ ءَايَاتُنَا بَيِّنَٰتٍ ۙ قَالَ ٱلَّذِينَ لَا يَرْجُونَ لِقَآءَنَا ٱئْتِ بِقُرْءَانٍ غَيْرِ هَٰذَآ أَوْ بَدِّلْهُ ۚ قُلْ مَا يَكُونُ لِىٓ أَنْ أُبَدِّلَهُۥ مِن تِلْقَآئِ نَفْسِىٓ ۖ إِنْ أَتَّبِعُ إِلَّا مَا يُوحَىٰٓ إِلَىَّ ۖ إِنِّىٓ أَخَافُ إِنْ عَصَيْتُ رَبِّى عَذَابَ يَوْمٍ عَظِيمٍ ۝ قُل لَّوْ شَآءَ ٱللَّهُ مَا تَلَوْتُهُۥ عَلَيْكُمْ وَلَآ أَدْرَىٰكُم بِهِۦ ۖ

فَقَدْ لَبِثْتُ فِيكُمْ عُمُرًا مِّن قَبْلِهِ ۚ أَفَلَا تَعْقِلُونَ ۝ فَمَنْ أَظْلَمُ مِمَّنِ افْتَرَىٰ عَلَى ٱللَّهِ كَذِبًا أَوْ كَذَّبَ بِـَٔايَـٰتِهِ ۚ إِنَّهُۥ لَا يُفْلِحُ ٱلْمُجْرِمُونَ ۝ وَيَعْبُدُونَ مِن دُونِ ٱللَّهِ مَا لَا يَضُرُّهُمْ وَلَا يَنفَعُهُمْ وَيَقُولُونَ هَـٰٓؤُلَآءِ شُفَعَـٰٓؤُنَا عِندَ ٱللَّهِ ۚ قُلْ أَتُنَبِّـُٔونَ ٱللَّهَ بِمَا لَا يَعْلَمُ فِى ٱلسَّمَـٰوَٰتِ وَلَا فِى ٱلْأَرْضِ ۚ سُبْحَـٰنَهُۥ وَتَعَـٰلَىٰ عَمَّا يُشْرِكُونَ ۝ وَمَا كَانَ ٱلنَّاسُ إِلَّآ أُمَّةً وَٰحِدَةً فَٱخْتَلَفُوا۟ ۚ وَلَوْلَا كَلِمَةٌ سَبَقَتْ مِن رَّبِّكَ لَقُضِىَ بَيْنَهُمْ فِيمَا فِيهِ يَخْتَلِفُونَ ۝ وَيَقُولُونَ لَوْلَآ أُنزِلَ عَلَيْهِ ءَايَةٌ مِّن رَّبِّهِۦ ۖ فَقُلْ إِنَّمَا ٱلْغَيْبُ لِلَّهِ فَٱنتَظِرُوٓا۟ إِنِّى مَعَكُم مِّنَ ٱلْمُنتَظِرِينَ ۝ وَإِذَآ أَذَقْنَا ٱلنَّاسَ رَحْمَةً مِّنۢ بَعْدِ ضَرَّآءَ مَسَّتْهُمْ إِذَا لَهُم مَّكْرٌ فِىٓ ءَايَاتِنَا ۚ قُلِ ٱللَّهُ أَسْرَعُ مَكْرًا ۚ إِنَّ رُسُلَنَا يَكْتُبُونَ مَا تَمْكُرُونَ ۝ هُوَ ٱلَّذِى يُسَيِّرُكُمْ فِى ٱلْبَرِّ وَٱلْبَحْرِ ۖ حَتَّىٰٓ إِذَا كُنتُمْ فِى ٱلْفُلْكِ وَجَرَيْنَ بِهِم بِرِيحٍ طَيِّبَةٍ وَفَرِحُوا۟ بِهَا جَآءَتْهَا رِيحٌ عَاصِفٌ وَجَآءَهُمُ ٱلْمَوْجُ مِن كُلِّ مَكَانٍ وَظَنُّوٓا۟ أَنَّهُمْ أُحِيطَ بِهِمْ ۙ دَعَوُا۟ ٱللَّهَ مُخْلِصِينَ لَهُ ٱلدِّينَ لَئِنْ أَنجَيْتَنَا مِنْ هَـٰذِهِۦ لَنَكُونَنَّ مِنَ ٱلشَّـٰكِرِينَ ۝ فَلَمَّآ أَنجَىٰهُمْ إِذَا هُمْ يَبْغُونَ فِى ٱلْأَرْضِ بِغَيْرِ ٱلْحَقِّ ۗ يَـٰٓأَيُّهَا ٱلنَّاسُ إِنَّمَا بَغْيُكُمْ عَلَىٰٓ أَنفُسِكُم ۖ مَّتَـٰعَ ٱلْحَيَوٰةِ ٱلدُّنْيَا ۖ ثُمَّ إِلَيْنَا مَرْجِعُكُمْ فَنُنَبِّئُكُم بِمَا كُنتُمْ تَعْمَلُونَ ۝ إِنَّمَا مَثَلُ ٱلْحَيَوٰةِ ٱلدُّنْيَا كَمَآءٍ أَنزَلْنَـٰهُ مِنَ ٱلسَّمَآءِ فَٱخْتَلَطَ بِهِۦ نَبَاتُ ٱلْأَرْضِ مِمَّا يَأْكُلُ ٱلنَّاسُ وَٱلْأَنْعَـٰمُ حَتَّىٰٓ إِذَآ أَخَذَتِ ٱلْأَرْضُ زُخْرُفَهَا وَٱزَّيَّنَتْ وَظَنَّ أَهْلُهَآ أَنَّهُمْ قَـٰدِرُونَ عَلَيْهَآ أَتَىٰهَآ أَمْرُنَا لَيْلًا أَوْ نَهَارًا فَجَعَلْنَـٰهَا حَصِيدًا كَأَن لَّمْ تَغْنَ بِٱلْأَمْسِ ۚ كَذَٰلِكَ نُفَصِّلُ ٱلْـَٔايَـٰتِ لِقَوْمٍ يَتَفَكَّرُونَ ۝ وَٱللَّهُ يَدْعُوٓا۟ إِلَىٰ دَارِ ٱلسَّلَـٰمِ وَيَهْدِى مَن يَشَآءُ إِلَىٰ صِرَٰطٍ مُّسْتَقِيمٍ ۝ لِّلَّذِينَ أَحْسَنُوا۟ ٱلْحُسْنَىٰ وَزِيَادَةٌ ۖ وَلَا يَرْهَقُ وُجُوهَهُمْ قَتَرٌ وَلَا ذِلَّةٌ ۚ أُو۟لَـٰٓئِكَ أَصْحَـٰبُ ٱلْجَنَّةِ ۖ هُمْ فِيهَا

خَالِدُونَ ۞ وَٱلَّذِينَ كَسَبُوا۟ ٱلسَّيِّـَٔاتِ جَزَآءُ سَيِّئَةٍۭ بِمِثْلِهَا وَتَرْهَقُهُمْ ذِلَّةٌ ۖ مَّا لَهُم مِّنَ ٱللَّهِ مِنْ عَاصِمٍ ۖ كَأَنَّمَآ أُغْشِيَتْ وُجُوهُهُمْ قِطَعًا مِّنَ ٱلَّيْلِ مُظْلِمًا ۚ أُو۟لَٰٓئِكَ أَصْحَٰبُ ٱلنَّارِ ۖ هُمْ فِيهَا خَٰلِدُونَ ۞ وَيَوْمَ نَحْشُرُهُمْ جَمِيعًا ثُمَّ نَقُولُ لِلَّذِينَ أَشْرَكُوا۟ مَكَانَكُمْ أَنتُمْ وَشُرَكَآؤُكُمْ ۚ فَزَيَّلْنَا بَيْنَهُمْ ۖ وَقَالَ شُرَكَآؤُهُم مَّا كُنتُمْ إِيَّانَا تَعْبُدُونَ ۞ فَكَفَىٰ بِٱللَّهِ شَهِيدًۢا بَيْنَنَا وَبَيْنَكُمْ إِن كُنَّا عَنْ عِبَادَتِكُمْ لَغَٰفِلِينَ ۞ هُنَالِكَ تَبْلُوا۟ كُلُّ نَفْسٍ مَّآ أَسْلَفَتْ ۚ وَرُدُّوٓا۟ إِلَى ٱللَّهِ مَوْلَىٰهُمُ ٱلْحَقِّ ۖ وَضَلَّ عَنْهُم مَّا كَانُوا۟ يَفْتَرُونَ ۞ قُلْ مَن يَرْزُقُكُم مِّنَ ٱلسَّمَآءِ وَٱلْأَرْضِ أَمَّن يَمْلِكُ ٱلسَّمْعَ وَٱلْأَبْصَٰرَ وَمَن يُخْرِجُ ٱلْحَىَّ مِنَ ٱلْمَيِّتِ وَيُخْرِجُ ٱلْمَيِّتَ مِنَ ٱلْحَىِّ وَمَن يُدَبِّرُ ٱلْأَمْرَ ۚ فَسَيَقُولُونَ ٱللَّهُ ۚ فَقُلْ أَفَلَا تَتَّقُونَ ۞ فَذَٰلِكُمُ ٱللَّهُ رَبُّكُمُ ٱلْحَقُّ ۖ فَمَاذَا بَعْدَ ٱلْحَقِّ إِلَّا ٱلضَّلَٰلُ ۖ فَأَنَّىٰ تُصْرَفُونَ ۞ كَذَٰلِكَ حَقَّتْ كَلِمَتُ رَبِّكَ عَلَى ٱلَّذِينَ فَسَقُوٓا۟ أَنَّهُمْ لَا يُؤْمِنُونَ ۞ قُلْ هَلْ مِن شُرَكَآئِكُم مَّن يَبْدَؤُا۟ ٱلْخَلْقَ ثُمَّ يُعِيدُهُۥ ۚ قُلِ ٱللَّهُ يَبْدَؤُا۟ ٱلْخَلْقَ ثُمَّ يُعِيدُهُۥ ۖ فَأَنَّىٰ تُؤْفَكُونَ ۞ قُلْ هَلْ مِن شُرَكَآئِكُم مَّن يَهْدِىٓ إِلَى ٱلْحَقِّ ۚ قُلِ ٱللَّهُ يَهْدِى لِلْحَقِّ ۗ أَفَمَن يَهْدِىٓ إِلَى ٱلْحَقِّ أَحَقُّ أَن يُتَّبَعَ أَمَّن لَّا يَهِدِّىٓ إِلَّآ أَن يُهْدَىٰ ۖ فَمَا لَكُمْ كَيْفَ تَحْكُمُونَ ۞ وَمَا يَتَّبِعُ أَكْثَرُهُمْ إِلَّا ظَنًّا ۚ إِنَّ ٱلظَّنَّ لَا يُغْنِى مِنَ ٱلْحَقِّ شَيْـًٔا ۚ إِنَّ ٱللَّهَ عَلِيمٌۢ بِمَا يَفْعَلُونَ ۞ وَمَا كَانَ هَٰذَا ٱلْقُرْءَانُ أَن يُفْتَرَىٰ مِن دُونِ ٱللَّهِ وَلَٰكِن تَصْدِيقَ ٱلَّذِى بَيْنَ يَدَيْهِ وَتَفْصِيلَ ٱلْكِتَٰبِ لَا رَيْبَ فِيهِ مِن رَّبِّ ٱلْعَٰلَمِينَ ۞ أَمْ يَقُولُونَ ٱفْتَرَىٰهُ ۖ قُلْ فَأْتُوا۟ بِسُورَةٍ مِّثْلِهِۦ وَٱدْعُوا۟ مَنِ ٱسْتَطَعْتُم مِّن دُونِ ٱللَّهِ إِن كُنتُمْ صَٰدِقِينَ ۞ بَلْ كَذَّبُوا۟ بِمَا لَمْ يُحِيطُوا۟ بِعِلْمِهِۦ وَلَمَّا يَأْتِهِمْ تَأْوِيلُهُۥ ۚ كَذَٰلِكَ كَذَّبَ ٱلَّذِينَ مِن قَبْلِهِمْ ۖ فَٱنظُرْ كَيْفَ كَانَ عَٰقِبَةُ ٱلظَّٰلِمِينَ ۞ وَمِنْهُم مَّن يُؤْمِنُ بِهِۦ وَمِنْهُم مَّن لَّا يُؤْمِنُ بِهِۦ ۚ وَرَبُّكَ أَعْلَمُ بِٱلْمُفْسِدِينَ ۞

وَإِن كَذَّبُوكَ فَقُل لِّى عَمَلِى وَلَكُمْ عَمَلُكُمْ أَنتُم بَرِيئُونَ مِمَّا أَعْمَلُ وَأَنَاْ بَرِىءٌ مِّمَّا تَعْمَلُونَ ۝ وَمِنْهُم مَّن يَسْتَمِعُونَ إِلَيْكَ أَفَأَنتَ تُسْمِعُ ٱلصُّمَّ وَلَوْ كَانُواْ لَا يَعْقِلُونَ ۝ وَمِنْهُم مَّن يَنظُرُ إِلَيْكَ أَفَأَنتَ تَهْدِى ٱلْعُمْىَ وَلَوْ كَانُواْ لَا يُبْصِرُونَ ۝ إِنَّ ٱللَّهَ لَا يَظْلِمُ ٱلنَّاسَ شَيْئًا وَلَكِنَّ ٱلنَّاسَ أَنفُسَهُمْ يَظْلِمُونَ ۝ وَيَوْمَ يَحْشُرُهُمْ كَأَن لَّمْ يَلْبَثُوٓاْ إِلَّا سَاعَةً مِّنَ ٱلنَّهَارِ يَتَعَارَفُونَ بَيْنَهُمْ قَدْ خَسِرَ ٱلَّذِينَ كَذَّبُواْ بِلِقَآءِ ٱللَّهِ وَمَا كَانُواْ مُهْتَدِينَ ۝ وَإِمَّا نُرِيَنَّكَ بَعْضَ ٱلَّذِى نَعِدُهُمْ أَوْ نَتَوَفَّيَنَّكَ فَإِلَيْنَا مَرْجِعُهُمْ ثُمَّ ٱللَّهُ شَهِيدٌ عَلَىٰ مَا يَفْعَلُونَ ۝ وَلِكُلِّ أُمَّةٍ رَّسُولٌ فَإِذَا جَآءَ رَسُولُهُمْ قُضِىَ بَيْنَهُم بِٱلْقِسْطِ وَهُمْ لَا يُظْلَمُونَ ۝ وَيَقُولُونَ مَتَىٰ هَـٰذَا ٱلْوَعْدُ إِن كُنتُمْ صَـٰدِقِينَ ۝ قُل لَّآ أَمْلِكُ لِنَفْسِى ضَرًّا وَلَا نَفْعًا إِلَّا مَا شَآءَ ٱللَّهُ لِكُلِّ أُمَّةٍ أَجَلٌ إِذَا جَآءَ أَجَلُهُمْ فَلَا يَسْتَـْٔخِرُونَ سَاعَةً وَلَا يَسْتَقْدِمُونَ ۝ قُلْ أَرَءَيْتُمْ إِنْ أَتَىٰكُمْ عَذَابُهُ بَيَـٰتًا أَوْ نَهَارًا مَّاذَا يَسْتَعْجِلُ مِنْهُ ٱلْمُجْرِمُونَ ۝ أَثُمَّ إِذَا مَا وَقَعَ ءَامَنتُم بِهِۦ ءَآلْـَٔـٰنَ وَقَدْ كُنتُم بِهِۦ تَسْتَعْجِلُونَ ۝ ثُمَّ قِيلَ لِلَّذِينَ ظَلَمُواْ ذُوقُواْ عَذَابَ ٱلْخُلْدِ هَلْ تُجْزَوْنَ إِلَّا بِمَا كُنتُمْ تَكْسِبُونَ ۝ وَيَسْتَنۢبِـُٔونَكَ أَحَقٌّ هُوَ قُلْ إِى وَرَبِّىٓ إِنَّهُۥ لَحَقٌّ وَمَآ أَنتُم بِمُعْجِزِينَ ۝ وَلَوْ أَنَّ لِكُلِّ نَفْسٍ ظَلَمَتْ مَا فِى ٱلْأَرْضِ لَٱفْتَدَتْ بِهِۦ وَأَسَرُّواْ ٱلنَّدَامَةَ لَمَّا رَأَوُاْ ٱلْعَذَابَ وَقُضِىَ بَيْنَهُم بِٱلْقِسْطِ وَهُمْ لَا يُظْلَمُونَ ۝ أَلَآ إِنَّ لِلَّهِ مَا فِى ٱلسَّمَـٰوَٰتِ وَٱلْأَرْضِ أَلَآ إِنَّ وَعْدَ ٱللَّهِ حَقٌّ وَلَـٰكِنَّ أَكْثَرَهُمْ لَا يَعْلَمُونَ ۝ هُوَ يُحْىِۦ وَيُمِيتُ وَإِلَيْهِ تُرْجَعُونَ ۝ يَـٰٓأَيُّهَا ٱلنَّاسُ قَدْ جَآءَتْكُم مَّوْعِظَةٌ مِّن رَّبِّكُمْ وَشِفَآءٌ لِّمَا فِى ٱلصُّدُورِ وَهُدًى وَرَحْمَةٌ لِّلْمُؤْمِنِينَ ۝ قُلْ بِفَضْلِ ٱللَّهِ وَبِرَحْمَتِهِۦ فَبِذَٰلِكَ فَلْيَفْرَحُواْ هُوَ خَيْرٌ مِّمَّا يَجْمَعُونَ ۝ قُلْ أَرَءَيْتُم مَّآ أَنزَلَ ٱللَّهُ لَكُم مِّن رِّزْقٍ فَجَعَلْتُم مِّنْهُ حَرَامًا

وَحَلَلًا قُلْ ءَآللَّهُ أَذِنَ لَكُمْ ۖ أَمْ عَلَى ٱللَّهِ تَفْتَرُونَ ۝ وَمَا ظَنُّ ٱلَّذِينَ يَفْتَرُونَ عَلَى ٱللَّهِ ٱلْكَذِبَ يَوْمَ ٱلْقِيَٰمَةِ ۗ إِنَّ ٱللَّهَ لَذُو فَضْلٍ عَلَى ٱلنَّاسِ وَلَٰكِنَّ أَكْثَرَهُمْ لَا يَشْكُرُونَ ۝ وَمَا تَكُونُ فِى شَأْنٍ وَمَا تَتْلُوا۟ مِنْهُ مِن قُرْءَانٍ وَلَا تَعْمَلُونَ مِنْ عَمَلٍ إِلَّا كُنَّا عَلَيْكُمْ شُهُودًا إِذْ تُفِيضُونَ فِيهِ ۚ وَمَا يَعْزُبُ عَن رَّبِّكَ مِن مِّثْقَالِ ذَرَّةٍ فِى ٱلْأَرْضِ وَلَا فِى ٱلسَّمَآءِ وَلَآ أَصْغَرَ مِن ذَٰلِكَ وَلَآ أَكْبَرَ إِلَّا فِى كِتَٰبٍ مُّبِينٍ ۝ أَلَآ إِنَّ أَوْلِيَآءَ ٱللَّهِ لَا خَوْفٌ عَلَيْهِمْ وَلَا هُمْ يَحْزَنُونَ ۝ ٱلَّذِينَ ءَامَنُوا۟ وَكَانُوا۟ يَتَّقُونَ ۝ لَهُمُ ٱلْبُشْرَىٰ فِى ٱلْحَيَوٰةِ ٱلدُّنْيَا وَفِى ٱلْءَاخِرَةِ ۚ لَا تَبْدِيلَ لِكَلِمَٰتِ ٱللَّهِ ۚ ذَٰلِكَ هُوَ ٱلْفَوْزُ ٱلْعَظِيمُ ۝ وَلَا يَحْزُنكَ قَوْلُهُمْ ۘ إِنَّ ٱلْعِزَّةَ لِلَّهِ جَمِيعًا ۚ هُوَ ٱلسَّمِيعُ ٱلْعَلِيمُ ۝ أَلَآ إِنَّ لِلَّهِ مَن فِى ٱلسَّمَٰوَٰتِ وَمَن فِى ٱلْأَرْضِ ۗ وَمَا يَتَّبِعُ ٱلَّذِينَ يَدْعُونَ مِن دُونِ ٱللَّهِ شُرَكَآءَ ۚ إِن يَتَّبِعُونَ إِلَّا ٱلظَّنَّ وَإِنْ هُمْ إِلَّا يَخْرُصُونَ ۝ هُوَ ٱلَّذِى جَعَلَ لَكُمُ ٱلَّيْلَ لِتَسْكُنُوا۟ فِيهِ وَٱلنَّهَارَ مُبْصِرًا ۚ إِنَّ فِى ذَٰلِكَ لَءَايَٰتٍ لِّقَوْمٍ يَسْمَعُونَ ۝ قَالُوا۟ ٱتَّخَذَ ٱللَّهُ وَلَدًا ۗ سُبْحَٰنَهُ ۖ هُوَ ٱلْغَنِىُّ ۖ لَهُ مَا فِى ٱلسَّمَٰوَٰتِ وَمَا فِى ٱلْأَرْضِ ۚ إِنْ عِندَكُم مِّن سُلْطَٰنٍ بِهَٰذَآ ۚ أَتَقُولُونَ عَلَى ٱللَّهِ مَا لَا تَعْلَمُونَ ۝ قُلْ إِنَّ ٱلَّذِينَ يَفْتَرُونَ عَلَى ٱللَّهِ ٱلْكَذِبَ لَا يُفْلِحُونَ ۝ مَتَٰعٌ فِى ٱلدُّنْيَا ثُمَّ إِلَيْنَا مَرْجِعُهُمْ ثُمَّ نُذِيقُهُمُ ٱلْعَذَابَ ٱلشَّدِيدَ بِمَا كَانُوا۟ يَكْفُرُونَ ۝ ۞ وَٱتْلُ عَلَيْهِمْ نَبَأَ نُوحٍ إِذْ قَالَ لِقَوْمِهِۦ يَٰقَوْمِ إِن كَانَ كَبُرَ عَلَيْكُم مَّقَامِى وَتَذْكِيرِى بِـَٔايَٰتِ ٱللَّهِ فَعَلَى ٱللَّهِ تَوَكَّلْتُ فَأَجْمِعُوٓا۟ أَمْرَكُمْ وَشُرَكَآءَكُمْ ثُمَّ لَا يَكُنْ أَمْرُكُمْ عَلَيْكُمْ غُمَّةً ثُمَّ ٱقْضُوٓا۟ إِلَىَّ وَلَا تُنظِرُونِ ۝ فَإِن تَوَلَّيْتُمْ فَمَا سَأَلْتُكُم مِّنْ أَجْرٍ ۖ إِنْ أَجْرِىَ إِلَّا عَلَى ٱللَّهِ ۖ وَأُمِرْتُ أَنْ أَكُونَ مِنَ ٱلْمُسْلِمِينَ ۝ فَكَذَّبُوهُ فَنَجَّيْنَٰهُ وَمَن مَّعَهُۥ فِى ٱلْفُلْكِ

وَجَعَلْنَـٰهُمْ خَلَـٰٓئِفَ وَأَغْرَقْنَا ٱلَّذِينَ كَذَّبُوا۟ بِـَٔايَـٰتِنَا ۖ فَٱنظُرْ كَيْفَ كَانَ عَـٰقِبَةُ ٱلْمُنذَرِينَ ۝ ثُمَّ بَعَثْنَا مِنۢ بَعْدِهِۦ رُسُلًا إِلَىٰ قَوْمِهِمْ فَجَآءُوهُم بِٱلْبَيِّنَـٰتِ فَمَا كَانُوا۟ لِيُؤْمِنُوا۟ بِمَا كَذَّبُوا۟ بِهِۦ مِن قَبْلُ ۚ كَذَٰلِكَ نَطْبَعُ عَلَىٰ قُلُوبِ ٱلْمُعْتَدِينَ ۝ ثُمَّ بَعَثْنَا مِنۢ بَعْدِهِم مُّوسَىٰ وَهَـٰرُونَ إِلَىٰ فِرْعَوْنَ وَمَلَإِي۟هِۦ بِـَٔايَـٰتِنَا فَٱسْتَكْبَرُوا۟ وَكَانُوا۟ قَوْمًا مُّجْرِمِينَ ۝ فَلَمَّا جَآءَهُمُ ٱلْحَقُّ مِنْ عِندِنَا قَالُوٓا۟ إِنَّ هَـٰذَا لَسِحْرٌ مُّبِينٌ ۝ قَالَ مُوسَىٰٓ أَتَقُولُونَ لِلْحَقِّ لَمَّا جَآءَكُمْ ۖ أَسِحْرٌ هَـٰذَا وَلَا يُفْلِحُ ٱلسَّـٰحِرُونَ ۝ قَالُوٓا۟ أَجِئْتَنَا لِتَلْفِتَنَا عَمَّا وَجَدْنَا عَلَيْهِ ءَابَآءَنَا وَتَكُونَ لَكُمَا ٱلْكِبْرِيَآءُ فِى ٱلْأَرْضِ وَمَا نَحْنُ لَكُمَا بِمُؤْمِنِينَ ۝ وَقَالَ فِرْعَوْنُ ٱئْتُونِى بِكُلِّ سَـٰحِرٍ عَلِيمٍ ۝ فَلَمَّا جَآءَ ٱلسَّحَرَةُ قَالَ لَهُم مُّوسَىٰٓ أَلْقُوا۟ مَآ أَنتُم مُّلْقُونَ ۝ فَلَمَّآ أَلْقَوْا۟ قَالَ مُوسَىٰ مَا جِئْتُم بِهِ ٱلسِّحْرُ ۖ إِنَّ ٱللَّهَ سَيُبْطِلُهُۥٓ ۖ إِنَّ ٱللَّهَ لَا يُصْلِحُ عَمَلَ ٱلْمُفْسِدِينَ ۝ وَيُحِقُّ ٱللَّهُ ٱلْحَقَّ بِكَلِمَـٰتِهِۦ وَلَوْ كَرِهَ ٱلْمُجْرِمُونَ ۝ فَمَآ ءَامَنَ لِمُوسَىٰٓ إِلَّا ذُرِّيَّةٌ مِّن قَوْمِهِۦ عَلَىٰ خَوْفٍ مِّن فِرْعَوْنَ وَمَلَإِي۟هِمْ أَن يَفْتِنَهُمْ ۚ وَإِنَّ فِرْعَوْنَ لَعَالٍ فِى ٱلْأَرْضِ وَإِنَّهُۥ لَمِنَ ٱلْمُسْرِفِينَ ۝ وَقَالَ مُوسَىٰ يَـٰقَوْمِ إِن كُنتُمْ ءَامَنتُم بِٱللَّهِ فَعَلَيْهِ تَوَكَّلُوٓا۟ إِن كُنتُم مُّسْلِمِينَ ۝ فَقَالُوا۟ عَلَى ٱللَّهِ تَوَكَّلْنَا رَبَّنَا لَا تَجْعَلْنَا فِتْنَةً لِّلْقَوْمِ ٱلظَّـٰلِمِينَ ۝ وَنَجِّنَا بِرَحْمَتِكَ مِنَ ٱلْقَوْمِ ٱلْكَـٰفِرِينَ ۝ وَأَوْحَيْنَآ إِلَىٰ مُوسَىٰ وَأَخِيهِ أَن تَبَوَّءَا لِقَوْمِكُمَا بِمِصْرَ بُيُوتًا وَٱجْعَلُوا۟ بُيُوتَكُمْ قِبْلَةً وَأَقِيمُوا۟ ٱلصَّلَوٰةَ ۗ وَبَشِّرِ ٱلْمُؤْمِنِينَ ۝ وَقَالَ مُوسَىٰ رَبَّنَآ إِنَّكَ ءَاتَيْتَ فِرْعَوْنَ وَمَلَأَهُۥ زِينَةً وَأَمْوَٰلًا فِى ٱلْحَيَوٰةِ ٱلدُّنْيَا رَبَّنَا لِيُضِلُّوا۟ عَن سَبِيلِكَ ۖ رَبَّنَا ٱطْمِسْ عَلَىٰٓ أَمْوَٰلِهِمْ وَٱشْدُدْ عَلَىٰ قُلُوبِهِمْ فَلَا يُؤْمِنُوا۟ حَتَّىٰ يَرَوُا۟ ٱلْعَذَابَ ٱلْأَلِيمَ ۝ قَالَ قَدْ أُجِيبَت دَّعْوَتُكُمَا فَٱسْتَقِيمَا وَلَا تَتَّبِعَآنِّ سَبِيلَ ٱلَّذِينَ لَا يَعْلَمُونَ ۝ ۞ وَجَـٰوَزْنَا

بِبَنِىٓ إِسْرَٰٓءِيلَ ٱلْبَحْرَ فَأَتْبَعَهُمْ فِرْعَوْنُ وَجُنُودُهُۥ بَغْيًا وَعَدْوًا ۖ حَتَّىٰٓ إِذَآ أَدْرَكَهُ ٱلْغَرَقُ قَالَ ءَامَنتُ أَنَّهُۥ لَآ إِلَٰهَ إِلَّا ٱلَّذِىٓ ءَامَنَتْ بِهِۦ بَنُوٓا۟ إِسْرَٰٓءِيلَ وَأَنَا۠ مِنَ ٱلْمُسْلِمِينَ ۝ ءَآلْـَٰٔنَ وَقَدْ عَصَيْتَ قَبْلُ وَكُنتَ مِنَ ٱلْمُفْسِدِينَ ۝ فَٱلْيَوْمَ نُنَجِّيكَ بِبَدَنِكَ لِتَكُونَ لِمَنْ خَلْفَكَ ءَايَةً ۚ وَإِنَّ كَثِيرًا مِّنَ ٱلنَّاسِ عَنْ ءَايَٰتِنَا لَغَٰفِلُونَ ۝ وَلَقَدْ بَوَّأْنَا بَنِىٓ إِسْرَٰٓءِيلَ مُبَوَّأَ صِدْقٍ وَرَزَقْنَٰهُم مِّنَ ٱلطَّيِّبَٰتِ فَمَا ٱخْتَلَفُوا۟ حَتَّىٰ جَآءَهُمُ ٱلْعِلْمُ ۚ إِنَّ رَبَّكَ يَقْضِى بَيْنَهُمْ يَوْمَ ٱلْقِيَٰمَةِ فِيمَا كَانُوا۟ فِيهِ يَخْتَلِفُونَ ۝ فَإِن كُنتَ فِى شَكٍّ مِّمَّآ أَنزَلْنَآ إِلَيْكَ فَسْـَٔلِ ٱلَّذِينَ يَقْرَءُونَ ٱلْكِتَٰبَ مِن قَبْلِكَ ۚ لَقَدْ جَآءَكَ ٱلْحَقُّ مِن رَّبِّكَ فَلَا تَكُونَنَّ مِنَ ٱلْمُمْتَرِينَ ۝ وَلَا تَكُونَنَّ مِنَ ٱلَّذِينَ كَذَّبُوا۟ بِـَٔايَٰتِ ٱللَّهِ فَتَكُونَ مِنَ ٱلْخَٰسِرِينَ ۝ إِنَّ ٱلَّذِينَ حَقَّتْ عَلَيْهِمْ كَلِمَتُ رَبِّكَ لَا يُؤْمِنُونَ ۝ وَلَوْ جَآءَتْهُمْ كُلُّ ءَايَةٍ حَتَّىٰ يَرَوُا۟ ٱلْعَذَابَ ٱلْأَلِيمَ ۝ فَلَوْلَا كَانَتْ قَرْيَةٌ ءَامَنَتْ فَنَفَعَهَآ إِيمَٰنُهَآ إِلَّا قَوْمَ يُونُسَ لَمَّآ ءَامَنُوا۟ كَشَفْنَا عَنْهُمْ عَذَابَ ٱلْخِزْىِ فِى ٱلْحَيَوٰةِ ٱلدُّنْيَا وَمَتَّعْنَٰهُمْ إِلَىٰ حِينٍ ۝ وَلَوْ شَآءَ رَبُّكَ لَءَامَنَ مَن فِى ٱلْأَرْضِ كُلُّهُمْ جَمِيعًا ۚ أَفَأَنتَ تُكْرِهُ ٱلنَّاسَ حَتَّىٰ يَكُونُوا۟ مُؤْمِنِينَ ۝ وَمَا كَانَ لِنَفْسٍ أَن تُؤْمِنَ إِلَّا بِإِذْنِ ٱللَّهِ ۚ وَيَجْعَلُ ٱلرِّجْسَ عَلَى ٱلَّذِينَ لَا يَعْقِلُونَ ۝ قُلِ ٱنظُرُوا۟ مَاذَا فِى ٱلسَّمَٰوَٰتِ وَٱلْأَرْضِ ۚ وَمَا تُغْنِى ٱلْءَايَٰتُ وَٱلنُّذُرُ عَن قَوْمٍ لَّا يُؤْمِنُونَ ۝ فَهَلْ يَنتَظِرُونَ إِلَّا مِثْلَ أَيَّامِ ٱلَّذِينَ خَلَوْا۟ مِن قَبْلِهِمْ ۚ قُلْ فَٱنتَظِرُوٓا۟ إِنِّى مَعَكُم مِّنَ ٱلْمُنتَظِرِينَ ۝ ثُمَّ نُنَجِّى رُسُلَنَا وَٱلَّذِينَ ءَامَنُوا۟ ۚ كَذَٰلِكَ حَقًّا عَلَيْنَا نُنجِ ٱلْمُؤْمِنِينَ ۝ قُلْ يَٰٓأَيُّهَا ٱلنَّاسُ إِن كُنتُمْ فِى شَكٍّ مِّن دِينِى فَلَآ أَعْبُدُ ٱلَّذِينَ تَعْبُدُونَ مِن دُونِ ٱللَّهِ وَلَٰكِنْ أَعْبُدُ ٱللَّهَ ٱلَّذِى يَتَوَفَّىٰكُمْ ۖ وَأُمِرْتُ أَنْ أَكُونَ مِنَ ٱلْمُؤْمِنِينَ ۝ وَأَنْ أَقِمْ وَجْهَكَ لِلدِّينِ حَنِيفًا

وَلَا تَكُونَنَّ مِنَ ٱلْمُشْرِكِينَ ۝ وَلَا تَدْعُ مِن دُونِ ٱللَّهِ مَا لَا يَنفَعُكَ وَلَا يَضُرُّكَ ۖ فَإِن فَعَلْتَ فَإِنَّكَ إِذًا مِّنَ ٱلظَّٰلِمِينَ ۝ وَإِن يَمْسَسْكَ ٱللَّهُ بِضُرٍّ فَلَا كَاشِفَ لَهُۥٓ إِلَّا هُوَ ۖ وَإِن يُرِدْكَ بِخَيْرٍ فَلَا رَآدَّ لِفَضْلِهِۦ ۚ يُصِيبُ بِهِۦ مَن يَشَآءُ مِنْ عِبَادِهِۦ ۚ وَهُوَ ٱلْغَفُورُ ٱلرَّحِيمُ ۝ قُلْ يَٰٓأَيُّهَا ٱلنَّاسُ قَدْ جَآءَكُمُ ٱلْحَقُّ مِن رَّبِّكُمْ ۖ فَمَنِ ٱهْتَدَىٰ فَإِنَّمَا يَهْتَدِى لِنَفْسِهِۦ ۖ وَمَن ضَلَّ فَإِنَّمَا يَضِلُّ عَلَيْهَا ۖ وَمَآ أَنَا۠ عَلَيْكُم بِوَكِيلٍ ۝ وَٱتَّبِعْ مَا يُوحَىٰٓ إِلَيْكَ وَٱصْبِرْ حَتَّىٰ يَحْكُمَ ٱللَّهُ ۚ وَهُوَ خَيْرُ ٱلْحَٰكِمِينَ ۝

Chapter (Surah) 11: Hud 001-005

بِسْمِ ٱللَّهِ ٱلرَّحْمَٰنِ ٱلرَّحِيمِ

الٓر ۚ كِتَٰبٌ أُحْكِمَتْ ءَايَٰتُهُۥ ثُمَّ فُصِّلَتْ مِن لَّدُنْ حَكِيمٍ خَبِيرٍ ۝ أَلَّا تَعْبُدُوٓا۟ إِلَّا ٱللَّهَ ۚ إِنَّنِى لَكُم مِّنْهُ نَذِيرٌ وَبَشِيرٌ ۝ وَأَنِ ٱسْتَغْفِرُوا۟ رَبَّكُمْ ثُمَّ تُوبُوٓا۟ إِلَيْهِ يُمَتِّعْكُم مَّتَٰعًا حَسَنًا إِلَىٰٓ أَجَلٍ مُّسَمًّى وَيُؤْتِ كُلَّ ذِى فَضْلٍ فَضْلَهُۥ ۖ وَإِن تَوَلَّوْا۟ فَإِنِّىٓ أَخَافُ عَلَيْكُمْ عَذَابَ يَوْمٍ كَبِيرٍ ۝ إِلَى ٱللَّهِ مَرْجِعُكُمْ ۖ وَهُوَ عَلَىٰ كُلِّ شَىْءٍ قَدِيرٌ ۝ أَلَآ إِنَّهُمْ يَثْنُونَ صُدُورَهُمْ لِيَسْتَخْفُوا۟ مِنْهُ ۚ أَلَا حِينَ يَسْتَغْشُونَ ثِيَابَهُمْ يَعْلَمُ مَا يُسِرُّونَ وَمَا يُعْلِنُونَ ۚ إِنَّهُۥ عَلِيمٌۢ بِذَاتِ ٱلصُّدُورِ ۝

CHAPTER (SURAH) 9: AT-TAWBA (REPENTANCE), VERSES 093 - 129

Surah: 9 Ayah: 91, Ayah: 92 (end of Part 10) & Ayah: 93 (start of Part 11)

﴿ لَّيْسَ عَلَى ٱلضُّعَفَآءِ وَلَا عَلَى ٱلْمَرْضَىٰ وَلَا عَلَى ٱلَّذِينَ لَا يَجِدُونَ مَا يُنفِقُونَ حَرَجٌ إِذَا نَصَحُواْ لِلَّهِ وَرَسُولِهِۦ ۚ مَا عَلَى ٱلْمُحْسِنِينَ مِن سَبِيلٍ ۚ وَٱللَّهُ غَفُورٌ رَّحِيمٌ ﴾

91. There is no blame on those who are weak or ill or who find no resources to spend (in holy fighting (Jihâd)) if they are sincere and true (in duty) to Allâh and His Messenger. No ground (of complaint) can there be against the Muhsinûn (good-doers). And Allâh is Oft-Forgiving, Most Merciful.

﴿ وَلَا عَلَى ٱلَّذِينَ إِذَا مَآ أَتَوْكَ لِتَحْمِلَهُمْ قُلْتَ لَآ أَجِدُ مَآ أَحْمِلُكُمْ عَلَيْهِ تَوَلَّواْ وَّأَعْيُنُهُمْ تَفِيضُ مِنَ ٱلدَّمْعِ حَزَنًا أَلَّا يَجِدُواْ مَا يُنفِقُونَ ﴾

92. Nor (is there blame) on those who came to you to be provided with mounts, when you said: "I can find no mounts for you," they turned back, while their eyes overflowing with tears of grief that they could not find anything to spend (for Jihâd).

﴿ ۞ إِنَّمَا ٱلسَّبِيلُ عَلَى ٱلَّذِينَ يَسْتَـْٔذِنُونَكَ وَهُمْ أَغْنِيَآءُ ۚ رَضُواْ بِأَن يَكُونُواْ مَعَ ٱلْخَوَالِفِ وَطَبَعَ ٱللَّهُ عَلَىٰ قُلُوبِهِمْ فَهُمْ لَا يَعْلَمُونَ ﴾

93. The ground (of complaint) is only against those who are rich, and yet ask exemption. They are content to be with (the women) who sit behind (at home) and Allâh has sealed up their hearts (from all kinds of goodness and right guidance) so that they know not (what they are losing).

Transliteration

91. Laysa AAala aldduAAafa-i wala AAala almarda wala AAala allatheena la yajidoona ma yunfiqoona harajun itha nasahoo lillahi warasoolihi ma AAala almuhsineena min sabeelin waAllahu ghafoorun raheemun   92. Wala AAala allatheena itha ma atawka litahmilahum qulta la ajidu ma ahmilukum AAalayhi tawallaw waaAAyunuhum tafeedu mina alddamAAi hazanan alla yajidoo ma yunfiqoona   93. Innama alssabeelu AAala allatheena yasta/thinoonaka wahum aghniyao radoo bi-an yakoonoo maAAa alkhawalifi watabaAAa Allahu AAala quloobihim fahum la yaAAlamoona

Tafsir Ibn Kathir

Legitimate Excuses for staying away from Jihad

Allah mentions here the valid excuses that permit one to stay away from fighting. He first mentions the excuses that remain with a person, the weakness in the body that disallows one from Jihad, such as blindness, limping, and so forth. He then mentions the excuses that are not permanent, such as an illness that would prevent one from fighting in the cause of Allah, or poverty that prevents preparing for Jihad. There is no sin in these cases if they remain behind, providing that when they remain behind, they do not spread malice or try to discourage Muslims from fighting, but all the while observing good behavior in this state, just as Allah said,

(No means (of complaint) can there be against the doers of good. And Allah is Oft-Forgiving, Most Merciful.) Al-Awza`i said, "The people went out for the Istisqa' (rain) prayer. Bilal bin Sa`d stood up, praised Allah and thanked Him then said, `O those who are present! Do you concur that wrong has been done' They said, `Yes, by Allah!' He said, `O Allah! We hear your statement,

(No means (of complaint) can there be against the doers of good.) O Allah! We admit our errors, so forgive us and give us mercy and rain.' He then raised his hands and the people also raised their hands, and rain was sent down on them." Mujahid said about Allah's statement,

(Nor (is there blame) on those who came to you to be provided with mounts) Mujahid said; "It was revealed about Bani Muqarrin from the tribe of Muzaynah. " Ibn Abi Hatim recorded that Al-Hasan said that the Messenger of Allah said,

«لَقَدْ خَلَّفْتُمْ بِالْمَدِينَةِ أَقْوَامًا مَا أَنْفَقْتُمْ مِنْ نَفَقَةٍ وَلَا قَطَعْتُمْ وَادِيًا وَلَا نِلْتُمْ مِنْ عَدُوٍّ نَيْلًا إِلَّا وَقَدْ شَرَكُوكُمْ فِي الْأَجْرِ»

(Some people have remained behind you in Al-Madinah; and you never spent anything, crossed a valley, or afflicted hardship on an enemy, but they were sharing the reward with you.) He then recited the Ayah,

(Nor (is there blame) on those who came to you to be provided with mounts, when you said: "I can find no mounts for you.") This Hadith has a basis in the Two Sahihs from Anas, the Messenger of Allah said,

«إِنَّ بِالْمَدِينَةِ أَقْوَامًا مَا قَطَعْتُمْ وَادِيًا وَلَا سِرْتُمْ سَيْرًا إِلَّا وَهُمْ مَعَكُمْ»

(Some people have remained behind in Al-Madinah and you never crossed a valley or marched forth, but they were with you.) They said, "While they are still at Al-Madinah" He said,

Chapter 9: At-Tawba (Repentance, Dispensation), Verses 093-129

《نَعَمْ حَبَسَهُمُ الْعُذْرِ》

(Yes, as they have been held back by a (legal) excuse.) Then, Allah criticized those who seek permission to remain behind while they are rich, admonishing them for wanting to stay behind with women who remained in their homes,

(and Allah has sealed up their hearts, so that they know not (what they are losing).)

Surah: 9 Ayah: 94, Ayah: 95 & Ayah: 96

﴿ يَعْتَذِرُونَ إِلَيْكُمْ إِذَا رَجَعْتُمْ إِلَيْهِمْ قُل لَّا تَعْتَذِرُواْ لَن نُّؤْمِنَ لَكُمْ قَدْ نَبَّأَنَا ٱللَّهُ مِنْ أَخْبَارِكُمْ وَسَيَرَى ٱللَّهُ عَمَلَكُمْ وَرَسُولُهُۥ ثُمَّ تُرَدُّونَ إِلَىٰ عَـٰلِمِ ٱلْغَيْبِ وَٱلشَّهَـٰدَةِ فَيُنَبِّئُكُم بِمَا كُنتُمْ تَعْمَلُونَ ﴾

94. They (the hypocrites) will present their excuses to you (Muslims), when you return to them. Say (O Muhammad (peace be upon him)) "Present no excuses, we shall not believe you. Allâh has already informed us of the news concerning you. Allâh and His Messenger will observe your deeds. In the end you will be brought back to the All-Knower of the unseen and the seen, then He (Allâh) will inform you of what you used to do." (Tafsir At-Tabari)

﴿ سَيَحْلِفُونَ بِٱللَّهِ لَكُمْ إِذَا ٱنقَلَبْتُمْ إِلَيْهِمْ لِتُعْرِضُواْ عَنْهُمْ فَأَعْرِضُواْ عَنْهُمْ إِنَّهُمْ رِجْسٌ وَمَأْوَىٰهُمْ جَهَنَّمُ جَزَآءًۢ بِمَا كَانُواْ يَكْسِبُونَ ﴾

95. They will swear by Allâh to you (Muslims) when you return to them, that you may turn away from them. So turn away from them. Surely, they are Rijs (i.e. Najas (impure) because of their evil deeds), and Hell is their dwelling place - a recompense for that which they used to earn.

﴿ يَحْلِفُونَ لَكُمْ لِتَرْضَوْاْ عَنْهُمْ فَإِن تَرْضَوْاْ عَنْهُمْ فَإِنَّ ٱللَّهَ لَا يَرْضَىٰ عَنِ ٱلْقَوْمِ ٱلْفَـٰسِقِينَ ﴾

96. They (the hypocrites) swear to you (Muslims) that you may be pleased with them, but if you are pleased with them, certainly Allâh is not pleased with the people who are Al-Fâsiqûn (rebellious, disobedient to Allâh).

Transliteration

94. YaAAtathiroona ilaykum itha rajaAAtum ilayhim qul la taAAtathiroo lan nu/mina lakum qad nabbaana Allahu min akhbarikum wasayara Allahu AAamalakum warasooluhu thumma turaddoona ila AAalimi alghaybi waalshshahadati fayunabbi-okum bima kuntum taAAmaloona   95. Sayahlifoona biAllahi lakum itha inqalabtum ilayhim lituAAridoo AAanhum faaAAridoo AAanhum innahum rijsun wama/wahum

jahannamu jazaan bima kanoo yaksiboona 96. Yahlifoona lakum litardaw AAanhum fa-in tardaw AAanhum fa-inna Allaha la yarda AAani alqawmi alfasiqeena

Tafsir Ibn Kathir

Exposing the Deceitful Ways of Hypocrites

Allah said that when the believers go back to Al-Madinah, the hypocrites will begin apologizing to them.

(Say "Present no excuses, we shall not believe you."), we shall not believe what you say,

(Allah has already informed us of the news concerning you.) Allah has exposed your news to us,

(Allah and His Messenger will observe your deeds.) your actions will be made public to people in this life,

(In the end you will be brought back to the All-Knower of the unseen and the seen, then He (Allah) will inform you of what you used to do.) Allah will inform you of your deeds, whether they were good or evil, and will recompense you for them. Allah said that the hypocrites will swear to the believers in apology, so that the believers turn away from them without admonishing them. Therefore, Allah ordered disgracing them by turning away from them, for they are,

(Rijs) meaning, impure inwardly and in their creed. Their destination in the end will be Jahannam,

(a recompense for that which they used to earn.) of sins and evil deeds. Allah said that if the believers forgive the hypocrites when they swear to them,

(certainly Allah is not pleased with the people who are Fasiqin.) who rebel against the obedience of Allah and His Messenger . `Fisq', means, `deviation'.

Surah: 9 Ayah: 97, Ayah: 98 & Ayah: 99

﴿ ٱلۡأَعۡرَابُ أَشَدُّ كُفۡرًا وَنِفَاقًا وَأَجۡدَرُ أَلَّا يَعۡلَمُواْ حُدُودَ مَآ أَنزَلَ ٱللَّهُ عَلَىٰ رَسُولِهِۦۗ وَٱللَّهُ عَلِيمٌ حَكِيمٌ ۝ ﴾

97. The bedouins are the worst in disbelief and hypocrisy, and more likely to be in ignorance of the limits (Allâh's Commandments and His Laws) which Allâh has revealed to His Messenger. And Allâh is All-Knower, All-Wise.

﴿ وَمِنَ ٱلۡأَعۡرَابِ مَن يَتَّخِذُ مَا يُنفِقُ مَغۡرَمٗا وَيَتَرَبَّصُ بِكُمُ ٱلدَّوَآئِرَۚ عَلَيۡهِمۡ دَآئِرَةُ ٱلسَّوۡءِۗ وَٱللَّهُ سَمِيعٌ عَلِيمٌ ۝ ﴾

98. And of the bedouins there are some who look upon what they spend (in Allâh's Cause) as a fine and watch for calamities for you, on them be the calamity of evil. And Allâh is All-Hearer, All-Knower.

﴿ وَمِنَ ٱلْأَعْرَابِ مَن يُؤْمِنُ بِٱللَّهِ وَٱلْيَوْمِ ٱلْأَخِرِ وَيَتَّخِذُ مَا يُنفِقُ قُرُبَٰتٍ عِندَ ٱللَّهِ وَصَلَوَٰتِ ٱلرَّسُولِ ۚ أَلَآ إِنَّهَا قُرْبَةٌ لَّهُمْ ۚ سَيُدْخِلُهُمُ ٱللَّهُ فِى رَحْمَتِهِۦٓ ۗ إِنَّ ٱللَّهَ غَفُورٌ رَّحِيمٌ ﴾

99. And of the bedouins there are some who believe in Allâh and the Last Day, and look upon what they spend in Allâh's Cause as means of nearness to Allâh, and a cause of receiving the Messenger's invocations. Indeed these (spendings in Allâh's Cause) are a means of nearness for them. Allâh will admit them to His Mercy. Certainly Allâh is Oft-Forgiving, Most Merciful.

Transliteration

97. Al-aAArabu ashaddu kufran wanifaqan waajdaru alla yaAAlamoo hudooda ma anzala Allahu AAala rasoolihi waAllahu AAaleemun hakeemun 98. Wamina al-aAArabi man yattakhithu ma yunfiqu maghraman wayatarabbasu bikumu alddawa-ira AAalayhim da-iratu alssaw-i waAllahu sameeAAun AAaleemun 99. Wamina al-aAArabi man yu/minu biAllahi waalyawmi al-akhiri wayattakhithu ma yunfiqu qurubatin AAinda Allahi wasalawati alrrasooli ala innaha qurbatun lahum sayudkhiluhumu Allahu fee rahmatihi inna Allaha ghafoorun raheemun

Tafsir Ibn Kathir

The Bedouins are the Worst in Disbelief and Hypocrisy

Allah states that there are disbelievers, hypocrites and believers among the bedouins. He also states that the disbelief and hypocrisy of the bedouins is worse and deeper than the disbelief and hypocrisy of others. They are the most likely of being ignorant of the commandments that Allah has revealed to His Messenger . Al-A`mash narrated that Ibrahim said, "A bedouin man sat next to Zayd bin Sawhan while he was speaking to his friends. Zayd had lost his hand during the battle of Nahawand. The bedouin man said, `By Allah! I like your speech. However, your hand causes me suspicion.' Zayd said, `Why are you suspicious because of my hand, it is the left hand (that is cut)' The bedouin man said, `By Allah! I do not know which hand they cut off (for committing theft), is it the right or the left' Zayd bin Sawhan said, `Allah has said the truth,

(The bedouins are the worst in disbelief and hypocrisy, and more likely to not know the limits which Allah has revealed to His Messenger.)" Imam Ahmad narrated that Ibn `Abbas said that the Messenger of Allah said,

«مَنْ سَكَنَ الْبَادِيَةَ جَفَا، وَمَنِ اتَّبَعَ الصَّيْدَ غَفَلَ، وَمَنْ أَتَى السُّلْطَانَ افْتُتِنَ»

(He who lives in the desert becomes hard-hearted, he who follows the game becomes heedless, and he who associates with the rulers falls into Fitnah.) Abu Dawud, At-Tirmidhi and An-Nasa'i collected this Hadith. At-Tirmidhi said, "Hasan Gharib." The Prophet once had to give a bedouin man many gifts because of what he gave him as a gift, until the bedouin became satisfied. The Prophet said,

«لَقَدْ هَمَمْتُ أَنْ لَا أَقْبَلَ هَدِيَّةً إِلَّا مِنْ قُرَشِيٍّ أَوْ ثَقَفِيٍّ أَوْ أَنْصَارِيٍّ أَوْ دَوْسِيٍّ»

(I almost decided not to accept a gift except from someone from Quraysh, Thaqafi, the Ansar or Daws.) This is because these people lived in cities, Makkah, At-Ta'if, Al-Madinah and Yemen, and therefore, their conduct and manners are nicer than that of the hard-hearted bedouins. Allah said next,

(And Allah is All-Knower, All-Wise.) Allah knows those who deserve to be taught faith and knowledge, He wisely distributes knowledge or ignorance, faith or disbelief and hypocrisy between His servants. He is never questioned as to what He does, for He is the All-Knower, All-Wise. Allah also said that among bedouins are those,

(who look upon what they spend), in the cause of Allah,

(as a fine), as a loss and a burden,

(and watch for calamities for you), awaiting afflictions and disasters to strike you,

(on them be the calamity of evil), evil will touch them instead,

(And Allah is All-Hearer, All-Knower.) Allah hears the invocation of His servants and knows who deserves victory, who deserve failure. Allah's said;

(And of the bedouins there are some who believe in Allah and the Last Day, and look upon what they spend (in Allah's cause) as means of nearness to Allah, and a cause of receiving the Messenger's invocations.) This is the type of praiseworthy bedouins. They give charity in Allah's cause as way of achieving nearness to Allah and seeking the Messenger's invocation for their benefit,

(Indeed these are a means of nearness for them.) they will attain what they sought,

(Allah will admit them to His mercy. Certainly Allah is Oft-Forgiving, Most Merciful.)

Surah: 9 Ayah: 100

﴿ وَٱلسَّٰبِقُونَ ٱلۡأَوَّلُونَ مِنَ ٱلۡمُهَٰجِرِينَ وَٱلۡأَنصَارِ وَٱلَّذِينَ ٱتَّبَعُوهُم بِإِحۡسَٰنٍ رَّضِيَ ٱللَّهُ عَنۡهُمۡ وَرَضُواْ عَنۡهُ وَأَعَدَّ لَهُمۡ جَنَّٰتٍ تَجۡرِي تَحۡتَهَا ٱلۡأَنۡهَٰرُ خَٰلِدِينَ فِيهَآ أَبَدٗاۚ ذَٰلِكَ ٱلۡفَوۡزُ ٱلۡعَظِيمُ ﴾

100. And the foremost to embrace Islâm of the Muhâjirûn (those who migrated from Makkah to Al-Madinah) and the Ansâr (the citizens of Al-Madinah who helped and gave aid to the Muhâjirûn) and also those who followed them exactly (in Faith). Allâh is well-pleased with them as they are well-pleased with Him. He has prepared for them Gardens under which rivers flow (Paradise), to dwell therein forever. That is the supreme success.

Transliteration

100. Waalssabiqoona al-awwaloona mina almuhajireena waal-ansari waallatheena ittabaAAoohum bi-ihsanin radiya Allahu AAanhum waradoo AAanhu waAAadda lahum jannatin tajree tahtaha al-anharu khalideena feeha abadan thalika alfawzu alAAatheemu

Tafsir Ibn Kathir

Virtues of the Muhajirin, Ansar and Those Who followed Them in Faith

Allah mentions that He is pleased foremost with the Muhajirin, Ansar and those who followed them in faith, and that they are well-pleased with Him, for He has prepared for them the gardens of delight and eternal joy. Ash-Sha`bi said that,

(The foremost Muhajirin and Ansar) are those who conducted the pledge of Ar-Ridwan in the year of Hudaybiyyah. Abu Musa Al-Ash`ari, Sa`id bin Al-Musayyib, Muhammad bin Sirin, Al-Hasan and Qatadah said that they are those who performed the prayer towards the two Qiblahs with the Messenger of Allah (first toward Jerusalem and later toward the Ka`bah). Allah, the Most Great, stated that He is pleased foremost with the Muhajirin, the Ansar and those who followed their lead with excellence. Therefore, woe to those who dislike or curse them, or dislike or curse any of them, especially their master after the Messenger, the best and most righteous among them, the Siddiq (the great truthful one) and the grand Khalifah, Abu Bakr bin Abi Quhafah, may Allah be pleased with him. The failure group, the Rafidah (a sect of Shiites), are the enemies of the best Companions, they hate and curse them, we seek refuge with Allah from such evil. This indicates that the minds of these people are twisted and their hearts turned upside down, for where are they in relation to believing in the Qur'an They curse those whom Allah stated He is pleased with! As for the followers of the Sunnah, they are pleased with those whom Allah is pleased with, curse whomever Allah and His Messenger curse, and give their loyalty to Allah's friends and show enmity to the enemies of Allah. They are followers not innovators, imitating (the Sunnah) they do not initiate it on their own. They are indeed the party of Allah, the successful, and Allah's faithful servants.

Surah: 9 Ayah: 101

﴿ وَمِمَّنْ حَوْلَكُم مِّنَ ٱلْأَعْرَابِ مُنَٰفِقُونَ ۖ وَمِنْ أَهْلِ ٱلْمَدِينَةِ ۖ مَرَدُواْ عَلَى ٱلنِّفَاقِ لَا تَعْلَمُهُمْ ۖ نَحْنُ نَعْلَمُهُمْ ۚ سَنُعَذِّبُهُم مَّرَّتَيْنِ ثُمَّ يُرَدُّونَ إِلَىٰ عَذَابٍ عَظِيمٍ

101. And among the bedouins round about you, some are hypocrites, and so are some among the people of Al-Madinah, who persist in hypocrisy; you (O Muhammad (peace be upon him)) know them not, We know them. We shall punish them twice, and thereafter they shall be brought back to a great (horrible) torment.

Transliteration

101. Wamimman hawlakum mina al-aAArabi munafiqoona wamin ahli almadeenati maradoo AAala alnnifaqi la taAAlamuhum nahnu naAAlamuhum sanuAAaththibuhum marratayni thumma yuraddoona ila AAathabin AAatheemin

Tafsir Ibn Kathir

Hypocrites among the Bedouins and Residents of Al-Madinah

Allah informs His Messenger, peace be upon him, that among the bedouins around Al-Madinah there are hypocrites and in Al-Madinah itself, those,

(who persist in hypocrisy;) meaning they insisted on hypocrisy and continued in it Allah's statement,

(you know them not, We know them), does not contradict His other statement,

(Had We willed, We could have shown them to you, and you should have known them by their marks; but surely, you will know them by the tone of their speech!)(47:30), because the latter Ayah describes them by their characteristics, not that the Messenger knows all those who have doubts and hypocrisy. The Messenger knew that some of those who associated with him from the people of Al-Madinah were hypocrites, and he used to see them day and night (but did not know who they were exactly). We mentioned before in the explanation of,

(...and they resolved that (plot) which they were unable to carry out...)(9:74) that the Prophet informed Hudhayfah of the names of fourteen or fifteen hypocrites. This knowledge is specific in this case, not that the Messenger of Allah was informed of all their names, and Allah knows best. `Abdur-Razzaq narrated that Ma`mar said that Qatadah commented on this Ayah (9:101), "What is the matter with some people who claim to have knowledge about other people, saying, `So-and-so is in Paradise and so-and-so is in the Fire.' If you ask any of these people about himself, he would say, `I do not know (if I will end up in Paradise or the Fire)!' Verily, you have more knowledge of yourself than other people. You have assumed a job that even the Prophets before you refrained from assuming. Allah's Prophet Nuh said,

(And what knowledge have I of what they used to do)(26:112) Allah's Prophet Shu`ayb said,

(That which is left by Allah for you (after giving the rights of the people) is better for you, if you are believers. And I am not a guardian over you)(11:86), while Allah said to His Prophet,

(you know them not, We know them.)" Mujahid said about Allah's statement,

(We shall punish them twice), "By killing and capture." In another narration he said, "By hunger and torment in the grave,

(and thereafter they shall be brought back to a great (horrible) torment.)" `Abdur-Rahman bin Zayd bin Aslam said, "The torment in this life strikes their wealth and offspring," and he recited this Ayah,

(So let not their wealth nor their children amaze you; Allah only wants to punish them with these things in the life of this world.) (9:55) These afflictions torment them, but will bring reward for the believers. As for the torment in the Hereafter, it is in the Fire,

(and thereafter they shall be brought back to a great (horrible) torment.)

Surah: 9 Ayah: 102

﴿ وَءَاخَرُونَ ٱعْتَرَفُواْ بِذُنُوبِهِمْ خَلَطُواْ عَمَلًا صَـٰلِحًا وَءَاخَرَ سَيِّئًا عَسَى ٱللَّهُ أَن يَتُوبَ عَلَيْهِمْ إِنَّ ٱللَّهَ غَفُورٌ رَّحِيمٌ ﴾

102. And (there are) others who have acknowledged their sins, they have mixed a deed that was righteous with another that was evil. Perhaps Allâh will turn unto them in forgiveness. Surely, Allâh is Oft-Forgiving, Most Merciful.

Transliteration

102. Waakharoona iAAtarafoo bithunoobihim khalatoo AAamalan salihan waakhara sayyi-an AAasa Allahu an yatooba AAalayhim inna Allaha ghafoorun raheemun

Tafsir Ibn Kathir

Some Believers stayed away from Battle because They were Lazy

After Allah explained the characteristics of the hypocrites who stayed away from battle because they sought to avoid it out of denial and doubt, He then mentioned the disobedient who stayed away from Jihad due to laziness and preferring comfort, even though they truely believed,

(And others who have acknowledged their sins,) These people admitted their error to themselves and their Lord. They had performed good deeds before, as well as, this evil deed that they committed. For them there was forgiveness and pardon of Allah. This Ayah is general, covering all sinners who combine good and evil deeds, thus becoming partly impure, even though it was revealed about some people in specific. Ibn `Abbas said that,

(And (there are) others), refers to Abu Lubabah and some of his friends who stayed away from the battle of Tabuk and the Messenger of Allah . When the Messenger of Allah returned from that battle, this group, Abu Lubabah and five, seven or nine with him, tied themselves to the pillars of the Masjid and refused to let anyone untie them except the Messenger of Allah . When this Ayah was revealed,

(And (there are) others who have acknowledged their sins,) the Messenger of Allah untied them and pardoned them. " Al-Bukhari recorded that Samurah bin Jundub said that the Messenger of Allah said to us,

«أَتَانِي اللَّيْلَةَ آتِيَانِ فَابْتَعَثَانِي، فَانْتَهَيَا بِي إِلَى مَدِينَةٍ مَبْنِيَّةٍ بِلَبِنِ ذَهَبٍ وَلَبِنِ فِضَّةٍ فَتَلَقَّانَا رِجَالٌ شَطْرٌ مِنْ خَلْقِهِمْ كَأَحْسَنِ مَا أَنْتَ رَاءٍ، وَشَطْرٌ كَأَقْبَحِ مَا أَنْتَ رَاءٍ، قَالَا لَهُمْ: اذْهَبُوا فَقَعُوا فِي ذَلِكَ النَّهْرِ فَوَقَعُوا فِيهِ ثُمَّ رَجَعُوا إِلَيْنَا قَدْ ذَهَبَ ذَلِكَ السُّوءُ عَنْهُمْ فَصَارُوا فِي أَحْسَنِ صُورَةٍ، قَالَا لِي: هَذِهِ جَنَّةُ عَدْنٍ وَهَذَا مَنْزِلُكَ، قَالَا: وَأَمَّا الْقَوْمُ الَّذِينَ كَانُوا شَطْرٌ مِنْهُمْ حَسَنٌ وَشَطْرٌ مِنْهُمْ قَبِيحٌ، فَإِنَّهُمْ خَلَطُوا عَمَلًا صَالِحًا وَآخَرَ سَيِّئًا تَجَاوَزَ اللهُ عَنْهُمْ»

(Last Night, two (angels) came to me (in a vision) and took me to a city, built with bricks made of gold and silver. We met some men who, part of their bodies were as handsome as you ever saw and the part as ugly as you ever saw. The two (angels) ordered these men to go to a river and submerge themselves in it; they did that and came back to us, and the ugliness went away from them, thus becoming the most beautiful form. The two said to me, `This is the garden of Eden, and this is your residence in it.' The two said, `As for the men who had part of their body handsome and part ugly, they have mixed a deed that was righteous with another that was evil. Allah has pardoned them.') Al-Bukhari recorded this Hadith in a short form upon the explanation of this Ayah.

Surah: 9 Ayah: 103 & 104

﴿ خُذْ مِنْ أَمْوَٰلِهِمْ صَدَقَةً تُطَهِّرُهُمْ وَتُزَكِّيهِم بِهَا وَصَلِّ عَلَيْهِمْ إِنَّ صَلَوٰتَكَ سَكَنٌ لَّهُمْ وَٱللَّهُ سَمِيعٌ عَلِيمٌ ﴾

103. Take Sadaqah (alms) from their wealth in order to purify them and sanctify them with it, and invoke Allâh for them. Verily! Your invocations are a source of security for them; and Allâh is All-Hearer, All-Knower.

﴿ أَلَمْ يَعْلَمُوٓا۟ أَنَّ ٱللَّهَ هُوَ يَقْبَلُ ٱلتَّوْبَةَ عَنْ عِبَادِهِۦ وَيَأْخُذُ ٱلصَّدَقَٰتِ وَأَنَّ ٱللَّهَ هُوَ ٱلتَّوَّابُ ٱلرَّحِيمُ ﴾

104. Know they not that Allâh accepts repentance from His slaves and takes the Sadaqât (alms, charity) and that Allah Alone is the One Who forgives and accepts repentance, Most Merciful?

Transliteration

103. Khuth min amwalihim sadaqatan tutahhiruhum watuzakkeehim biha wasalli AAalayhim inna salataka sakanun lahum waAllahu sameeAAun AAaleemun

104. Alam yaAAlamoo anna Allaha huwa yaqbalu alttawbata AAan AAibadihi waya/khuthu alssadaqati waanna Allaha huwa alttawwabu alrraheemu

Tafsir Ibn Kathir

The Command to collect the Zakah and Its Benefits

Allah commanded His Messenger to take Sadaqah from the Muslims' money to purify and sanctify them with it. This Ayah is general, even though some said that it refers specifically to those who mixed good and evil deeds, who admitted to their errors. Some bedouin later thought that paying Zakah to the Leader was not legislated except to the Messenger himself, using this Ayah as evidence,

(Take Sadaqah from their wealth.) Abu Bakr As-Siddiq and other Companions refuted this ill comprehension and fought against them until they paid the Zakah to the Khalifah, just as they used to pay it to the Messenger of Allah . As-Siddiq said, "By Allah! If they abstain from paying a bridle that they used to pay to the Messenger of Allah , I will fight them for refraining from paying it." Allah's statement,

(and Salli for them), means, supplicate for them, and ask Allah to forgive them. In the Sahih, Muslim recorded that `Abdullah bin Abi Awfa said, "Whenever the Prophet was brought charity, he used to invoke Allah for those who brought it. My father also brought his charity and the Prophet said,

«اللَّهُمَّ صَلِّ عَلَى آلِ أَبِي أَوْفَى»

(O Allah! I invoke You for the family of Abu Awfa.)" Allah's statement,

(Verily, your Salat are a Sakan for them), means, a mercy for them, according to Ibn `Abbas. Allah said next,

(and Allah is All-Hearer,) of your invocation (O Muhammad),

(All-Knower.) in those who deserve your invocation on their behalf, who are worthy of it. Allah said,

(Know they not that Allah accepts repentance from His servants and accepts the Sadaqat) This Ayah encourages reverting to repentance and giving charity, for each of these actions erases, deletes and eradicate sins. Allah states that He accepts the repentance of those who repent to Him, as well as charity from pure resources, for Allah accepts it with His Right Hand and raises it for its giver until even a date becomes as large as Mount Uhud. Abu Hurayrah narrated that the Messenger of Allah said,

> «إِنَّ اللهَ يَقْبَلُ الصَّدَقَةَ وَيَأْخُذُهَا بِيَمِينِهِ فَيُرَبِّيهَا لِأَحَدِكُمْ كَمَا يُرَبِّي أَحَدُكُمْ مُهْرَهُ، حَتَّى إِنَّ اللُّقْمَةَ لَتَكُونُ مِثْلَ أُحُدٍ»

(Verily, Allah accepts charity, receives it in His Right Hand and develops it for its giver, just as one of you raises his pony, until the bite (of food) becomes as large as Uhud.) The Book of Allah, the Exalted and Most Honored, testifies to this Hadith,

(Know they not that Allah accepts repentance from His servants and accepts the Sadaqat), and,

(Allah will destroy Riba and will give increase for Sadaqat.) (2:276) `Abdullah bin Mas`ud said, "Charity falls in Allah's Hand before it falls in the needy's hand," he then recited this Ayah,

(Know they not that Allah accepts repentance from His servants and accepts the Sadaqat).

Surah: 9 Ayah: 105

﴿ وَقُلِ ٱعْمَلُوا۟ فَسَيَرَى ٱللَّهُ عَمَلَكُمْ وَرَسُولُهُۥ وَٱلْمُؤْمِنُونَ ۖ وَسَتُرَدُّونَ إِلَىٰ عَٰلِمِ ٱلْغَيْبِ وَٱلشَّهَٰدَةِ فَيُنَبِّئُكُم بِمَا كُنتُمْ تَعْمَلُونَ ﴾

105. And say (O Muhammad (peace be upon him)) "Do deeds! Allâh will see your deeds, and (so will) His Messenger and the believers. And you will be brought back to the All-Knower of the unseen and the seen. Then He will inform you of what you used to do."

Transliteration

105. Waquli iAAmaloo fasayara Allahu AAamalakum warasooluhu waalmu/minoona wasaturaddoona ila AAalimi alghaybi waalshshahadati fayunabbi-okum bima kuntum taAAmaloona

Tafsir Ibn Kathir

Warning the Disobedient

Mujahid said that this Ayah carries a warning from Allah to those who defy His orders. Their deeds will be shown to Allah, Blessed and Most Honored, and to the Messenger and the believers. This will certainly occur on the Day of Resurrection, just as Allah said,

(That Day shall you be brought to Judgement, not a secret of you will be hidden.) (69:18),

(The Day when all the secrets will be examined.)(86:9), and,

(And that which is in the breasts (of men) shall be made known.)(100:10) Allah might also expose some deeds to the people in this life. Al-Bukhari said that `Aishah said, "If the good deeds of a Muslim person please you, then say,

(Do deeds! Allah will see your deeds, and (so will) His Messenger and the believers.)" There is a Hadith that carries a similar meaning. Imam Ahmad recorded that Anas said that the Messenger of Allah said,

«لَا عَلَيْكُمْ أَنْ تُعْجَبُوا بِأَحَدٍ حَتَّى تَنْظُرُوا بِمَ يُخْتَمُ لَهُ، فَإِنَّ الْعَامِلَ يَعْمَلُ زَمَانًا مِنْ عُمْرِهِ أَوْ بَرْهَةً مِنْ دَهْرِهِ . بِعَمَلٍ صَالِحٍ لَوْ مَاتَ عَلَيْهِ دَخَلَ الْجَنَّةَ ثُمَّ يَتَحَوَّلُ فَيَعْمَلُ عَمَلًا سَيِّئًا، وَإِنَّ الْعَبْدَ لَيَعْمَلُ الْبُرْهَةَ مِنْ دَهْرِهِ بِعَمَلٍ سَيِّءٍ، لَوْ مَاتَ عَلَيْهِ دَخَلَ النَّارَ ثُمَّ يَتَحَوَّلُ فَيَعْمَلُ عَمَلًا صَالِحًا، وَإِذَا أَرَادَ اللهُ بِعَبْدِهِ خَيْرًا اسْتَعْمَلَهُ قَبْلَ مَوْتِهِ»

(Do not be pleased with someone's deeds until you see what his deeds in the end will be like. Verily, one might work for some time of his life with good deeds, so that if he dies while doing it, he will enter Paradise. However, he changes and commits evil deeds. one might commit evil deeds for some time in his life, so that if he dies while doing them he will enter the Fire. However, he changes and performs good deeds. If Allah wants the good of a servant He employs him before he dies.) He was asked, "How would Allah employ him, O Allah's Messenger" He said,

«يُوَفِّقُهُ لِعَمَلٍ صَالِحٍ ثُمَّ يَقْبِضُهُ عَلَيْهِ»

(He directs him to perform good deeds and takes his life in that condition.) Only Imam Ahmad collected this Hadith.

Surah: 9 Ayah: 106

﴿وَءَاخَرُونَ مُرْجَوْنَ لِأَمْرِ ٱللَّهِ إِمَّا يُعَذِّبُهُمْ وَإِمَّا يَتُوبُ عَلَيْهِمْ وَٱللَّهُ عَلِيمٌ حَكِيمٌ﴾

106. And others are made to await Allâh's Decree, whether He will punish them or will forgive them. And Allâh is All-Knowing, All-Wise.

Transliteration

106. Waakharoona murjawna li-amri Allahi imma yuAAaththibuhum wa-imma yatoobu AAalayhim waAllahu AAaleemun hakeemun

Tafsir Ibn Kathir

Delaying the Decision about the Three Companions Who stayed away from the Battle of Tabuk

Ibn `Abbas, Mujahid, `Ikrimah, Ad-Dahhak and several others said that those mentioned in the Ayah are the three who were made to wait to know if their repentance was accepted; Mararah bin Ar-Rabi`, Ka`b bin Malik and Hilal bin Umayyah. Some Companions stayed behind from the battle of Tabuk due to laziness, preferring comfort, ease, ripe fruits and shade. They did not lag behind because of hypocrisy or doubts. Some of them tied themselves to the pillars (of the Masjid) like Abu Lubabah and several of his friends did. Some of them did not do that, and they are the three mentioned here. Those who tied themselves received their pardon before these three men whose pardon was delayed, until this Ayah was revealed,

(Allah has forgiven the Prophet, the Muhajirin and the Ansar...)

(And the three who stayed behind, until for them the earth, vast as it is, was straitened...) We will mention the Hadith about this story from Ka`b bin Malik. Allah said,

(whether He will punish them or will forgive them.) meaning, they are at Allah's mercy, if He wills, He pardons them or punishes them. However, Allah's mercy comes before His anger,

(And Allah is All-Knowing, All-Wise.) (9:106) Allah knows those who deserve the punishment and those who deserve the pardon. He is All-Wise in His actions and statements, there is no deity worthy of worship nor Lord besides Him.

Surah: 9 Ayah: 107 & Ayah: 108

﴿ وَٱلَّذِينَ ٱتَّخَذُواْ مَسْجِدًا ضِرَارًا وَكُفْرًا وَتَفْرِيقًۢا بَيْنَ ٱلْمُؤْمِنِينَ وَإِرْصَادًا لِّمَنْ حَارَبَ ٱللَّهَ وَرَسُولَهُۥ مِن قَبْلُ ۚ وَلَيَحْلِفُنَّ إِنْ أَرَدْنَآ إِلَّا ٱلْحُسْنَىٰ ۖ وَٱللَّهُ يَشْهَدُ إِنَّهُمْ لَكَٰذِبُونَ ﴾

107. And as for those who put up a mosque by way of harm and disbelief and to disunite the believers, and as an outpost for those who warred against Allâh and His Messenger (Muhammad (peace be upon him)) aforetime, they will indeed swear that their intention is nothing but good. Allâh bears witness that they are certainly liars.

﴿ لَا تَقُمْ فِيهِ أَبَدًا ۚ لَّمَسْجِدٌ أُسِّسَ عَلَى ٱلتَّقْوَىٰ مِنْ أَوَّلِ يَوْمٍ أَحَقُّ أَن تَقُومَ فِيهِ ۚ فِيهِ رِجَالٌ يُحِبُّونَ أَن يَتَطَهَّرُواْ ۚ وَٱللَّهُ يُحِبُّ ٱلْمُطَّهِّرِينَ ﴾

108. Never stand you therein. Verily, the mosque whose foundation was laid from the first day on piety is more worthy that you stand therein (to pray). In it are men

who love to clean and to purify themselves. And Allâh loves those who make themselves clean and pure (i.e. who clean their private parts with dust (which has the properties of soap) and water from urine and stools, after answering the call of nature).

Transliteration

107. Waallatheena ittakhathoo masjidan diraran wakufran watafreeqan bayna almu/mineena wa-irsadan liman haraba Allaha warasoolahu min qablu walayahlifunna in aradna illa alhusna waAllahu yashhadu innahum lakathiboona   108. La taqum feehi abadan lamasjidun ossisa AAala alttaqwa min awwali yawmin ahaqqu an taqooma feehi feehi rijalun yuhibboona an yatatahharoo waAllahu yuhibbu almuttahhireena

Tafsir Ibn Kathir

Masjid Ad-Dirar and Masjid At-Taqwa

The reason behind revealing these honorable Ayat is that before the Messenger of Allah migrated to Al-Madinah, there was a man from Al-Khazraj called "Abu `Amir Ar-Rahib (the Monk)." This man embraced Christianity before Islam and read the Scriptures. During the time of Jahiliyyah, Abu `Amir was known for being a worshipper and being a notable person among Al-Khazraj. When the Messenger of Allah arrived at Al-Madinah after the Hijrah, the Muslims gathered around him and the word of Islam was triumphant on the day of Badr, causing Abu `Amir, the cursed one, to choke on his own saliva and announce his enmity to Islam. He fled from Al-Madinah to the idolators of Quraysh in Makkah to support them in the war against the Messenger of Allah . The Quraysh united their forces and the bedouins who joined them for the battle of Uhud, during which Allah tested the Muslims, but the good end is always for the pious and righteous people. The rebellious Abu `Amir dug many holes in the ground between the two camps, into one of which the Messenger fell, injuring his face and breaking one of his right lower teeth. He also sustained a head injury. Before the fighting started, Abu `Amir approached his people among the Ansar and tried to convince them to support and agree with him. When they recognized him, they said, "May Allah never burden an eye by seeing you, O Fasiq one, O enemy of Allah!" They cursed him and he went back declaring, "By Allah! Evil has touched my people after I left." The Messenger of Allah called Abu `Amir to Allah and recited the Qur'an to him before his flight to Makkah, but he refused to embrace Islam and rebelled. The Messenger invoked Allah that Abu `Amir die as an outcast in an alien land, and his invocation came true. After the battle of Uhud was finished, Abu `Amir realized that the Messenger's call was still rising and gaining momentum, so he went to Heraclius, the emperor of Rome, asking for his aid against the Prophet . Heraclius gave him promises and Abu `Amir remained with him. He also wrote to several of his people in Al-Madinah, who embraced hypocrisy, promising and insinuating to them that he will lead an army to fight the Messenger of Allah to defeat him and his call. He ordered them to establish a stronghold where he could send his emissaries and to serve as an outpost when he joins them later on. These hypocrites built a Masjid next to the Masjid in Quba', and they finished building it before the Messenger went to Tabuk. They went to the Messenger inviting him to pray in their Masjid so that it would be a proof that the Messenger approved of their Masjid. They told him that they built the Masjid for the weak and ill persons on rainy nights. However, Allah prevented His Messenger from praying in that Masjid. He said to them,

$$\text{«إِنَّا عَلَى سَفَرٍ وَلَكِنْ إِذَا رَجَعْنَا إِنْ شَاءَ اللهُ»}$$

(If we come back from our travel, Allah willing.)" When the Messenger of Allah came back from Tabuk and was approximately one or two days away from Al-Madinah, Jibril came down to him with the news about Masjid Ad-Dirar and the disbelief and division between the believers, who were in Masjid Quba' (which was built on piety from the first day), that Masjid Ad-Dirar was meant to achieve. Therefore, the Messenger of Allah sent some people to Masjid Ad-Dirar to bring it down before he reached Al-Madinah. `Ali bin Abi Talhah reported that Ibn `Abbas said about this Ayah (9:107), "They are some people of the Ansar to whom Abu `Amir said, `Build a Masjid and prepare whatever you can of power and weapons, for I am headed towards Caesar, emperor of Rome, to bring Roman soldiers with whom I will expel Muhammad and his companions.' When they built their Masjid, they went to the Prophet and said to him, "We finished building our Masjid and we would like you pray in it and invoke Allah for us for His blessings." Allah revealed this verse,

(Never stand you therein), until,

(...wrongdoers)" Allah said next,

(they will indeed swear), those who built it,

(that their intention is nothing but good.) by building this Masjid we sought the good and the comfort of the people. Allah replied,

(Allah bears witness that they are certainly liars) for they only built it to harm Masjid Quba', and out of disbelief in Allah, and to divide the believers. They made it an outpost for those who warred against Allah and His Messenger, such as Abu `Amir the Fasiq who used to be called Ar-Rahib, may Allah curse him! Allah said,

(Never stand you therein), prohibiting His Prophet and his Ummah from ever standing in it in prayer.

Virtues of Masjid Quba

Allah encouraged His Prophet to pray in Masjid Quba' which, from the first day, was built on Taqwa, obedience to Allah and His Messenger, for gathering the word of the believers and as an outpost and a fort for Islam and its people. This is why Allah the Exalted said,

(Verily, the Masjid whose foundation was laid from the first day on Taqwa is more worthy that you stand therein (to pray).) in reference to the Masjid of Quba'. An authentic Hadith records that the Messenger of Allah said,

«صَلَاةٌ فِي مَسْجِدِ قُبَاءٍ كَعُمْرَةٍ»

(One prayer in Masjid Quba' is just like an `Umrah.) It is recorded in the Sahih that the Messenger of Allah used to visit Masjid Quba' while riding and walking. Imam Ahmad recorded that `Uwaym bin Sa`idah Al-Ansari said that the Prophet went to Masjid Quba' and asked,

«إِنَّ اللهَ تَعَالَى قَدْ أَحْسَنَ عَلَيْكُمُ الثَّنَاءَ فِي الطُّهُورِ فِي قِصَّةِ مَسْجِدِكُمْ، فَمَا هَذَا الطُّهُورُ الَّذِي تَطَهَّرُونَ بِهِ؟»

(In the story about your Masjid, Allah the Exalted has praised you concerning the purification that you perform. What is the purification that you perform) They said, "By Allah, O Allah's Messenger! We do not know except that we had neighbors from the Jews who used to use water to wash with after answering the call of nature, and we washed as they washed." Ibn Khuzaymah collected this Hadith in his Sahih. Allah's statement,

(Verily, the Masjid whose foundation was laid from the first day on Taqwa is more worthy that you stand therein (to pray). In it are men who love to clean and purify themselves. And Allah loves those who make themselves clean and pure.) This encourages praying in old Masjids that were built for the purpose of worshipping Allah alone, without partners. It is also recommended to join the prayer with the believing group and worshippers who implement their faith, those who perform Wudu' perfectly and preserve themselves from impure things. Imam Ahmad recorded that one of the Companions of the Messenger of Allah said that the Messenger of Allah led them in a Dawn (Subh) prayer in which he recited Surat Ar-Rum (chapter 30) and made mistakes in the recitation. When he finished the prayer, he said,

«إِنَّهُ يَلْبِسُ عَلَيْنَا الْقُرْآنَ أَنَّ أَقْوَامًا مِنْكُمْ يُصَلُّونَ مَعَنَا لَا يُحْسِنُونَ الْوُضُوءَ، فَمَنْ شَهِدَ الصَّلَاةَ مَعَنَا فَلْيُحْسِنِ الْوُضُوءَ»

(We sometimes make mistakes in reciting the Qur'an, there are people among you who attend the prayer with us, but do not perform Wudu' perfectly. Therefore, whoever attends the prayer with us let him make perfect Wudu'.) This Hadith indicates that complete purification helps in the performance of acts of worship and aids in preserving and completing them.

Surah: 9 Ayah: 109 & Ayah: 110

﴿ أَفَمَنْ أَسَّسَ بُنْيَـٰنَهُ عَلَىٰ تَقْوَىٰ مِنَ ٱللَّهِ وَرِضْوَٰنٍ خَيْرٌ أَم مَّنْ أَسَّسَ بُنْيَـٰنَهُ عَلَىٰ شَفَا جُرُفٍ هَارٍ فَٱنْهَارَ بِهِ فِى نَارِ جَهَنَّمَ وَٱللَّهُ لَا يَهْدِى ٱلْقَوْمَ ٱلظَّـٰلِمِينَ ﴿١٠٩﴾ ﴾

109. Is it then he, who laid the foundation of his building on piety to Allâh and His Good Pleasure, better, or he who laid the foundation of his building on an undetermined brink of a precipice ready to crumble down, so that it crumbled to pieces with him into the Fire of Hell. And Allâh guides not the people who are the Zâlimûn (cruel, violent, proud, polytheist and wrong-doer).

﴿ لَا يَزَالُ بُنْيَـٰنُهُمُ ٱلَّذِى بَنَوْاْ رِيبَةً فِى قُلُوبِهِمْ إِلَّا أَن تَقَطَّعَ قُلُوبُهُمْ وَٱللَّهُ عَلِيمٌ حَكِيمٌ ﴿١١٠﴾ ﴾

110. The building which they built will never cease to be a cause of hypocrisy and doubt in their hearts, unless their hearts are cut to pieces. (i.e. till they die). And Allâh is All-Knowing, All-Wise.

Transliteration

109. Afaman assasa bunyanahu AAala taqwa mina Allahi waridwanin khayrun am man assasa bunyanahu AAala shafa jurufin harin fainhara bihi fee nari jahannama waAllahu la yahdee alqawma alththalimeena   110. La yazalu bunyanuhumu allathee banaw reebatan fee quloobihim illa an taqattaAAa quloobuhum waAllahu AAaleemun hakeemun

Tafsir Ibn Kathir

The Difference between Masjid At-Taqwa and Masjid Ad-Dirar

Allah the Exalted says that the Masjid that has been built on the basis of Taqwa of Allah and His pleasure is not the same as a Masjid that was been built based on causing harm, disbelief and causing division among the believers, and as an outpost for those who warred against Allah and His Messenger . The latter built their Masjid on the edge of a steep hole,

(into the fire of Hell. And Allah guides not the people who are the wrongdoers.), Allah does not bring aright the works of those who commit mischief. Jabir bin `Abdullah said, "I saw the Masjid that was built to cause harm with smoke rising up from it, during the time of the Messenger of Allah ." Allah's statement,

(The building which they built will never cease to be a cause of doubt in their hearts) and hypocrisy. Because of this awful action that they committed, they inherited hypocrisy in their hearts, just as those who worshipped the calf were inclined to adoring it. Allah said next, (unless their hearts are cut to pieces.) until they die, according to Ibn `Abbas, Mujahid, Qatadah, Zayd bin Aslam, As-Suddi, Habib bin Abi Thabit, Ad-Dahhak, `Abdur-Rahman bin Zayd bin Aslam and several other scholars of the Salaf.

(And Allah is All-Knowing,) of the actions of His creation,

(All-Wise.) in compensating them for their good or evil actions.

Surah: 9 Ayah: 111

﴿ ۞ إِنَّ ٱللَّهَ ٱشْتَرَىٰ مِنَ ٱلْمُؤْمِنِينَ أَنفُسَهُمْ وَأَمْوَٰلَهُم بِأَنَّ لَهُمُ ٱلْجَنَّةَ ۚ يُقَٰتِلُونَ فِى سَبِيلِ ٱللَّهِ فَيَقْتُلُونَ وَيُقْتَلُونَ ۖ وَعْدًا عَلَيْهِ حَقًّا فِى ٱلتَّوْرَىٰةِ وَٱلْإِنجِيلِ وَٱلْقُرْءَانِ ۚ وَمَنْ أَوْفَىٰ بِعَهْدِهِۦ مِنَ ٱللَّهِ ۚ فَٱسْتَبْشِرُوا۟ بِبَيْعِكُمُ ٱلَّذِى بَايَعْتُم بِهِۦ ۚ وَذَٰلِكَ هُوَ ٱلْفَوْزُ ٱلْعَظِيمُ ﴿١١١﴾ ﴾

111. Verily, Allâh has purchased of the believers their lives and their properties for (the price) that theirs shall be the Paradise. They fight in Allâh's Cause, so they kill (others) and are killed. It is a promise in truth which is binding on Him in the Taurât (Torah) and the Injeel (Gospel) and the Qur'ân. And who is truer to his covenant than Allâh? Then rejoice in the bargain which you have concluded. That is the supreme success.

Transliteration

111. Inna Allaha ishtara mina almu/mineena anfusahum waamwalahum bi-anna lahumu aljannata yuqatiloona fee sabeeli Allahi fayaqtuloona wayuqtaloona waAAdan AAalayhi haqqan fee alttawrati waal-injeeli waalqur-ani waman awfa biAAahdihi mina Allahi faistabshiroo bibayAAikumu allathee bayaAAtum bihi wathalika huwa alfawzu alAAatheemu

Tafsir Ibn Kathir

Allah has purchased the Souls and Wealth of the Mujahidin in Return for Paradise

Allah states that He has compensated His believing servants for their lives and wealth -- if they give them up in His cause -- with Paradise. This demonstrates Allah's favor, generosity and bounty, for He has accepted the good that He already owns and bestowed, as a price from His faithful servants. Al-Hasan Al-Basri and Qatadah commented, "By Allah! Allah has purchased them and raised their worth." Shimr bin `Atiyyah said, "There is not a Muslim but has on his neck a sale that he must conduct with Allah; he either fulfills its terms or dies without doing that." He then recited this Ayah. This is why those who fight in the cause of Allah are said to have conducted the sale with Allah, meaning, accepted and fulfilled his covenant. Allah's statement,

(They fight in Allah's cause, so they kill and are killed.) indicates that whether they were killed or they kill the enemy, or both, then Paradise will be theirs. The Two Sahihs recorded the Hadith,

«وَتَكَفَّلَ اللهُ لِمَنْ خَرَجَ فِي سَبِيلِهِ لَا يُخْرِجُهُ إِلَّا جِهَادٌ فِي سَبِيلِي وَتَصْدِيقٌ بِرُسُلِي بِأَنْ تَوَفَّاهُ أَنْ يُدْخِلَهُ الْجَنَّةَ، أَوْ يَرْجِعَهُ إِلَى مَنْزِلِهِ الَّذِي خَرَجَ مِنْهُ، نَائِلًا مَا نَالَ مِنْ أَجْرٍ أَوْ غَنِيمَة»

(Allah has made a promise to the person who goes out (to fight) in His cause; `And nothing compels him to do so except Jihad in My Cause and belief in My Messengers.' He will either be admitted to Paradise if he dies, or compensated by Allah, either with a reward or booty if He returns him to the home which he departed from.) Allah's statement,

(It is a promise in truth which is binding on Him in the Tawrah and the Injil and the Qur'an.) affirms this promise and informs us that Allah has decreed this for His Most Honorable Self, and revealed it to His Messengers in His Glorious Books, the Tawrah that He sent down to Musa, the Injil that He sent down to `Isa, and the Qur'an that was sent down to Muhammad, may Allah's peace and blessings be on them all. Allah said next,

(And who is truer to his covenant than Allah) affirming that He never breaks a promise. Allah said in similar statements,

(And who is truer in statement than Allah)(4:87), and,

(And whose words can be truer than those of Allah)(4:122). Allah said next,

(Then rejoice in the bargain which you have concluded. That is the supreme success.), meaning, let those who fulfill the terms of this contract and uphold this covenant receive the good news of great success and everlasting delight.

Surah: 9 Ayah: 112

﴿ٱلتَّٰٓئِبُونَ ٱلۡعَٰبِدُونَ ٱلۡحَٰمِدُونَ ٱلسَّٰٓئِحُونَ ٱلرَّٰكِعُونَ ٱلسَّٰجِدُونَ ٱلۡءَامِرُونَ بِٱلۡمَعۡرُوفِ وَٱلنَّاهُونَ عَنِ ٱلۡمُنكَرِ وَٱلۡحَٰفِظُونَ لِحُدُودِ ٱللَّهِۗ وَبَشِّرِ ٱلۡمُؤۡمِنِينَ ﴾

112. (The believers whose lives Allâh has purchased are) those who repent to Allâh (from polytheism and hypocrisy, etc.), who worship Him, who praise Him, who fast (or go out in Allâh's Cause), who bow down (in prayer), who prostrate themselves (in prayer), who enjoin (on people) Al-Ma'rûf (i.e. Islâmic Monotheism and all what Islâm has ordained) and forbid (people) from Al-Munkar

(i.e. disbelief, polytheism of all kinds and all that Islâm has forbidden), and who observe the limits set by Allâh (do all that Allâh has ordained and abstain from all kinds of sins and evil deeds which Allâh has forbidden). And give glad tidings to the believers.

Transliteration

112. Altta-iboona alAAabidoona alhamidoona alssa-ihoona alrrakiAAoona alssajidoona al-amiroona bialmaAAroofi waalnnahoona AAani almunkari waalhafithoona lihudoodi Allahi wabashshiri almu/mineena

Tafsir Ibn Kathir

This is the description of the believers from whom Allah has purchased their souls and wealth, who have these beautiful and honorable qualities,

(who repent) from all sins and shun all evils,

(who worship), their Lord and preserve the acts of worship that include statements and actions. Praising Allah is among the best statements. This is why Allah said next,

(who praise (Him)). Fasting is among the best actions, involving abstaining from the delights of food, drink and sexual intercourse, this is the meaning hereby,

(As-Sa'ihun (who fast)) (9: 112). Allah also described the Prophet's wives that they are,

(Sa'ihat) (66:5), meaning, they fast. As for prostrating and bowing down, they are acts of the prayer,

(who bow down, who prostrate themselves,) These believers also benefit Allah's creation and direct them to His obedience by ordaining righteousness and forbidding evil. They have knowledge about what should be performed and what should be shunned. This includes abiding by Allah's limits in knowledge and action, meaning, what He allowed and what He prohibited. Therefore, they worship the True Lord and advise creation. This is why Allah said next,

(And give glad tidings to the believers.) since faith includes all of this, and the supreme success is for those who have faith.

Surah: 9 Ayah: 113 & Ayah: 114

﴿ مَا كَانَ لِلنَّبِيِّ وَٱلَّذِينَ ءَامَنُوٓاْ أَن يَسْتَغْفِرُواْ لِلْمُشْرِكِينَ وَلَوْ كَانُوٓاْ أُوْلِى قُرْبَىٰ مِنۢ بَعْدِ مَا تَبَيَّنَ لَهُمْ أَنَّهُمْ أَصْحَٰبُ ٱلْجَحِيمِ ۝ ﴾

113. It is not (proper) for the Prophet and those who believe to ask Allâh's Forgiveness for the Mushrikûn (polytheists, idolaters, pagans, disbelievers in the Oneness of Allâh) even though they be of kin, after it has become clear to them that they are the dwellers of the Fire (because they died in a state of disbelief).

$$\textit{﴿ وَمَا كَانَ ٱسْتِغْفَارُ إِبْرَٰهِيمَ لِأَبِيهِ إِلَّا عَن مَّوْعِدَةٍ وَعَدَهَآ إِيَّاهُ فَلَمَّا تَبَيَّنَ لَهُۥٓ أَنَّهُۥ عَدُوٌّ لِّلَّهِ تَبَرَّأَ مِنْهُ إِنَّ إِبْرَٰهِيمَ لَأَوَّٰهٌ حَلِيمٌ ۝ ﴾}$$

114. And Ibrahîm's (Abraham) invoking (of Allâh) for his father's forgiveness was only because of a promise he (Ibrahîm (Abraham)) had made to him (his father). But when it became clear to him (Ibrahîm (Abraham)) that he (his father) is an enemy of Allâh, he dissociated himself from him. Verily Ibrahîm (Abraham) was Awwah (one who invokes Allah with humility, glorifies Him and remembers Him much) and was forbearing. (Tafsir Al-Qurtubî).

Transliteration

113. Ma kana lilnnabiyyi waallatheena amanoo an yastaghfiroo lilmushrikeena walaw kanoo olee qurba min baAAdi ma tabayyana lahum annahum as-habu aljaheemi 114. Wama kana istighfaru ibraheema li-abeehi illa AAan mawAAidatin waAAadaha iyyahu falamma tabayyana lahu annahu AAaduwwun lillahi tabarraa minhu inna ibraheema laawwahun haleemun

Tafsir Ibn Kathir

The Prohibition of supplicating for Polytheists

Imam Ahmad recorded that Ibn Al-Musayyib said that his father Al-Musayyib said, "When Abu Talib was dying, the Prophet went to him and found Abu Jahl and `Abdullah bin Abi Umayyah present. The Prophet said,

«أَيْ عَمِّ، قُلْ لَا إِلَهَ إِلَّا اللهُ كَلِمَةً أُحَاجُّ لَكَ بِهَا عِنْدَ اللهِ عَزَّ وَجَل»

(O uncle! Say, `La ilaha illa-llah,' a word concerning which I will plea for you with Allah, the Exalted and Most Honored.) Abu Jahl and `Abdullah bin Abi Umayyah said, `O Abu Talib! Would you leave the religion of Abdul-Muttalib' Abu Talib said, `Rather, I will remain on the religion of Abdul-Muttalib.' The Prophet said,

«لَأَسْتَغْفِرَنَّ لَكَ مَا لَمْ أُنْهَ عَنْك»

(I will invoke Allah for forgiveness for you, as long as I am not prohibited from doing so.) This verse was revealed,

(It is not (proper) for the Prophet and those who believe to ask Allah's forgiveness for the Mushrikin, even though they be of kin, after it has become clear to them that they are the dwellers of the Fire.) Concerning Abu Talib, this Ayah was revealed,

(Verily, you guide not whom you like, but Allah guides whom He wills) (28:56)." This Hadith is recorded in the Two Sahihs. Ibn Jarir recorded that Sulayman bin Buraydah said that his father said, "When the Prophet came to Makkah, he went to a grave, sat next to it, started talking and then stood up with tears in his eyes. We said, `O Allah's Messenger! We saw what you did.' He said,

$$\text{«إِنِّي اسْتَأْذَنْتُ رَبِّي فِي زِيَارَةِ قَبْرِ أُمِّي فَأَذِنَ لِي، وَاسْتَأْذَنْتُهُ فِي الْاسْتِغْفَارِ لَهَا فَلَمْ يَأْذَنْ لِي»}$$

(I asked my Lord for permission to visit the grave of my mother and He gave me permission. I asked for His permission to invoke Him for forgiveness for her, but He did not give me permission.) We never saw him more tearful than on that day.''' Al-`Awfi narrated from Ibn `Abbas about Allah's statement,

(It is not (proper) for the Prophet and those who believe to ask Allah's forgiveness for the Mushrikin) "The Prophet wanted to invoke Allah for forgiveness for his mother, but Allah did not allow him. The Prophet said,

$$\text{«إِنَّ إِبْرَاهِيمَ خَلِيلَ اللهِ صلى الله عليه وسلّم قَدِ اسْتَغْفَرَ لِأَبِيهِ»}$$

(Ibrahim, Allah's Khalil, invoked Allah for his father.) Allah revealed,

(And Ibrahim's invoking (of Allah) for his father's forgiveness was only because of a promise he (Ibrahim) had made to him (his father)). " `Ali bin Abi Talhah narrated that Ibn `Abbas commented on this Ayah, "They used to invoke Allah for them (pagans) until this Ayah was revealed. They then refrained from invoking Allah to forgive the dead among them, but were not stopped from invoking Allah for the living among them until they die. Allah sent this Ayah,

(And Ibrahim's invoking (of Allah) for his father's forgiveness was only...) (9:114)." Allah said next,

(But when it became clear to him (Ibrahim) that he (his father) is an enemy of Allah, he dissociated himself from him) (9:114). Ibn `Abbas commented, "Ibrahim kept asking Allah to forgive his father until he died, when he realized that he died as an enemy to Allah, he disassociated himself from him." In another narration, he said, "When his father died he realized that he died as an enemy of Allah." Similar was said by Mujahid, Ad-Dahhak, Qatadah and several others. `Ubayd bin `Umayr and Sa`id bin Jubayr said, "Ibrahim will disown his father on the Day of Resurrection, but he will meet his father and see dust and fatigue on his face. He will say, `O Ibrahim! I disobeyed you, but today, I will not disobey you.' Ibrahim will say, `O Lord! You promised me that You will not disgrace me on the Day they are resurrected. What more disgrace than witnessing my father being disgraced' He will be told, `Look behind you,' where he will see a bloody hyena -- for his father will have been transformed into that -- and it will be dragged from its feet and thrown in the Fire.''' Allah's statement,

(Verily, Ibrahim was Awwah and was forbearing.) means, he invoked Allah always, according to `Abdullah bin Mas`ud. Several narrations report this from Ibn Mas`ud. It was also said that, `Awwah', means, `who invokes Allah with humility', `merciful', `who believes with certainty', `who praises (Allah)', and so forth.

Surah: 9 Ayah: 115 & Ayah: 116

﴿ وَمَا كَانَ ٱللَّهُ لِيُضِلَّ قَوْمًۢا بَعْدَ إِذْ هَدَىٰهُمْ حَتَّىٰ يُبَيِّنَ لَهُم مَّا يَتَّقُونَ إِنَّ ٱللَّهَ بِكُلِّ شَىْءٍ عَلِيمٌ ﴾

115. And Allâh will never lead a people astray after He has guided them until He makes clear to them as to what they should avoid. Verily, Allâh is the All-Knower of everything.

﴿ إِنَّ ٱللَّهَ لَهُۥ مُلْكُ ٱلسَّمَٰوَٰتِ وَٱلْأَرْضِ يُحْىِۦ وَيُمِيتُ وَمَا لَكُم مِّن دُونِ ٱللَّهِ مِن وَلِىٍّ وَلَا نَصِيرٍ ﴾

116. Verily, Allâh! Unto Him belongs the dominion of the heavens and the earth, He gives life and He causes death. And besides Allâh you have neither any Walî (protector or guardian) nor any helper.

Transliteration

115. Wama kana Allahu liyudilla qawman baAAda ith hadahum hatta yubayyina lahum ma yattaqoona inna Allaha bikulli shay-in AAaleemun   116. Inna Allaha lahu mulku alssamawati waal-ardi yuhyee wayumeetu wama lakum min dooni Allahi min waliyyin wala naseerin

Tafsir Ibn Kathir

Recompense comes after Proof is established

Allah describes His Honorable Self and just judgment in that He does not lead a people astray but after the Message comes to them, so that the proof is established against them. For instance, Allah said,

(And as for Thamud, We showed and made clear to them the path of truth ...) (41:17). Mujahid commented on Allah's saying;

(And Allah will never lead a people astray after He has guided them) "Allah the Mighty and Sublime is clarifying to the believers about not seeking forgiveness for the idolators in particular, and in general, it is an exhortation to beware of disobeying Him, and encouragement to obey Him. So either do or suffer." Ibn Jarir commented, "Allah says that He would not direct you to misguidance, so that you invoke Him for forgiveness for your dead idolators, after He gave you guidance and directed you to believe in Him and in His Messenger! First, He will inform you of what you should avoid, so that you avoid it. Before He informs you that this action is not allowed, you would not have disobeyed Him and fallen into what He prohibited for you (if you

Chapter 9: At-Tawba (Repentance, Dispensation), Verses 093-129

indulge in this action). Therefore, in this case, He will not allow you to be misguided. Verily, guidance or misguidance occurs after commands and prohibitions are established. As for those who were neither commanded nor prohibited, they can neither be obedient nor disobedient in doing what they were neither ordered nor prohibited from doing." Allah said,

(Indeed to Allah belongs the dominion of the heavens and the earth, He gives life and He causes death. And besides Allah you have neither any protector nor any helper.) Ibn Jarir commented, "This is an encouragement from Allah for His believing servants to fight the idolators and chiefs of disbelief. It is also a command for them to trust in Allah's aid, for He is the Owner of the heavens and earth, and not to fear His enemies. Verily, they have no protector besides Allah, nor a supporter other than Him."

Surah: 9 Ayah: 117

﴿ لَّقَد تَّابَ ٱللَّهُ عَلَى ٱلنَّبِيِّ وَٱلْمُهَٰجِرِينَ وَٱلْأَنصَارِ ٱلَّذِينَ ٱتَّبَعُوهُ فِى سَاعَةِ ٱلْعُسْرَةِ مِنۢ بَعْدِ مَا كَادَ يَزِيغُ قُلُوبُ فَرِيقٍ مِّنْهُمْ ثُمَّ تَابَ عَلَيْهِمْ إِنَّهُۥ بِهِمْ رَءُوفٌ رَّحِيمٌ ﴾ ۝

117. Allâh has forgiven the Prophet (peace be upon him), the Muhajirûn (Muslim emigrants who left their homes and came to Al-Madinah) and the Ansar (Muslims of Al-Madinah) who followed him (Muhammad (peace be upon him)) in the time of distress (Tabûk expedition), after the hearts of a party of them had nearly deviated (from the Right Path), but He accepted their repentance. Certainly, He is unto them full of Kindness, Most Merciful.

Transliteration

117. Laqad taba Allahu AAala alnnabiyyi waalmuhajireena waal-ansari allatheena ittabaAAoohu fee saAAati alAAusrati min baAAdi ma kada yazeeghu quloobu fareeqin minhum thumma taba AAalayhim innahu bihim raoofun raheemun

Tafsir Ibn Kathir

Battle of Tabuk

Mujahid and several others said, "This Ayah was revealed concerning the battle of Tabuk. They left for that battle during a period of distress. It was a year with little rain, intense heat and scarcity of supplies and water." Qatadah said, "They went to Ash-Sham during the year of the battle of Tabuk at a time when the heat was intense. Allah knew how hard things were, and they suffered great hardship. We were told that two men used to divide a date between themselves. Some of them would take turns in sucking on a date and drinking water, then give it to another man to suck on. Allah forgave them and allowed them to come back from that battle." Ibn Jarir reported that `Abdullah bin `Abbas said that `Umar bin Al-Khattab was reminded of the battle of distress (Tabuk) and `Umar said, "We went with the Messenger of Allah in the intense heat for Tabuk. We camped at a place in which we were stricken so hard by thirst that we thought that our necks would be severed. One of us used to go out in search of water and did not return until he feared that his neck would be severed. One would slaughter his camel, squeeze its intestines and drink its content, placing whatever was left on his kidney. Abu Bakr As-Siddiq said, `O Allah's Messenger! Allah, the Exalted and Most Honored, has always accepted your invocation, so invoke Allah for us.' The Prophet said,

«تُحِبُّ ذَلِكَ؟»

(Would you like me to do that) Abu Bakr said, `Yes.' The Prophet raised his hands and did not put them down until rain fell from the sky in abundance. It rained and then stopped raining for a while, then rained again, so they filled their containers. We went out to see where the rain reached and found that it did not rain beyond our camp.'" Ibn Jarir said about Allah's statement,

(Allah has forgiven the Prophet, the Muhajirin and the Ansar who followed him in the time of distress,) meaning "With regards to expenditures, transportation, supplies and water,

(after the hearts of a party of them had nearly deviated,) away from the truth, thus falling prey to doubting the Messenger's religion because of the distress and hardships they suffered during their travel and battle,

(but He accepted their repentance.) He directed them to repent to their Lord and renew their firmness on His religion,

(Certainly, He is unto them full of kindness, Most Merciful.)"

Surah: 9 Ayah: 118 & Ayah: 119

﴿ وَعَلَى ٱلثَّلَٰثَةِ ٱلَّذِينَ خُلِّفُوا۟ حَتَّىٰٓ إِذَا ضَاقَتْ عَلَيْهِمُ ٱلْأَرْضُ بِمَا رَحُبَتْ وَضَاقَتْ عَلَيْهِمْ أَنفُسُهُمْ وَظَنُّوٓا۟ أَن لَّا مَلْجَأَ مِنَ ٱللَّهِ إِلَّآ إِلَيْهِ ثُمَّ تَابَ عَلَيْهِمْ لِيَتُوبُوٓا۟ إِنَّ ٱللَّهَ هُوَ ٱلتَّوَّابُ ٱلرَّحِيمُ ﴿١١٨﴾ ﴾

118. And (He did forgive also) the three (who did not join the Tabûk expedition whose case was deferred (by the Prophet (peace be upon him))) (for Allâh's Decision) till for them the earth, vast as it is, was straitened and their own selves were straitened to them, and they perceived that there is no fleeing from Allâh, and no refuge but with Him. Then, He forgave them (accepted their repentance), that they might beg for His pardon (repent (unto Him)) Verily, Allâh is the One Who forgives and accepts repentance, Most Merciful.

﴿ يَٰٓأَيُّهَا ٱلَّذِينَ ءَامَنُوا۟ ٱتَّقُوا۟ ٱللَّهَ وَكُونُوا۟ مَعَ ٱلصَّٰدِقِينَ ﴿١١٩﴾ ﴾

119. O you who believe! Be afraid of Allâh, and be with those who are true (in words and deeds).

Transliteration

118. WaAAala alththalathati allatheena khullifoo hatta itha daqat AAalayhimu al-ardu bima rahubat wadaqat AAalayhim anfusuhum wathannoo an la maljaa mina Allahi illa ilayhi thumma taba AAalayhim liyatooboo inna Allaha huwa alttawwabu alrraheemu
119. Ya ayyuha allatheena amanoo ittaqoo Allaha wakoonoo maAAa alssadiqeena

Tafsir Ibn Kathir

The Three, Whose Decision was deferred by the Messenger of Allah

Imam Ahmad recorded that `Abdullah bin Ka`b bin Malik, who used to guide Ka`b after he became blind, said that he heard Ka`b bin Malik narrate his story when he did not join the battle of Tabuk with the Messenger of Allah . Ka`b bin Malik said, "I did not remain behind Allah's Messenger in any battle that he fought except the battle of Tabuk. I failed to take part in the battle of Badr, but Allah did not admonish anyone who did not participate in it, for in fact, Allah's Messenger had gone out in search of the caravan of Quraysh, until Allah made the Muslims and their enemies meet without any appointment. I witnessed the night of Al-`Aqabah pledge with Allah's Messenger when we pledged for Islam, and I would not exchange it for the Badr Battle, even though the Badr Battle is more popular among the people than the `Aqabah pledge. As for my news of this battle of Tabuk, I was never stronger or wealthier than I was when I remained behind Allah's Messenger in that battle. By Allah, never had I two she-camels before, but I did at the time of that battle. Whenever Allah's Messenger wanted to go to a battle, he used to hide his intention by referring to different battles, until it was the time of that battle (of Tabuk) which Allah's Messenger fought in intense heat, facing a long journey, the desert, and the great number of enemy soldiers. So the Prophet clearly announced the destination to the Muslims, so that they could prepare for their battle, and he told them about his intent. Allah's Messenger was accompanied by such a large number of Muslims that they could not be listed in a book by name, nor registered." Ka`b added, "Any man who intended not to attend the battle would think that the matter would remain hidden, unless Allah revealed it through divine revelation. Allah's Messenger fought that battle at a time when the fruits had ripened and the shade was pleasant, and I found myself inclined towards that. Allah's Messenger and his Companions prepared for the battle and I started to go out in order to get myself ready along with them, but I returned without doing anything. I would say to myself, `I can do that if I want.' So I kept on delaying it every now and then until the people were prepared, and Allah's Messenger , and the Muslims along with him, departed. But I had not prepared anything for my departure. I said, `I will prepare myself (for departure) one or two days after him, and then join them.' In the morning following their departure, I went out to get myself ready but returned having done nothing. Then again, the next morning, I went out to get ready but returned without doing anything. Such was the case with me until they hurried away and I missed the battle. Even then I intended to depart to catch up to them. I wish I had done so! But such was not the case. So, after the departure of Allah's Messenger , whenever I went out and walked among the people (who remained behind), it grieved me that I could see none around me, but one accused of hypocrisy or one of those weak men whom Allah had excused. Allah's Messenger did not remember me until he reached Tabuk. So while he was sitting among the people in Tabuk, he said,

«مَا فَعَلَ كَعْبُ بْنُ مَالِكٍ؟»

(What did Ka`b bin Malik do) A man from Banu Salimah said, `O Allah's Messenger! He has been stopped by his two Burdah (garments) and looking at his own flanks with pride.' Mu`adh bin Jabal said, `What a bad thing you have said! By Allah! O Allah's Messenger! We know nothing about him but that which is good.' Allah's Messenger kept silent."' Ka`b bin Malik added, "When I heard that Allah's Messenger was on his way back to Al-Madinah, I was overcome by concern and began to think of false excuses. I said to myself, `How can I escape from his anger tomorrow' I started looking for advice from wise members of my family in this matter. When it was said that Allah's Messenger had approached (Al-Madinah) all evil and false excuses abandoned my mind and I knew well that I could never come out of this problem by forging a false statement. Then I decided firmly to speak the truth. Allah's Messenger arrived in the morning, and whenever he returned from a journey, he used to visit the Masjid first, and offer a two Rak`ah prayer, then sit for the people. So when he had done all that (this time), those who failed to join the battle came and started offering (false) excuses and taking oaths before him. They were over eighty men. Allah's Messenger accepted the excuses they expressed outwardly, asked for Allah's forgiveness for them and left the secrets of their hearts for Allah to judge. Then I came to him, and when I greeted him, he smiled a smile of an angry person and then said,

«تَعَالَ»

(Come) So I came walking until I sat before him. He said to me,

«مَا خَلَّفَكَ أَلَمْ تَكُنْ قَدِ اشْتَرَيْتَ ظَهْرًا»

(What stopped you from joining us Had you not purchased an animal for carrying you) I answered, `Yes, O Allah's Messenger! By Allah, if I were sitting before any person from among the people of the world other than you, I would have escaped from his anger with an excuse. By Allah, I have been bestowed with the power of speaking fluently and eloquently, but by Allah, I knew well that if I tell you a lie today to seek your favor, Allah would surely make you angry with me in the near future. But if I tell you the truth, though you will get angry because of it, I hope for Allah's forgiveness. By Allah, I had never been stronger or wealthier than I was when I remained behind you.' Allah's Messenger said,

Chapter 9: At-Tawba (Repentance, Dispensation), Verses 093-129

«أَمَّا هَذَا فَقَدْ صَدَقَ فَقُمْ حَتَّى يَقْضِيَ اللهُ فِيكَ»

(As regards to this man, he has surely told the truth. So get up until Allah decides your case.) I got up, and many men of Banu Salimah followed me and said to me, `By Allah, we never witnessed you commit any sin before this! Surely, you failed to offer an excuse to Allah's Messenger like the others who did not join him. The invocation of Allah's Messenger to Allah to forgive you would have been sufficient for your sin.' By Allah, they continued blaming me so much that I intended to return (to the Prophet) and accuse myself of having told a lie, but I said to them, `Is there anybody else who has met the same end as I have' They replied, `Yes, there are two men who have said the same thing as you have, and to both of them was given the same order as given to you.' I said, `Who are they' They replied, `Murarah bin Ar-Rabi` Al-`Amiri and Hilal bin Umayyah Al-Waqifi.' They mentioned to me two pious men who had attended the battle of Badr and in whom there was an example for me. So I did not change my mind when they mentioned them to me. Allah's Messenger forbade all the Muslims from talking to us, the three aforesaid persons, out of all those who remained behind for that battle. So we kept away from the people and they changed their attitude towards us until the very land (where I lived) appeared strange to me as if I did not know it. We remained in that condition for fifty nights. As for my two companions, they remained in their houses and kept on weeping, but I was the youngest and the firmest of them. So I would go out and attend the prayer along with the Muslims and roam the markets, but none would talk to me. I would come to Allah's Messenger and greet him while he was sitting in his gathering after the prayer, and I would wonder whether he even moved his lips in return of my greeting or not. Then I would offer my prayer near him and look at him carefully.

When I was busy with my prayer, he would turn his face towards me, but when I turned my face to him, he would turn his face away from me. When this harsh attitude and boycott of the people continued for a long time, I walked until I scaled the wall of the garden of Abu Qatadah who was my cousin and the dearest person to me. I offered my greeting to him. By Allah, he did not return my greetings. I said, `O Abu Qatadah! I beseech you by Allah! Do you know that I love Allah and His Messenger' He kept quiet. I asked him again, beseeching him by Allah, but he remained silent. I asked him again in the Name of Allah and he said, `Allah and His Messenger know better.' Thereupon my eyes flowed with tears and I returned and jumped over the wall. tWhile I was walking in the market of Al-Madinah, suddenly I saw that a Nabatean from Ash-Sham came to sell his grains in Al-Madinah, saying, `Who will lead me to Ka`b bin Malik' The people began to point (me) out for him, until he came to me and handed me a letter from the king of Ghassan (who ruled Syria for Caesar), for I knew how to read and write. In that letter, the following was written: `To proceed, I have been informed that your friend (the Prophet) has treated you harshly. Anyhow, Allah does not make you live in a place where you feel inferior and your right is lost. So, join us, and we will console you.' When I read it, I said to myself, `This is also a sort of test.' I took the letter to the oven and made a fire burning it. When forty out of the fifty nights elapsed, behold! There came to me a messenger of Allah's Messenger saying `Allah's Messenger orders you to keep away from your wife.' I said, `Should I divorce her; or else what should I do' He said, `No, only keep aloof from her and do not mingle with her.' The Prophet sent the same message to my two fellows. I said to my wife, `Go to your parents and remain with them until Allah gives His verdict in this matter.'" Ka`b added, "The wife of Hilal bin Umayyah came to Allah's Messenger and said, `O Allah's Messenger! Hilal bin Umayyah is a helpless old man who has no servant to attend on him. Do you dislike that I should serve him' He said,

$$«لَا وَلَكِنْ (لَا يَقْرَبَكَ)»$$

(`No (you can serve him), but he should not come near you (sexually)).' She said, `By Allah! He has no desire for anything. By Allah, he has never ceased weeping since his case began until this day of his.' On that, some of my family members said to me, `Will you also ask Allah's Messenger to permit your wife (to serve you) as he has permitted the wife of Hilal bin Umayyah to serve him' I said, `By Allah, I will not ask permission of Allah's Messenger regarding her, for I do not know what Allah's Messenger would say if I asked him to permit her (to serve me) while I am a young man.' We remained in that state for ten more nights, until the period of fifty nights was completed, starting from the time when Allah's Messenger prohibited the people from talking to us. When I had finished the Fajr prayer on the fiftieth morning on the roof of one of our houses, while sitting in the condition in which Allah described (in the Qur'an): my very soul seemed straitened to me and even the earth seemed narrow to me for all its spaciousness. There I heard the voice of a man who had ascended the mountain of Sal` calling with his loudest voice, `O Ka`b bin Malik! Be happy (by receiving good tidings).' I fell down in prostration before Allah, realizing that relief has come with His forgiveness for us. Allah's Messenger announced the acceptance of our repentance by Allah after Fajr prayer. The people went out to congratulate us. Some bearers of good news went to my two companions, a horseman came to me in haste, while a man from Banu Aslam came running and ascended the mountain and his voice was swifter than the horse. When the man whose voice I had heard, came to me conveying the good news, I took off my garments and dressed him with them; and by Allah, I owned no other than them on that day. Then I borrowed two garments, wore them and went to Allah's Messenger. The people started receiving me in batches, congratulating me on Allah's acceptance of my repentance, saying, `We congratulate you on Allah's acceptance of your repentance.'" Ka`b further said, "When I entered the Masjid, I saw Allah's Messenger sitting in the Masjid with the people around him. Talhah bin `Ubaydullah swiftly came to me, shook my hands and congratulated me. By Allah, none of the Muhajirun got up for me except Talhah; I will never forget Talhah for this." Ka`b added, "When I greeted Allah's Messenger, his face was bright with joy. He said,

$$«أَبْشِرْ بِخَيْرِ يَوْمٍ مَرَّ عَلَيْكَ مُنْذُ وَلَدَتْكَ أُمُّكَ»$$

(`Be happy with the best day you have ever seen since your mother gave birth to you.) I said to the Prophet, `Is this forgiveness from you or from Allah' He said,

Chapter 9: At-Tawba (Repentance, Dispensation), Verses 093-129   43

«لَا بَلْ مِنْ عِنْدِ اللهِ»

(No, it is from Allah). Whenever Allah's Messenger became happy, his face would shine as if it was a piece of the moon, and we all knew that characteristic of him. When I sat before him, I said, `O Allah's Messenger! Because of the acceptance of my repentance I will give up all my wealth as alms for the sake of Allah and His Messenger.' Allah's Messenger said,

«أَمْسِكْ عَلَيْكَ بَعْضَ مَالِكَ فَهْوَ خَيْرٌ لَكَ»

(Keep some of your wealth, as it will be better for you). I said, `So I will keep my share from Khaybar with me.' I added, `O Allah's Messenger! Allah has saved me for telling the truth; so it is part of my repentance not to tell but the truth as long as I am alive.' By Allah, I do not know of any Muslim, whom Allah has helped to tell the truth more than I. Ever since I have mentioned the truth to Allah's Messenger , I have never intended to tell a lie, until today. I hope that Allah will also save me (from telling lies) the rest of my life. So Allah revealed the Ayah,

(Allah has forgiven the Prophet, the Muhajirin and the Ansar who followed him in the time of distress, after the hearts of a party of them had nearly deviated, but He accepted their repentance. Certainly, He is unto them full of kindness, Most Merciful. And the three who stayed behind, until for them the earth, vast as it is, was straitened and their souls were straitened to them, and they perceived that there is no fleeing from Allah, and no refuge but with Him. Then, He forgave them, that they might beg for His pardon. Verily, Allah is the One Who forgives and accepts repentance, Most Merciful. O you who believe! Have Taqwa of Allah, and be with those who are true (in words and deeds).) Ka`b said; "By Allah! Allah has never bestowed upon me, apart from His guiding me to Islam, a greater blessing than the fact that I did not tell a lie to Allah's Messenger which would have caused me to perish, just as those who had told a lie have perished. Allah described those who told lies with the worst descriptions He ever attributed to anyone. Allah said,

(They will swear by Allah to you when you return to them, that you may turn away from them. So turn away from them. Surely, they are Rijs (impure), and Hell is their dwelling place -- a recompense for that which they used to earn. They swear to you that you may be pleased with them, but if you are pleased with them, certainly Allah is not pleased with the people who are rebellious.) Ka`b added, "We, the three persons, differed altogether from those whose excuses Allah's Messenger accepted when they swore to him. He took their pledge and asked Allah to forgive them, but Allah's Messenger left our case pending until Allah gave us His judgement about it. As for that Allah said,

(And (He did forgive also) the three who stayed behind...) What Allah said does not discuss our failure to take part in the battle, but to the deferment of making a decision by the Prophet about our case, in contrast to the case of those who had taken an oath before him, and he excused them by accepting their excuses." This is an authentic Hadith collected in the Two Sahihs (Al-Bukhari and Muslim) and as such, its authenticity is agreed upon. This Hadith contains the explanation of this honorable Ayah in the best, most comprehensive way. Similar explanation was given by several among the Salaf. For instance, Al-A`mash narrated from Abu Sufyan, from Jabir bin `Abdullah about Allah's statement,

(And (He did forgive also) the three who stayed behind...) "They are Ka`b bin Malik, Hilal bin Umayyah and Murarah bin Ar-Rabi`, all of them from the Ansar."

The Order to speak the Truth

Allah sent His relief from the distress and grief that struck these three men, because Muslims ignored them for fifty days and nights, until they themselves, and the earth -- vast as it is -- were straitened for them. As vast as the earth is, its ways and paths were closed for them, and they did not know what action to take. They were patient for Allah's sake and awaited humbly for His decree. They remained firm, until Allah sent His relief to them since they told the Messenger of Allah the truth about why they remained behind, declaring that they did not have an excuse for doing so. They were requited for this period, then Allah forgave them. Therefore, the consequence of being truthful was better for them, for they gained forgiveness. Hence Allah's statement next,

(O you who believe! Have Taqwa of Allah, and be with those who are true.) The Ayah says, adhere to and always say the truth so that you become among its people and be saved from destruction. Allah will make a way for you out of your concerns and a refuge. Imam Ahmad recorded that `Abdullah bin Mas`ud said that the Messenger of Allah said,

«عَلَيْكُمْ بِالصِّدْقِ فَإِنَّ الصِّدْقَ يَهْدِي إِلَى الْبِرِّ، وَإِنَّ الْبِرَّ يَهْدِي إِلَى الْجَنَّةِ، وَلَا يَزَالُ الرَّجُلُ يَصْدُقُ وَيَتَحَرَّى الصِّدْقَ حَتَّى يُكْتَبَ عِنْدَ اللهِ صِدِّيقًا، وَإِيَّاكُمْ وَالْكَذِبَ فَإِنَّ الْكَذِبَ يَهْدِي إِلَى الْفُجُورِ وَإِنَّ الْفُجُورَ يَهْدِي إِلَى النَّارِ، وَلَا يَزَالُ الرَّجُلُ يَكْذِبُ وَيَتَحَرَّى الْكَذِبَ حَتَّى يُكْتَبَ عِنْدَ اللهِ كَذَّابًا»

(Hold on to truth, for being truthful leads to righteousness, and righteousness leads to Paradise. Verily, a man will keep saying the truth and striving for truth, until he is written before Allah as very truthful (Siddiq). Beware of lying, for lying leads to sin, and sin leads to the Fire. Verily, the man will keep lying and striving for falsehood until he is written before Allah as a great liar.) This Hadith is recorded in the Two Sahihs.

Surah: 9 Ayah: 120

$$ \text{﴿ مَا كَانَ لِأَهْلِ ٱلْمَدِينَةِ وَمَنْ حَوْلَهُم مِّنَ ٱلْأَعْرَابِ أَن يَتَخَلَّفُوا۟ عَن رَّسُولِ ٱللَّهِ وَلَا يَرْغَبُوا۟ بِأَنفُسِهِمْ عَن نَّفْسِهِۦ ۚ ذَٰلِكَ بِأَنَّهُمْ لَا يُصِيبُهُمْ ظَمَأٌ وَلَا نَصَبٌ وَلَا مَخْمَصَةٌ فِى سَبِيلِ ٱللَّهِ وَلَا يَطَـُٔونَ مَوْطِئًا يَغِيظُ ٱلْكُفَّارَ وَلَا يَنَالُونَ مِنْ عَدُوٍّ نَّيْلًا إِلَّا كُتِبَ لَهُم بِهِۦ عَمَلٌ صَـٰلِحٌ ۚ إِنَّ ٱللَّهَ لَا يُضِيعُ أَجْرَ ٱلْمُحْسِنِينَ ۝ ﴾} $$

120. It was not becoming of the people of Al-Madinah and the bedouins of the neighborhood to remain behind Allâh's Messenger (Muhammad (peace be upon him) when fighting in Allâh's Cause) and (it was not becoming of them) to prefer their own lives to his life. That is because they suffer neither thirst nor fatigue, nor hunger in the Cause of Allâh, nor they take any step to raise the anger of disbelievers nor inflict any injury upon an enemy but is written to their credit as a deed of righteousness. Surely, Allâh wastes not the reward of the Muhsinûn

Transliteration

120. Ma kana li-ahli almadeenati waman hawlahum mina al-aAArabi an yatakhallafoo AAan rasooli Allahi wala yarghaboo bi-anfusihim AAan nafsihi thalika bi-annahum la yuseebuhum thamaon wala nasabun wala makhmasatun fee sabeeli Allahi wala yataoona mawti-an yagheethu alkuffara wala yanaloona min AAaduwwin naylan illa kutiba lahum bihi AAamalun salihun inna Allaha la yudeeAAu ajra almuhsineena

Tafsir Ibn Kathir

Rewards of Jihad

Allah, the Exalted and Most Honored, criticizes the people of Al-Madinah and the bedouins around it, who did not participate in the battle of Tabuk with the Messenger of Allah . They sought to preserve themselves rather than comfort the Messenger during the hardship that he suffered in that battle. They incurred a loss in their share of the reward, since,

(they suffer neither Zama'), thirst,

(nor Nasab), fatigue,

(nor Makhmasah), hunger,

(nor they take any step to raise the anger of disbelievers), by strategies of war that would terrify their enemy,

(nor inflict), a defeat on the enemy,

(but is written to their credit) as compensation for these steps that are not under their control, but a consequence of performing good deeds that earn them tremendous rewards,

(Surely, Allah wastes not the reward of the doers of good.) Allah said in a similar Ayah,

(Certainly We shall not make the reward of anyone who does his (righteous) deeds in the most perfect manner to be lost)

Surah: 9 Ayah: 121

﴿ وَلَا يُنفِقُونَ نَفَقَةً صَغِيرَةً وَلَا كَبِيرَةً وَلَا يَقْطَعُونَ وَادِيًا إِلَّا كُتِبَ لَهُمْ لِيَجْزِيَهُمُ ٱللَّهُ أَحْسَنَ مَا كَانُوا۟ يَعْمَلُونَ ﴾

121. Nor do they spend anything (in Allâh's Cause) - small or great - nor cross a valley, but is written to their credit, that Allâh may recompense them with the best of what they used to do (i.e. Allâh will reward their good deeds according to the reward of their best deeds which they did in the most perfect manner).

Transliteration

121. Wala yunfiqoona nafaqatan sagheeratan wala kabeeratan wala yaqtaAAoona wadiyan illa kutiba lahum liyajziyahumu Allahu ahsana ma kanoo yaAAmaloona

Tafsir Ibn Kathir

Allah said next,

(Neithr do they spend), in reference to the fighters in Allah's cause,

(any contribution -- small or great --), with regards to its amount,

(nor cross a valley), while marching towards the enemy,

(but is written to their credit), for these actions that they take (and which are under their control),

(that Allah may recompense them with the best of what they used to do.) Certainly, the Leader of the faithful, `Uthman bin `Affan, may Allah be pleased with him, acquired a tremendous share of the virtues mentioned in this honorable Ayah. He spent large amounts and tremendous wealth on this battle (Tabuk). Abdullah, the son of Imam Ahmad recorded that `Abdur-Rahman bin Khabbab As-Sulami said; "The Messenger of Allah gave a speech in which he encouraged spending on the army of distress (for Tabuk). I`Uthman bin `Affan, may Allah be pleased with him said; `I will give one hundred camels with their saddles and supplies.' Then he exhorted them some more. So `Uthman said; `I will give one hundred more camels with their saddles and supplies.' Then he descended one step of the Minbar and exhorted them some more. So `Uthman bin `Affan said; `I will give one hundred more camels with

Chapter 9: At-Tawba (Repentance, Dispensation), Verses 093-129

their saddles and supplies.' Then I saw Allah's Messenger with his hand moving like this - and `Abdus-Samad's (one of the narrators) hand went out like one in amazement - he said,

«مَا عَلَى عُثْمَانَ مَا عَمِلَ بَعْدَ هَذَا»

(It does not matter what `Uthman does after.) It is also recorded in the Musnad that `Abdur-Rahman bin Samurah said, "`Uthman brought a thousand Dinars in his garment so that the Prophet could prepare supplies for the army of distress. `Uthman poured the money on the Prophet's lap, and the Prophet started turning it around with his hand and declaring repeatedly,

«مَا ضَرَّ ابْنَ عَفَّانَ مَا عَمِلَ بَعْدَ الْيَوْمِ»

(The son of `Affan (i.e., `Uthman) will never be harmed by anything he does after today.)" Qatadah commented on Allah's statement,

(nor cross a valley, but is written to their credit), "The farther any people march forth away from their families in the cause of Allah, the nearer they will be to Allah."

Surah: 9 Ayah: 122

﴿ ۞ وَمَا كَانَ ٱلْمُؤْمِنُونَ لِيَنفِرُواْ كَآفَّةً ۚ فَلَوْلَا نَفَرَ مِن كُلِّ فِرْقَةٍ مِّنْهُمْ طَآئِفَةٌ لِّيَتَفَقَّهُواْ فِى ٱلدِّينِ وَلِيُنذِرُواْ قَوْمَهُمْ إِذَا رَجَعُوٓاْ إِلَيْهِمْ لَعَلَّهُمْ يَحْذَرُونَ ۝ ﴾

122. And it is not (proper) for the believers to go out to fight (Jihâd) all together. Of every troop of them, a party only should go forth, that they (who are left behind) may get instructions in (Islâmic) religion, and that they may warn their people when they return to them, so that they may beware (of evil).

Transliteration

122. Wama kana almu/minoona liyanfiroo kaffatan falawla nafara min kulli firqatin minhum ta-ifatun liyatafaqqahoo fee alddeeni waliyunthiroo qawmahum itha rajaAAoo ilayhim laAAallahum yahtharoona

Tafsir Ibn Kathir

Allah the Exalted here explains His order to Muslims to march forth with the Messenger of Allah for the battle of Tabuk.

We should first mention that a group of the Salaf said that marching along with the Messenger, when he went to battle, was at first obliged on all Muslims, because, as they say, Allah said,

(March forth, whether you are light or heavy) (9:41), and,

(It was not becoming of the people of Al-Madinah and the bedouins of the neighborhood...) (9:120). However, they said, Allah abrogated this ruling (9:41 and 9:120) when He revealed this Ayah, (9:122). However, we could say that this Ayah explains Allah's order to participate in battle on all Arab neighborhoods, that at least a group of every tribe should march for Jihad. Those who went with the Messenger would gain instructions and studies in the revelation that came down to him, and warn their people about that battle when they returned to them. This way, the group that went with the Prophet will achieve both goals (Jihad and learning the revelation from the Prophet). After the Prophet , a group of every tribe or neighborhood should seek religious knowledge or perform Jihad, for in this case, Jihad is required from at least a part of each Muslim community. `Ali bin Abi Talhah reported from Ibn `Abbas about the Ayah,

(And it is not (proper) for the believers to go out (to fight - Jihad) all together.) "The believers should not all go to battle and leave the Prophet alone,

(Of every troop of them, a party only should go forth) in the expeditions that the Prophet sent. When these armies returned to the Prophet, who in the meantime received revealed parts of the Qur'an from Allah, the group who remained with the Prophet would have learned that revelation from him. They would say, `Allah has revealed some parts of the Qur'an to your Prophet and we learned it.' So they learned from them what Allah revealed to His Prophet in their absence, while the Prophet sent some other men into military expeditions. Hence Allah's statement,

(that they may get instructions in religion,) so that they learn what Allah has revealed to their Prophet and teach the armies when they return,

(so that they may beware.)" Mujahid said, "This Ayah was revealed about some of the Companions of the Prophet who went to the desert and were helped by its residents, had a good rainy year and called whomever they met to guidance. The people said to them, `We see that you left your companions and came to us.' They felt bad in themselves because of this and they all came back from the desert to the Prophet . Allah said,

(Of every troop of them, a party only should go forth,) those who seek righteousness (such as to spread the call of Islam, while others remain behind),

(that they may get instructions in (Islamic) religion,) and learn what Allah has revealed,

(and that they may warn their people), when those who went forth returned to them,

(so that they may beware (of evil).)" Qatadah said about this Ayah, "It is about when the Messenger of Allah sent an army; Allah commanded them to go into battle, while another group remained with the Messenger of Allah to gain instructions in the religion. Another group returns to its own people to call them (to Allah) and warn them against Allah's punishment of those who were before them." It was also said that this verse,

(And it is not (proper) for the believers to go out all together.) is not about joining Jihad. They say that the Messenger of Allah invoked Allah against Mudar to try them with years of famine, and their lands were struck by famine. The various tribes among them started to come, entire tribes at a time, to Al-Madinah, because of the hardship they faced and they would falsely claim that they are Muslims. This caused hardship for the Companions of the Messenger and Allah revealed to him that they are not believers. The Messenger of Allah sent them back to their tribes and warned their people not to repeat what they did. Hence Allah's statement,

(and that they may warn their people when they return to them,)

Surah: 9 Ayah: 123

﴿ يَٰٓأَيُّهَا ٱلَّذِينَ ءَامَنُوا۟ قَٰتِلُوا۟ ٱلَّذِينَ يَلُونَكُم مِّنَ ٱلْكُفَّارِ وَلْيَجِدُوا۟ فِيكُمْ غِلْظَةً ۚ وَٱعْلَمُوٓا۟ أَنَّ ٱللَّهَ مَعَ ٱلْمُتَّقِينَ ﴾

123. O you who believe! Fight those of the disbelievers who are close to you, and let them find harshness in you; and know that Allâh is with those who are the Al-Muttaqûn (the pious - see V.2:2).

Transliteration

123. Ya ayyuha allatheena amanoo qatiloo allatheena yaloonakum mina alkuffari walyajidoo feekum ghilthatan waiAAlamoo anna Allaha maAAa almuttaqeena

Tafsir Ibn Kathir

The Order for Jihad against the Disbelievers, the Closest, then the Farthest Areas

Allah commands the believers to fight the disbelievers, the closest in area to the Islamic state, then the farthest. This is why the Messenger of Allah started fighting the idolators in the Arabian Peninsula. When he finished with them and Allah gave him control over Makkah, Al-Madinah, At-Ta'if, Yemen, Yamamah, Hajr, Khaybar, Hadramawt and other Arab provinces, and the various Arab tribes entered Islam in large crowds, he then started fighting the People of the Scriptures. He began preparations to fight the Romans who were the closest in area to the Arabian Peninsula, and as such, had the most right to be called to Islam, especially since they were from the People of the Scriptures. The Prophet marched until he reached Tabuk and went back because of the extreme hardship, little rain and little supplies. This battle occurred on the ninth year after his Hijrah. In the tenth year, the Messenger of Allah was busy with the Farewell Hajj. The Messenger died eighty-one days after he returned from that Hajj, Allah chose him for what He had prepared for him (in Paradise). After his death, his executor, friend, and Khalifah, Abu Bakr As-Siddiq, may Allah be pleased with him, became the leader. At that time, the religion came under attack and would have been defeated, if it had not been for the fact that Allah gave the religion firmness through Abu Bakr, who established its basis and made its foundations firm. He brought those who strayed from the religion back to it, and made those who reverted from Islam return. He took the Zakah from the evil people who did not want to pay it, and explained the truth to those who were unaware of it. On behalf of the Prophet , Abu Bakr delivered what he was entrusted with. Then, he started preparing the Islamic armies to fight the Roman cross worshippers, and the Persian fire worshippers. By the blessing of his mission, Allah opened the lands for him and brought down Caesar and Kisra and those who obeyed them among the servants. Abu Bakr spent their treasures in the cause of Allah, just as the Messenger of Allah had foretold would happen. This mission continued after Abu Bakr at the hands of he whom Abu Bakr chose to be his successor, Al-Faruq, the Martyr of the Mihrab, Abu Hafs, `Umar bin Al-Khattab, may Allah be pleased with him. With `Umar, Allah humiliated the disbelievers, suppressed the tyrants and hypocrites, and opened the eastern and western parts of the world. The treasures of various countries were brought to `Umar from near and far provinces, and he divided them according to the legitimate and accepted method. `Umar then died as a martyr after he lived a praise worthy life. Then, the Companions among the Muhajirin and Ansar agreed to chose after `Umar, `Uthman bin `Affan, Leader of the faithful and Martyr of the House, may Allah be pleased with him. During `Uthman's reign, Islam wore its widest garment and Allah's unequivocal proof was established in various parts of the world over the necks of the servants. Islam appeared in the eastern and western parts of the world and Allah's Word was elevated and His religion apparent. The pure religion reached its deepest aims against Allah's enemies, and whenever Muslims overcame an Ummah, they moved to the next one, and then the next one, crushing the tyranical evil doers. They did this in reverence to Allah's statement,

(O you who believe! Fight those of the disbelievers who are close to you,) Allah said next,

(and let them find harshness in you), meaning, let the disbelievers find harshness in you against them in battle. The complete believer is he who is kind to his believing brother, and harsh with his disbelieving enemy. Allah said in other Ayah,

(Allah will bring a people whom He will love and they will love Him; humble towards the believers, stern towards the disbelievers...)(5:54),

(Muhammad is the Messenger of Allah. And those who are with him are severe against the disbelievers, and merciful among themselves.)(48:29), and,

(O Prophet! Strive hard against the disbelievers and the hypocrites, and be harsh against them.)(9:73) Allah said,

(And know that Allah is with those who have Taqwa), meaning, fight the disbelievers and trust in Allah knowing that Allah is with you if you fear and obey Him. This was the case in the first three blessed generations of Islam, the best members of this Ummah. Since they were firm on the religion and reached an unsurpassed level of obedience to Allah, they consistently prevailed over their enemies. During that era, victories were abundant, and enemies were ever more in a state of utter loss and degradation. However, after the turmoil began, desires and divisions became prevalent between various Muslim kings, the enemies were eager to attack the outposts of Islam and marched into its territory without much opposition. Then, the Muslim kings were too busy with their enmity for each other. The disbelievers then marched to the capital cities of the Islamic states, after gaining control over many of its areas, in addition to entire Islamic lands. Verily, ownership of all affairs is with Allah in the beginning and in the end. Whenever a just Muslim king stood up and obeyed Allah's orders, all the while trusting in Allah, Allah helped him regain control over some Muslim lands and took back from the enemy what was compatible to his obedience and support to Allah. We ask Allah to help the Muslims gain control over the forelocks of His disbeliever enemies and to raise high the word of Muslims over all lands. Verily, Allah is Most Generous, Most Giving.

Surah: 9 Ayah: 124 & Ayah: 125

﴿ وَإِذَا مَا أُنزِلَتْ سُورَةٌ فَمِنْهُم مَّن يَقُولُ أَيُّكُمْ زَادَتْهُ هَٰذِهِۦٓ إِيمَٰنًا ۚ فَأَمَّا ٱلَّذِينَ ءَامَنُوا۟ فَزَادَتْهُمْ إِيمَٰنًا وَهُمْ يَسْتَبْشِرُونَ ﴾

124. And whenever there comes down a Sûrah (chapter from the Qur'ân), some of them (hypocrites) say: "Which of you has had his Faith increased by it?" As for those who believe, it has increased their Faith, and they rejoice.

﴿ وَأَمَّا ٱلَّذِينَ فِى قُلُوبِهِم مَّرَضٌ فَزَادَتْهُمْ رِجْسًا إِلَىٰ رِجْسِهِمْ وَمَاتُوا۟ وَهُمْ كَٰفِرُونَ ﴾

125. But as for those in whose hearts is a disease (of doubt, disbelief and hypocrisy), it will add suspicion and doubt to their suspicion, disbelief and doubt; and they die while they are disbelievers.

Transliteration

124. Wa-itha ma onzilat sooratun faminhum man yaqoolu ayyukum zadat-hu hathihi eemanan faamma allatheena amanoo fazadat-hum eemanan wahum yastabshiroona
125. Waamma allatheena fee quloobihim maradun fazadat-hum rijsan ila rijsihim wamatoo wahum kafiroona

Tafsir Ibn Kathir

Faith of the Believers increases, while Hypocrites increase in Doubts and Suspicion

Allah said,

(And whenever there comes down a Surah), then among the hypocrites are,

(some who say: "Which of you has had his faith increased by it") They say to each other, who among you had his faith increased by this Surah (from the Qur'an) Allah the Exalted said,

(As for those who believe, it has increased their faith, and they rejoice.) This Ayah is one of the mightiest evidences that faith increases and decreases, as is the belief of most of the Salaf and later generations of scholars and Imams. Many scholars said that there is a consensus on this ruling. We explained this subject in detail in the beginning of the explanation of Sahih Al-Bukhari, may Allah grant him His mercy. rAllah said next,

(But as for those in whose hearts is a disease, it will add Rijs to their Rijs.) the Surah increases them in doubt, and brings more suspicion on top of the doubts and suspicion that they had before. Allah said in another Ayah,

(And We send down in the Qur'an that which is a healing) (17:82), and,

(Say: "It is for those who believe, a guide and a healing. And as for those who disbelieve, there is heaviness (deafness) in their ears, and it (the Qur'an) is blindness for them. They are those who are called from a place far away (so they neither listen nor understand)".)(41:44) This indicates the misery of the hypocrites and disbelievers, since, what should bring guidance to their hearts is instead a cause of misguidance and destruction for them. Similarly, those who get upset by a type of food, for instance, will be upset and anxious even more if they are fed that food!

Surah: 9 Ayah: 126 & Ayah: 127

﴿ أَوَلَا يَرَوْنَ أَنَّهُمْ يُفْتَنُونَ فِى كُلِّ عَامٍ مَّرَّةً أَوْ مَرَّتَيْنِ ثُمَّ لَا يَتُوبُونَ وَلَا هُمْ يَذَّكَّرُونَ ﴿١٢٦﴾ ﴾

126. See they not that they are tried once or twice every year (with different kinds of calamities, disease, famine)? Yet, they turn not in repentance, nor do they learn a lesson (from it).

﴿ وَإِذَا مَآ أُنزِلَتْ سُورَةٌ نَّظَرَ بَعْضُهُمْ إِلَىٰ بَعْضٍ هَلْ يَرَاكُم مِّنْ أَحَدٍ ثُمَّ انصَرَفُواْ صَرَفَ ٱللَّهُ قُلُوبَهُم بِأَنَّهُمْ قَوْمٌ لَّا يَفْقَهُونَ ﴿١٢٧﴾ ﴾

127. And whenever there comes down a Sûrah (chapter from the Qur'ân), they look at one another (saying): "Does any one see you?" Then they turn away. Allâh has turned their hearts (from the light) because they are a people that understand not.

Transliteration

126. Awa la yarawna annahum yuftanoona fee kulli AAamin marratan aw marratayni thumma la yatooboona wala hum yaththakkaroona 127. Wa-itha ma onzilat sooratun nathara baAAduhum ila baAAdin hal yarakum min ahadin thumma insarafoo sarafa Allahu quloobahum bi-annahum qawmun la yafqahoona

Tafsir Ibn Kathir

Hypocrites suffer Afflictions

Allah says, do not these hypocrites see,

(that they are put in trial), being tested,

(once or twice every year Yet, they turn not in repentance, nor do they learn a lesson.) They neither repent from their previous sins nor learn a lesson for the future. Mujahid said that hypocrites are tested with drought and hunger. Allah said;

(And whenever there comes down a Surah, they look at one another (saying): "Does any one see you" Then they turn away. Allah has turned their hearts because they are a people that understand not.) This describes the hypocrites that when a Surah is revealed to the Messenger of Allah ,

(they look at one another), they turn their heads, right and left, saying,

("Does any one see you" Then they turn away. ..) turning away from, and shunning the truth. This is the description of hypocrites in this life, for they do not remain where the truth is being declared, neither accepting nor understanding it, just as Allah said in other Ayat,

(Then what is wrong with them that they turn away from admonition As if they were wild donkeys. Fleeing from a lion.)(74:49-51), and,

(So what is the matter with those who disbelieve that they hasten to hear from you. (Sitting) in groups on the right and on the left.)(70:36-37). This Ayah also means, what is the matter with these people who turn away from you to the right and to the left, to escape from truth and revert to falsehood Allah's statement,

(Then they turn away. Allah has turned their hearts (from Truth)) is similar to,

(So when they turned away, Allah turned their hearts away.) (61:5). Allah said next,

(because they are a people that understand not.) They neither understand Allah's Word nor attempt to comprehend it nor want it. Rather, they are too busy, turning away from it. This is why they ended up in this condition.

Surah: 9 Ayah: 128 & Ayah: 129

﴿ لَقَدْ جَاءَكُمْ رَسُولٌ مِّنْ أَنفُسِكُمْ عَزِيزٌ عَلَيْهِ مَا عَنِتُّمْ حَرِيصٌ عَلَيْكُم بِالْمُؤْمِنِينَ رَءُوفٌ رَّحِيمٌ ۝ ﴾

128. Verily, there has come unto you a Messenger (Muhammad (peace be upon him)) from amongst yourselves (i.e. whom you know well). It grieves him that you should receive any injury or difficulty. He (Muhammad (peace be upon him)) is anxious over you (to be rightly guided, to repent to Allâh, and beg Him to pardon and forgive your sins, in order that you may enter Paradise and be saved from the punishment of the Hell-fire); for the believers (he peace be upon him is) full of pity, kind, and merciful.

$$\left\{ \text{فَإِن تَوَلَّوْا۟ فَقُلْ حَسْبِىَ ٱللَّهُ لَآ إِلَـٰهَ إِلَّا هُوَ ۖ عَلَيْهِ تَوَكَّلْتُ ۖ وَهُوَ رَبُّ ٱلْعَرْشِ ٱلْعَظِيمِ } \right\}$$

129. But if they turn away, say (O Muhammad (peace be upon him)) "Allâh is sufficient for me. Lâ ilâha illa Huwa (none has the right to be worshipped but He) in Him I put my trust and He is the Lord of the Mighty Throne."

Transliteration

128. Laqad jaakum rasoolun min anfusikum AAazeezun AAalayhi ma AAanittum hareesun AAalaykum bialmu/mineena raoofun raheemun   129. Fa-in tawallaw faqul hasbiya Allahu la ilaha illa huwa AAalayhi tawakkaltu wahuwa rabbu alAAarshi alAAatheemi

Tafsir Ibn Kathir

$$\text{«بُعِثْتُ بِالْحَنِيفِيَّةِ السَّمْحَةِ»}$$

(I was sent with the easy Hanifiyah (monotheism) way.) An authenic Hadith mentions,

$$\text{«إِنَّ هَذَا الدِّينَ يُسْرٌ»}$$

(Verily, this religion is easy) and its Law is all easy, lenient and perfect. It is easy for those whom Allah the Exalted makes it easy.) (He is eager for you), that you gain guidance and acquire benefits in this life and the Hereafter. Imam Ahmad recorded that `Abdullah bin Mas`ud said that the Messenger of Allah said,

$$\text{«إِنَّ اللهَ لَمْ يُحَرِّمْ حُرْمَةً إِلَّا وَقَدْ عَلِمَ أَنَّهُ سَيَطَّلِعُهَا مِنْكُمْ مُطَّلِعٌ، أَلَا وَإِنِّي آخِذٌ بِحُجَزِكُمْ أَنْ تَهَافَتُوا فِي النَّارِ كَتَهَافُتِ الْفَرَاشِ أَوِ الذُّبَابِ»}$$

(Verily, every matter that Allah has prohibited, He knows that some among you will breach it; but I am indeed holding you by the waist so that you do not fall in the Fire, just like butterflies and flies.) Allah's statement next, (for the believers (he is) full of pity, kind, and merciful.) (9:128), is similar to His other statement,

(And be kind and humble to the believers who follow you. Then if they disobey you, say: "I am innocent of what you do." And put your trust in the All-Mighty, the Most Merciful) (26:215-217). Allah the Exalted commanded His Messenger in this honorable Ayah,

(But if they turn away), from the glorious, pure, perfect and encompassing Law that you -- O Muhammad -- brought them, (then say: "Allah is sufficient for me. There is no God but He,) Allah is sufficient for me, there is no deity worthy of worship except Him, and in Him I put my trust. Similarly, Allah said,

((He alone is) the Lord of the east and the west; there is no God but He. So take Him alone as a guardian.) (73:9). Allah said next,

(and He is the Lord of the Mighty Throne) (9:129). He is the King and Creator of all things, and He is the Lord of the Mighty Throne (`Arsh), which is above all creation; all that is in and between the heavens and earths is under the Throne (`Arsh) and subservient to Allah's power. His knowledge encompasses all things, and His decision will certainly come to pass over all matters. He is the guardian of all things. Imam Ahmad recorded that Ibn `Abbas said that Ubayy bin Ka`b said, "The last Ayah revealed from the Qur'an was this Ayah,

(Verily, there has come unto you a Messenger from among yourselves ...) (9:128)" until the end of the Surah It is recorded in the Sahih that Zayd bin Thabit said, "I found the last Ayah in Surah Bara'ah with Khuzaymah bin Thabit." This is the end of Surah Bara'ah, all praise is due to Allah.

CHAPTER (SURAH) 10: YUNUS (JONAH), VERSES 001-109

﴿ بِسْمِ ٱللَّهِ ٱلرَّحْمَٰنِ ٱلرَّحِيمِ ﴾

In the Name of Allâh, the Most Gracious, the Most Merciful.

Surah: 10 Ayah: 1 & Ayah: 2

﴿ الٓر تِلْكَ ءَايَٰتُ ٱلْكِتَٰبِ ٱلْحَكِيمِ ﴾

1. Alif-Lâm-Râ. (These letters are one of the miracles of the Qur'ân, and none but Allâh (Alone) knows their meanings). These are the Verses of the Book (the Qur'ân) Al-Hakîm.

﴿ أَكَانَ لِلنَّاسِ عَجَبًا أَنْ أَوْحَيْنَآ إِلَىٰ رَجُلٍ مِّنْهُمْ أَنْ أَنذِرِ ٱلنَّاسَ وَبَشِّرِ ٱلَّذِينَ ءَامَنُوٓا۟ أَنَّ لَهُمْ قَدَمَ صِدْقٍ عِندَ رَبِّهِمْ قَالَ ٱلْكَٰفِرُونَ إِنَّ هَٰذَا لَسَٰحِرٌ مُّبِينٌ ﴾

2. Is it wonder for mankind that We have sent Our Inspiration to a man from among themselves (i.e. Prophet Muhammad (peace be upon him)) (saying): "Warn mankind (of the coming torment in Hell), and give good news to those who believe (in the Oneness of Allâh and in His Prophet Muhammad (peace be upon him)) that they shall have with their Lord the rewards of their good deeds?" (But) the disbelievers say: "This is indeed an evident sorcerer (i.e. Prophet Muhammad (peace be upon him) and the Qur'ân)!

Transliteration

1. Alif-lam-ra tilka ayatu alkitabi alhakeemi 2. Akana lilnnasi AAajaban an awhayna ila rajulin minhum an anthiri alnnasa wabashshiri allatheena amanoo anna lahum qadama sidqin AAinda rabbihim qala alkafiroona inna hatha lasahirun mubeenun

Tafsir Ibn Kathir

The isolated letters in the beginning of this Surah, as well as in others, have been previously discussed at the beginning of Surat Al-Baqarah. Allah said:

(These are the verses of the Book (the Qur'an) Al-Hakim.) This indicates that these are verses of the Qur'an, in which the wisdom of judgment is clear.

The Messenger cannot be but a Human Being

Allah rebukes the attitude of the disbelievers with the words

(Is it a wonder for mankind...) They have always found it strange that Allah would send Messengers to them from among mankind. Allah also tells us about other people from previous nations who said,

(Shall mere men guide us) (64:6) Hud and Salih said to their people:

(Do you wonder that there has come to you a reminder from your Lord through a man from among you.) (7:63) Allah also told us what the disbelievers from Quraysh said:

(Has he made the gods into one God Verily, this is a curious thing!) (38:5) Ad-Dahhak reported Ibn `Abbas that he said: "When Allah sent Muhammad as a Messenger, most of the Arabs denied him and his message and said: Allah is greater than sending a human Messenger like Muhammad. " Ibn `Abbas said, "So Allah revealed:

(Is it a wonder for mankind...)" Allah's statement;

(that they shall have with their Lord the rewards of their good deeds) Scholars have differed over the meaning of the reward for the good deeds in this Ayah:

(and give good news to those who believe that they shall have with their Lord the rewards of their good deeds.) `Ali bin Abi Talhah reported that Ibn `Abbas said about this Ayah, "Eternal happiness has been written for them." Al-`Awfi reported that Ibn `Abbas said: "It is the good reward for what they have done." Mujahid said: "It is their good deeds -- their prayers, fasting, charity, and glorification." He then said, "And Muhammad will intercede for them." Allah said:

((But) the disbelievers say: "This is indeed an evident sorcerer!") This means that the disbelievers said this although Allah has sent a Messenger from among themselves to them, a man of their own race as a bearer of good news and as a warner. But they are the liars in saying that.

Chapter 10: Yunus (Jonah), Verses 001-109

Surah: 10 Ayah: 3

﴿ إِنَّ رَبَّكُمُ ٱللَّهُ ٱلَّذِى خَلَقَ ٱلسَّمَـٰوَٰتِ وَٱلْأَرْضَ فِى سِتَّةِ أَيَّامٍ ثُمَّ ٱسْتَوَىٰ عَلَى ٱلْعَرْشِ ۖ يُدَبِّرُ ٱلْأَمْرَ ۖ مَا مِن شَفِيعٍ إِلَّا مِنۢ بَعْدِ إِذْنِهِۦ ۚ ذَٰلِكُمُ ٱللَّهُ رَبُّكُمْ فَٱعْبُدُوهُ ۚ أَفَلَا تَذَكَّرُونَ ﴾ ۞

3. Surely, your Lord is Allâh Who created the heavens and the earth in six Days and then rose over (Istawâ) the Throne (really in a manner that suits His Majesty), disposing the affair of all things. No intercessor (can plead with Him) except after His Leave. That is Allâh, your Lord; so worship Him (Alone). Then, will you not remember?

Transliteration

3. Inna rabbakumu Allahu allathee khalaqa alssamawati waal-arda fee sittati ayyamin thumma istawa AAala alAAarshi yudabbiru al-amra ma min shafeeAAin illa min baAAdi ithnihi thalikumu Allahu rabbukum faoAAbudoohu afala tathakkaroona

Tafsir Ibn Kathir

Allah is the Creator Who arranges the Affairs of the Universe

Allah tells us that He is the Lord of the entire existence. He tells us that He created the heavens and the earth in six days. It was said: "Like these days (meaning our worldly days)." It was also said: "Every day is like a thousand years of what we reckon." Later, this will be discussed further.

(and then rose over (Istawa) the Throne.)" The Throne is the greatest of the creatures and is like a ceiling for them. Allah's statement:

(arranging the affair (of all things).) means that He controls the affairs of the creatures.

(Not even the weight of a speck of dust escapes His Knowledge in the heavens or in the earth.) (34:3) No affair distracts Him from other affairs. No matter troubles Him. The persistent requests of His creatures do not annoy Him. He governs big things as He governs small things everywhere, on the mountains, in the oceans, in populated areas, or in wastelands.

(And no moving creature is there on earth but its provision is due from Allah.) (11:6)

(Not a leaf falls, but He knows it. There is not a grain in the darkness of the earth nor anything fresh or dry, but is written in a Clear Record.) (6:59) Ad-Darawardi narrated from Sa`d bin Ishaq bin Ka`b bin `Ujrah that he said: "When this Ayah was revealed,

(Surely, your Lord is Allah Who created the heavens and the earth) they met a great caravan whom they thought should be Arabs. They said to them: `Who are you' They replied: 'We are Jinns. We left Al-Madinah because of this Ayah.'" This was recorded by Ibn Abi Hatim. Allah said:

(No intercessor (can plead with Him) except after He permits.) This is similar to what is in the following Ayat:

(Who is he that can intercede with Him except with His permission) (2:255) and,

(And there are many angels in the heavens, whose intercession will avail nothing except after Allah has given leave for whom He wills and is pleased with.)(53:26), and;

(Intercession with Him profits not except for him whom He permits.)(34:23). Allah then said:

(That is Allah, your Lord; so worship Him (alone). Then, will you not remember) meaning worship Him alone with no partners.

(Then will you not remember) meaning "O idolators, you worship gods with Allah while you know that He alone is the Creator," as He said:

(And if you ask them who created them, they will surely say: "Allah.")(43:87),

("Say: "Who is (the) Lord of the seven heavens, and (the) Lord of the Great Throne They will say: "Allah." Say: "Will you not then have Taqwa") (23:86-87), Similar is mentioned in the Ayah before this Ayah and after it.

Surah: 10 Ayah: 4

﴿إِلَيْهِ مَرْجِعُكُمْ جَمِيعًا ۖ وَعْدَ ٱللَّهِ حَقًّا ۚ إِنَّهُۥ يَبْدَؤُا۟ ٱلْخَلْقَ ثُمَّ يُعِيدُهُۥ لِيَجْزِىَ ٱلَّذِينَ ءَامَنُوا۟ وَعَمِلُوا۟ ٱلصَّـٰلِحَـٰتِ بِٱلْقِسْطِ ۚ وَٱلَّذِينَ كَفَرُوا۟ لَهُمْ شَرَابٌ مِّنْ حَمِيمٍ وَعَذَابٌ أَلِيمٌۢ بِمَا كَانُوا۟ يَكْفُرُونَ﴾

4. To Him is the return of all of you. The Promise of Allâh is true. It is He Who begins the creation and then will repeat it, that He may reward with justice those who believed (in the Oneness of Allâh - Islâmic Monotheism) and did deeds of righteousness. But those who disbelieved will have a drink of boiling fluids and painful torment because they used to disbelieve.

Transliteration

4. Ilayhi marjiAAukum jameeAAan waAAda Allahi haqqan innahu yabdao alkhalqa thumma yuAAeeduhu liyajziya allatheena amanoo waAAamiloo alssalihati bialqisti waallatheena kafaroo lahum sharabun min hameemin waAAathabun aleemun bima kanoo yakfuroona

Chapter 10: Yunus (Jonah), Verses 001-109

Tafsir Ibn Kathir

The Return of Everything is to Allah

Allah tells us that the return of the creatures on the Day of Resurrection is to Him. He will not leave anyone of them without bringing everyone into being as He brought them in the beginning. Then Allah states that He is going to bring all the creatures into being.

(And He it is Who originates the creation, then He will repeat it (after it has perished); and this is easier for Him.) (30:27),

(that He may reward with justice those who believed and did deeds of righteousness.) meaning, the reward will be with justice and complete recompense.

(But those who disbelieved will have a drink of boiling fluids and painful torment because they used to disbelieve.) meaning, because of their disbelief they will be punished on the Day of Resurrection by different forms of torment, such as fierce hot winds, boiling water, and the shadow of black smoke.

(This is so! Then let them taste it; a boiling fluid and dirty wound discharges. And other (torments) of similar kind all together!) (38: 57-58)

(This is the Hell which the criminals denied. They will go between it (Hell) and the fierce boiling water!) (55:43-44)

Surah: 10 Ayah: 5 & Ayah: 6

﴿ هُوَ ٱلَّذِى جَعَلَ ٱلشَّمْسَ ضِيَآءً وَٱلْقَمَرَ نُورًا وَقَدَّرَهُۥ مَنَازِلَ لِتَعْلَمُوا۟ عَدَدَ ٱلسِّنِينَ وَٱلْحِسَابَ ۚ مَا خَلَقَ ٱللَّهُ ذَٰلِكَ إِلَّا بِٱلْحَقِّ ۚ يُفَصِّلُ ٱلْءَايَٰتِ لِقَوْمٍ يَعْلَمُونَ ﴾

5. It is He Who made the sun a shining thing and the moon as a light and measured out for it stages that you might know the number of years and the reckoning. Allâh did not create this but in truth. He explains the Ayât (proofs, evidences, verses, lessons, signs, revelations, etc.) in detail for people who have knowledge.

﴿ إِنَّ فِى ٱخْتِلَٰفِ ٱلَّيْلِ وَٱلنَّهَارِ وَمَا خَلَقَ ٱللَّهُ فِى ٱلسَّمَٰوَٰتِ وَٱلْأَرْضِ لَءَايَٰتٍ لِّقَوْمٍ يَتَّقُونَ ﴾

6. Verily, in the alternation of the night and the day and in all that Allâh has created in the heavens and the earth are Ayât (proofs, evidences, verses, lessons, signs, revelations, etc.) for those people who keep their duty to Allâh, and fear Him much.

Transliteration

5. Huwa allathee jaAAala alshshamsa diyaan waalqamara nooran waqaddarahu manazila litaAAlamoo AAadada alssineena waalhisaba ma khalaqa Allahu thalika illa bialhaqqi yufassilu al-ayati liqawmin yaAAlamoona   6. Inna fee ikhtilafi allayli waalnnahari wama khalaqa Allahu fee alssamawati waal-ardi laayatin liqawmin yattaqoona

Tafsir Ibn Kathir

Everything is a Witness to the Power of Allah.

Allah tells us about the signs He created that are indicative of His complete power and great might. He made the rays that come forth from the bright sun as the source of light, and made the beams that come forth from the moon as light. He made them of two different natures so they would not be confused with one another. Allah made the dominion of the sun in the daytime and the moon in the night. He ordained phases for the moon, where it starts small then its light increases until it completes a full moon. Then it begins to decrease until it returns to its first phase at the conclusion of the month. Allah said:

(And the moon, We have measured for it mansions (to traverse) till it returns like the old dried curved date stalk. It is not for the sun to overtake the moon, nor does the night outstrip the day. They all float, each in an orbit.) (36:39-40) And He said:

(And the sun and the moon for counting) And in this Ayah He said:

(and measured) that is the moon, Allah said:

(And measured out for it stages that you might know the number of years and the reckoning. ") The days are revealed by the action of the sun, and the months and the years by the moon. Allah then stated

(Allah did not create this but in truth.) He didn't create that for amusement but with great wisdom and perfect reasoning. With a similar meaning, Allah said:

(And We created not the heaven and the earth and all that is between them without purpose! That is the consideration of those who disbelieve! Then woe to those who disbelieve from the Fire!) (38:27) He also said:

("Did you think that We had created you in play (without any purpose), and that you would not be brought back to Us" So Exalted be Allah, the True King: None has the right to be worshipped but He, the Lord of the Supreme Throne!) (23:115-116) Allah said:

(He explains the Ayat in detail for people who have knowledge.) In other words, He explained the signs and proofs for people who know. Allah further stated:

(Verily, in the alternation of the night and the day) The day and the night alternate, when one arrives, the other goes, and so on, with no errors. This is similar to the meaning indicated in the following Ayat:

Chapter 10: Yunus (Jonah), Verses 001-109

(He brings the night as a cover over the day, seeking it rapidly...).

(It is not for the sun to overtake the moon.) (36:40), and

((He is the) Cleaver of the daybreak. He has appointed the night for resting). (6:96) Allah continued:

(and in all that Allah has created in the heavens and the earth) meaning the signs that indicate His greatness. This is similar to Allah's statements:

(And how many a sign in the heavens and the earth...) (12:105),

("Say: "Behold all that is in the heavens and the earth," but neither Ayat nor warners benefit those who believe not.)(10:101)

(See they not what is before them and what is behind them, of the heaven and the earth.) (34:9).

(Verily, in the creation of the heavens and the earth, and in the alternation of night and day, there are indeed signs for men of understanding.) (3:190) means intelligent men. Allah said here,

(Ayat for those who have Taqwa.) meaning fear Allah's punishment, wrath and torment.

Surah: 10 Ayah: 7 & Ayah: 8

﴿ إِنَّ ٱلَّذِينَ لَا يَرْجُونَ لِقَآءَنَا وَرَضُوا۟ بِٱلْحَيَوٰةِ ٱلدُّنْيَا وَٱطْمَأَنُّوا۟ بِهَا وَٱلَّذِينَ هُمْ عَنْ ءَايَٰتِنَا غَٰفِلُونَ ۝ ﴾

7. Verily, those who hope not for their meeting with Us, but are pleased and satisfied with the life of the present world, and those who are heedless of Our Ayât (proofs, evidences, verses, lessons, signs, revelations, etc.),

﴿ أُو۟لَٰٓئِكَ مَأْوَىٰهُمُ ٱلنَّارُ بِمَا كَانُوا۟ يَكْسِبُونَ ۝ ﴾

8. Those, their abode will be the Fire, because of what they used to earn.

Transliteration

7. Inna allatheena la yarjoona liqaana waradoo bialhayati alddunya waitmaannoo biha waallatheena hum AAan ayatina ghafiloona 8. Ola-ika ma/wahumu alnnaru bima kanoo yaksiboona Translation

Tafsir Ibn Kathir

The Abode of Those Who deny the Hour is Hell-Fire

Allah describes the state of the wretched who disbelieved in the meeting with Allah on the Day of Resurrection and did not look forward to it, who were well-pleased with the life of this world and at rest in it. Al-Hasan said: "They adorned it and praised it until they were well pleased with it. Whereas they were heedless of Allah's signs in the universe, they did not contemplate them. They were also heedless of Allah's Laws, for they didn't abide by them. Their abode on the Day of Return is Fire, a reward for what they have earned in their worldly life from among their sins and crimes. That is beside their disbelief in Allah, His Messenger and the Last Day."

Surah: 10 Ayah: 9 & Ayah: 10

﴿ إِنَّ ٱلَّذِينَ ءَامَنُواْ وَعَمِلُواْ ٱلصَّـٰلِحَـٰتِ يَهْدِيهِمْ رَبُّهُم بِإِيمَـٰنِهِمْ تَجْرِى مِن تَحْتِهِمُ ٱلْأَنْهَـٰرُ فِى جَنَّـٰتِ ٱلنَّعِيمِ ﴾

9. Verily, those who believe and do deeds of righteousness, their Lord will guide them through their Faith; under them will flow rivers in the Gardens of delight (Paradise).

﴿ دَعْوَىٰهُمْ فِيهَا سُبْحَـٰنَكَ ٱللَّهُمَّ وَتَحِيَّتُهُمْ فِيهَا سَلَـٰمٌ وَءَاخِرُ دَعْوَىٰهُمْ أَنِ ٱلْحَمْدُ لِلَّهِ رَبِّ ٱلْعَـٰلَمِينَ ﴾

10. Their way of request therein will be Subhânaka Allâhumma (Glory to You, O Allâh!) and Salâm (peace, safe from evil) will be their greetings therein (Paradise)! and the close of their request will be: Al-Hamdu Lillâhi Rabbil-'Alamîn (all the praises and thanks are to Allâh, the Lord of 'Alamîn (mankind, jinn and all that exists))

Transliteration

9. Inna allatheena amanoo waAAamiloo alssalihati yahdeehim rabbuhum bi-eemanihim tajree min tahtihimu al-anharu fee jannati alnnaAAeemi 10. DaAAwahum feeha subhanaka allahumma watahiyyatuhum feeha salamun waakhiru daAAwahum ani alhamdu lillahi rabbi alAAalameena

Tafsir Ibn Kathir

The Good Reward is for the People of Faith and Good Deeds

In these two Ayat, Allah promises the happy blessings for those who believed in Allah and His Messengers. And for those that have complied with what they were commanded to follow. The promise is that He will guide them because of their faith, or it may mean through their faith. As to the first interpretation, the meaning is that Allah will guide them on the Day of Resurrection to the straight path until they pass into Paradise because of their faith in this world. The other meaning is that their faith will assist them on the Day of Resurrection as Mujahid said:

(Their Lord will guide them through their faith) meaning "Their faith will be a light in which they will walk."

Chapter 10: Yunus (Jonah), Verses 001-109

(Their way of request therein will be: "Glory to You, O Allah!" And Salam (peace, safety from evil) will be their greetings therein! And the close of their request will be: "All praise is due to Allah, the Lord of all that exists.") meaning this is the condition of the people of Paradise. This is similar to what is found in the following Ayat:

(Their greeting on the Day they shall meet Him will be "Salam (Peace)!") (33:44),

(No Laghw (dirty, false, evil vain talk) will they hear therein, nor any sinful speech. But only the saying of: Salam! Salam!!") (56:25-26),

((It will be said to them): "Salam" -- a Word from the Lord, Most Merciful.) (36:58),

(And angels shall enter unto them from every gate (saying): "Salamun `Alaykum (peace be upon you)!") (13:23-24) In Allah's statement,

(And the close of their request will be: All praise is due to Allah, the Lord of all that exists.") There is an indication that Allah Almighty is the Praised One always, the Worshipped at all times. This is why He praised Himself at the beginning and the duration of His creation. He also praised Himself in the beginning of His Book and the beginning of its revelation. Allah said:

(All the praises and thanks be to Allah, Who has sent down to His servant the Book (the Qur'an).) (18:1),

(All praise is due to Allah, Who (alone) created the heavens and the earth,) (6:1), and many other citations with this meaning. The Ayah also indicates that Allah is the Praised One in this world and in the Hereafter and in all situations. In a Hadith recorded by Muslim:

«إِنَّ أَهْلَ الْجَنَّةِ يُلْهَمُونَ التَّسْبِيحَ وَالتَّحْمِيدَ كَمَا يُلْهَمُونَ النَّفَسَ»

(The people of Paradise will be inspired to glorify Allah and praise Him as they instinctively breath.) This will be their nature because of the increasing bounties of Allah upon them. These bounties are repeated and brought back again and increased with no limit or termination. So praise be to Allah for there is no God but He and no Lord save He.

Surah: 10 Ayah: 11

﴿ ۞ وَلَوْ يُعَجِّلُ ٱللَّهُ لِلنَّاسِ ٱلشَّرَّ ٱسْتِعْجَالَهُم بِٱلْخَيْرِ لَقُضِىَ إِلَيْهِمْ أَجَلُهُمْ ۖ فَنَذَرُ ٱلَّذِينَ لَا يَرْجُونَ لِقَآءَنَا فِى طُغْيَـٰنِهِمْ يَعْمَهُونَ ﴾

11. And were Allâh to hasten for mankind the evil (they invoke for themselves and for their children, while in a state of anger) as He hastens for them the good (they invoke) then they would have been ruined. So We leave those who expect not their meeting with Us, in their trespasses, wandering blindly in distraction. (Tafsir At-Tabarî)

Transliteration

11. Walaw yuAAajjilu Allahu lilnnasi alshsharra istiAAjalahum bialkhayri laqudiya ilayhim ajaluhum fanatharu allatheena la yarjoona liqaana fee tughyanihim yaAAmahoona Translation

Tafsir Ibn Kathir

Allah does not respond to the Requests for Evil like He does with the Requests for Good

Allah tells us about His Forbearance and Benevolence with His servants. He does not respond to them when they pray with evil intentions against themselves, their wealth or their children during times of grief or anger. He knows that they do not truly intend evil for themselves so He doesn't respond to them. This is in reality kindness and mercy. On the other hand, He responds to them when they pray for themselves, wealth and money, with good, blessing and growth. Allah has said,

(And were Allah to hasten for mankind the evil as He hastens for them the good then they would have been ruined.) This means that if He had responded to all of their evil requests, He would have destroyed them. However, people should avoid praying for evil as much as they can. Abu Bakr Al-Bazzar recorded in his Musnad that Jabir said, "Allah's Messenger said:

«لَا تَدْعُوا عَلَى أَنْفُسِكُمْ، لَا تَدْعُوا عَلَى أَوْلَادِكُمْ، لَا تَدْعُوا عَلَى أَمْوَالِكُمْ، لَا تُوَافِقُوا مِنَ اللهِ سَاعَةً فِيهَا إِجَابَةٌ فَيَسْتَجِيبَ لَكُمْ»

(Do not pray against yourselves, do not pray against your children, do not pray against your wealth, for your prayer may coincide with a time of response from Allah and Allah will respond to you.) This Hadith was also recorded by Abu Dawud. This is similar to what is understood from the following Ayah:

(And man invokes (Allah) for evil as he invokes (Allah) for good.)(17:11) In regard to the interpretation of this Ayah,

(And were Allah to hasten for mankind the evil as He hastens for them the good) Mujahid said: "It is the man saying to his son or money when he is angry, `O Allah don't bless him (or it) and curse him (or it).' Should Allah respond to this man in this request as He responds to him with good, He would destroy them."

Surah: 10 Ayah: 12

﴿ وَإِذَا مَسَّ ٱلْإِنسَـٰنَ ٱلضُّرُّ دَعَانَا لِجَنۢبِهِۦٓ أَوْ قَاعِدًا أَوْ قَآئِمًا فَلَمَّا كَشَفْنَا عَنْهُ ضُرَّهُۥ مَرَّ كَأَن لَّمْ يَدْعُنَآ إِلَىٰ ضُرٍّ مَّسَّهُۥ ۚ كَذَٰلِكَ زُيِّنَ لِلْمُسْرِفِينَ مَا كَانُوا۟ يَعْمَلُونَ ﴾ ⟨١٢⟩

12. And when harm touches man, he invokes Us, lying down on his side, or sitting or standing. But when We have removed his harm from him, he passes on his way as if he had never invoked Us for a harm that touched him! Thus it is made fair-seeming to the Musrifûn that which they used to do.

Transliteration

12. Wa-itha massa al-insana alddurru daAAana lijanbihi aw qaAAidan aw qa-iman falamma kashafna AAanhu durrahu marra kaan lam yadAAuna ila durrin massahu kathalika zuyyina lilmusrifeena ma kanoo yaAAmaloona Translation

Tafsir Ibn Kathir

Man remembers Allah at Times of Adversity and forgets Him at Times of Prosperity

Allah tells us about man and how he becomes annoyed and worried when he is touched with distress.

(but when evil touches him, then he has recourse to long supplications.)(41:51) `Long supplications' also means many supplications. When man suffers adversity he becomes worried and anxious. So he supplicates more. He prays to Allah to lift and remove the adversity. He prays while standing, sitting or laying down. When Allah removes his adversity and lifts his distress, he turns away and becomes arrogant. He goes on as if nothing were wrong with him before.

(He passes on as if he had never invoked Us for a harm that touched him!) Allah then criticized and condemned those who have these qualities or act this way, so He said:

(Thus it is made fair seeming to the wasteful that which they used to do.) But those on whom Allah has bestowed good guidance and support are an exception.

(Except those who have patience believe and do righteous good deeds.) (11:11) The Prophet said:

«عَجَبًا (لِأَمْرِ) الْمُؤْمِنِ لَا يَقْضِي اللهُ لَهُ قَضَاءً إِلَّا كَانَ خَيْرًا لَهُ، إِنْ أَصَابَتْهُ ضَرَّاءُ فَصَبَرَ كَانَ خَيْرًا لَهُ، وَإِنْ أَصَابَتْهُ سَرَّاءُ فَشَكَرَ كَانَ خَيْرًا لَهُ، وَلَيْسَ ذَلِكَ لِأَحَدٍ إِلَّا لِلْمُؤْمِنِ»

(How wonderful is the case of a believer; there is good for him in everything and this is not the case with anyone except a believer. If prosperity attends him, he expresses gratitude to Allah, and that is good for him. And if adversity befalls him, he endures it patiently and that is also good for him.)

Surah: 10 Ayah: 13 & Ayah: 14

﴿ وَلَقَدْ أَهْلَكْنَا ٱلْقُرُونَ مِن قَبْلِكُمْ لَمَّا ظَلَمُوا۟ وَجَآءَتْهُمْ رُسُلُهُم بِٱلْبَيِّنَـٰتِ وَمَا كَانُوا۟ لِيُؤْمِنُوا۟ ۚ كَذَٰلِكَ نَجْزِى ٱلْقَوْمَ ٱلْمُجْرِمِينَ ﴾

13. And indeed, We destroyed generations before you, when they did wrong, while their Messengers came to them with clear proofs, but they were not such as to believe! Thus do We requite the people who are Mujrimûn (disbelievers, polytheists, sinners, criminals, etc.).

﴿ ثُمَّ جَعَلْنَـٰكُمْ خَلَـٰٓئِفَ فِى ٱلْأَرْضِ مِنۢ بَعْدِهِمْ لِنَنظُرَ كَيْفَ تَعْمَلُونَ ﴾

14. Then We made you successors after them, generations after generations in the land, that We might see how you would work!

Transliteration

13. Walaqad ahlakna alquroona min qablikum lamma thalamoo wajaat-hum rusuluhum bialbayyinati wama kanoo liyu/minoo kathalika najzee alqawma almujrimeena 14. Thumma jaAAalnakum khala-ifa fee al-ardi min baAAdihim linanthura kayfa taAAmaloona

Tafsir Ibn Kathir

The Admonition held in the Destruction of the Previous Generations

Allah tells us about what happened to past generations when they belied the Messengers and the clear signs and proofs the latter brought to them. Allah then made this nation successors after them. He sent to them a Messenger to test their obedience to Him and following His Messenger. Muslim recorded that Abu Nadrah reported from Abu Sa`id that he said: "Allah's Messenger said:

> «إِنَّ الدُّنْيَا حُلْوَةٌ خَضِرَةٌ، وَإِنَّ اللهَ مُسْتَخْلِفُكُمْ فِيهَا، فَنَاظِرٌ كَيْفَ تَعْمَلُونَ، فَاتَّقُوا الدُّنْيَا وَاتَّقُوا النِّسَاءَ، فَإِنَّ أَوَّلَ فِتْنَةِ بَنِي إِسْرَائِيلَ كَانَتْ فِي النِّسَاءِ»

(The world is indeed sweet and green; and verily Allah is going to install you generations after generations in it in order to see how you act. So safeguard yourselves against the world and avoid (the trial caused by) women. For the first trial of the Children of Israel was due to women..) Ibn Jarir reported from `Abdur-Rahman from Ibn Abi Layla that `Awf bin Malik said to Abu Bakr: "In a dream, I saw a rope hanging from the sky and Allah's Messenger was being raised. The rope was suspended again and Abu Bakr was raised. Then people were given different measurements around the Minbar, and `Umar was favored with three forearm measurements." `Umar said: "Keep your dream away from us, we have no need for it." When `Umar succeeded, he called for `Awf and said to him, "Tell me about your dream" `Awf said: "Do you need to hear about my dream now Did you not scold me before" He then said, "Woe unto you! I hated for you to announce it to the successor of Allah's Messenger himself." So `Awf related his dream until he got to the three forearms, he said: "One that he was Khalifah, second he did not -- for the sake of Allah -- fear the blame of blamers, and third he was a martyr." Allah said:

(Then We made you successors after them, generations after generations in the land, that We might see how you would work.)(10:14) Then he said: "Son of the mother of `Umar, you have been appointed as Khalifah, so look at what you will do! About not fearing the blame of blamers, that is Allah's will. About becoming a martyr, how can `Umar reach that when the Muslims are in support of him"

Surah: 10 Ayah: 15 & Ayah: 16

﴿ وَإِذَا تُتْلَىٰ عَلَيْهِمْ ءَايَاتُنَا بَيِّنَاتٍ قَالَ ٱلَّذِينَ لَا يَرْجُونَ لِقَآءَنَا ٱئْتِ بِقُرْءَانٍ غَيْرِ هَٰذَآ أَوْ بَدِّلْهُ ۚ قُلْ مَا يَكُونُ لِىٓ أَنْ أُبَدِّلَهُۥ مِن تِلْقَآئِ نَفْسِىٓ ۖ إِنْ أَتَّبِعُ إِلَّا مَا يُوحَىٰٓ إِلَىَّ ۖ إِنِّىٓ أَخَافُ إِنْ عَصَيْتُ رَبِّى عَذَابَ يَوْمٍ عَظِيمٍ ﴾

15. And when Our Clear Verses are recited unto them, those who hope not for their meeting with Us, say: "Bring us a Qur'ân other than this, or change it." Say (O Muhammad (peace be upon him)) "It is not for me to change it on my own accord; I only follow that which is revealed unto me. Verily, I fear the torment of the Great Day (i.e. the Day of Resurrection) if I were to disobey my Lord."

﴿ قُل لَّوْ شَآءَ ٱللَّهُ مَا تَلَوْتُهُۥ عَلَيْكُمْ وَلَآ أَدْرَىٰكُم بِهِۦ ۖ فَقَدْ لَبِثْتُ فِيكُمْ عُمُرًا مِّن قَبْلِهِۦٓ ۚ أَفَلَا تَعْقِلُونَ ﴾

16. Say (O Muhammad (peace be upon him)) "If Allâh had so willed, I should not have recited it to you nor would He have made it known to you. Verily, I have stayed amongst you a life time before this. Have you then no sense?"

Transliteration

15. Wa-itha tutla AAalayhim ayatuna bayyinatin qala allatheena la yarjoona liqaana i/ti biqur-anin ghayri hatha aw baddilhu qul ma yakoonu lee an obaddilahu min tilqa-i nafsee in attabiAAu illa ma yooha ilayya innee akhafu in AAasaytu rabbee AAathaba yawmin AAatheemin 16. Qul law shaa Allahu ma talawtuhu AAalaykum wala adrakum bihi faqad labithtu feekum AAumuran min qablihi afala taAAqiloona

Tafsir Ibn Kathir

Obstinance of the Chiefs of the Quraysh

Allah tells us about the obstinance of the disbelievers of the Quraysh, who were opposed to the message and denied Allah. When the Messenger read to them from the Book of Allah and His clear evidence they said to him: "Bring a Qur'an other than this." They wanted the Prophet to take back this Book and bring them another book of a different style or change it to a different form. So Allah said to His Prophet:

(Say: "It is not for me to change it on my own accord;) This means that it is not up to me to do such a thing. I am but a servant who receives commands. I am a Messenger conveying from Allah.

(I only follow that which is revealed unto me. Verily, I fear the torment of the Great Day (the Day of Resurrection) if I were to disobey my Lord.)

The Evidence of the Truthfulness of the Qur'an. Muhammad then argued with supporting evidence to the truthfulness of what he had brought them:

(Say: "If Allah had so willed, I should not have recited it to you nor would He have made it known to you...") This indicates that he brought this only with the permission and will of Allah for him to do so. The proof of this was that he had not fabricated it himself and that they were incapable of refuting it, and that they should be fully aware of his truthfulness and honesty since he grew up among them, until Allah sent the Message to him. The Prophet was never criticized for anything or held in contempt. So he said,

(Verily, I have stayed among you a lifetime before this. Have you then no sense) Which meant "don't you have brains with which you may distinguish the truth from falsehood" When Heraclius, the Roman king, asked Abu Sufyan and those who were in his company about the Prophet, he said: "Have you ever accused him of telling lies before his claim" Abu Sufyan replied: "No." Abu Sufyan was then the head of the disbelievers and the leader of the idolators, but he still admitted the truth. This is a clear and irrefutable testimony since it came from the enemy. Heraclius then said: "I wondered how a person who does not tell a lie about others could ever tell a lie about Allah." Ja`far bin Abu Talib said to An-Najashi, the king of Ethiopia: "Allah has sent to

Chapter 10: Yunus (Jonah), Verses 001-109

us a Messenger that we know his truthfulness, ancestral lineage, and honesty. He stayed among us before the prophethood for forty years."

Surah: 10 Ayah: 17

﴿ فَمَنْ أَظْلَمُ مِمَّنِ ٱفْتَرَىٰ عَلَى ٱللَّهِ كَذِبًا أَوْ كَذَّبَ بِـَٔايَـٰتِهِۦٓ ۚ إِنَّهُۥ لَا يُفْلِحُ ٱلْمُجْرِمُونَ ﴾

17. So who does more wrong than he who forges a lie against Allâh or denies His Ayât (proofs, evidences, verses, lessons, signs, revelations, etc.)? Surely, the Mujrimûn (criminals, sinners, disbelievers and polytheists) will never be successful!

Transliteration

17. Faman athlamu mimmani iftara AAala Allahi kathiban aw kaththaba bi-ayatihi innahu la yuflihu almujrimoona Translation

Tafsir Ibn Kathir

Allah says that no one is more wrong, unjust and arrogant than he who invented a lie against Allah, forged claims about Allah, or claimed that Allah has sent a message to him but his claim was not true.

No one is more of a criminal or has committed greater wrong than such a person. Liars cannot be confused with Prophets. Anyone who claims such a thing, whether lying or telling the truth, will necessarily be supported by Allah with proofs and signs of his falsehood or truthfulness. The difference between Muhammad and Musaylamah the liar, was clearer to those who met both of them than the difference between forenoon and midnight when it is extremely dark. Those who are clear-sighted can distinguish via signs and proofs between the truthfulness of Muhammad and the falsehood of Musaylamah the liar, Sajah and Al-Aswad Al-`Ansi. Abdullah bin Salam said: "When Allah's Messenger arrived at Al-Madinah, people were scared away and I was one of them. But when I saw him, I realized that his face could never be the face of a liar. The first thing I heard from him was his statement:

«يَا أَيُّهَا النَّاسُ أَفْشُوا السَّلَامَ، وَأَطْعِمُوا الطَّعَامَ، وَصِلُوا الْأَرْحَامَ، وَصَلُّوا بِاللَّيْلِ وَالنَّاسُ نِيَامٌ، تَدْخُلُوا الْجَنَّةَ بِسَلَام»

(O people, spread the greetings of peace, feed others, be dutiful to your relatives and offer prayers in the night when others are asleep so that you will enter Paradise in peace.)" When Dimam bin Tha`labah came to Allah's Messenger and asked him in the presence of his people -- Banu Sa`d bin Bakr: "Who raised this heaven" He replied, ١. (Allah). He asked: "And who erected these mountains" He replied, ١. (Allah). He asked: "Who spread out this earth" He replied, ١. (Allah). Then he asked: "I ask you in the name of the One, Who raised the heavens, erected the mountains, and spread out this earth, has Allah sent you as a Messenger to all mankind" He said,

«اللَّهُمَّ نَعَم»

(By Allah, Yes!) Then Dimam asked him about Salah, Zakah, Hajj and fasting. With every question he swore by Allah and with every response the Prophet swore also. Dimam then said: "You indeed are telling the truth. By the One Who sent you with the truth I will not increase or decrease from what you have told me." This man was content with the few responses of the Prophet . He was convinced of the Prophet's truthfulness by the signs that he saw and witnessed. It was narrated that `Amr bin Al-`As went to Musaylamah. `Amr was not a Muslim at that time and he was a friend of Musaylamah. Musaylamah said: "Woe unto you `Amr. What was revealed unto your friend -- meaning Allah's Messenger -- during this period" `Amr replied: "I heard his companions reading a short but great Surah." He asked, "And what was that" He recited:

(By Al-`Asr (the time). Verily, man is in loss.) (103:1-2) until the end of the Surah. Musaylamah thought for a while and then said: "Something similar to that was also revealed to me." `Amr asked: "And what is it" He then recited: "O Wabr, O Wabr! You are only two ears and a breast. The rest of you is hollow.' What do you think, `Amr" `Amr then said: "By Allah, you know that I know that you are a liar." This was a statement made by an idolator in judgment of Musaylamah. He knew Muhammad and his truthfulness. He also knew Musaylamah and his tendency toward falsehood and lying. People who think and have insight know even better. Allah said: (And who does more aggression and wrong than he who invents a lie against Allah or rejects His Ayat.) (6:21) (So who does more wrong than he who forges a lie against Allah or denies His Ayat Surely, the criminals will never be successful!) (10:17) No one is more unjust than he who belies the truth which the Messengers have brought supported with evidence and proof.

Surah: 10 Ayah: 18 & Ayah: 19

﴿ وَيَعْبُدُونَ مِن دُونِ ٱللَّهِ مَا لَا يَضُرُّهُمْ وَلَا يَنفَعُهُمْ وَيَقُولُونَ هَٰٓؤُلَآءِ شُفَعَٰٓؤُنَا عِندَ ٱللَّهِ ۚ قُلْ أَتُنَبِّـُٔونَ ٱللَّهَ بِمَا لَا يَعْلَمُ فِى ٱلسَّمَٰوَٰتِ وَلَا فِى ٱلْأَرْضِ ۚ سُبْحَٰنَهُۥ وَتَعَٰلَىٰ عَمَّا يُشْرِكُونَ ﴾

18. And they worship besides Allâh things that hurt them not, nor profit them, and they say: "These are our intercessors with Allâh." Say: "Do you inform Allâh of that which He knows not in the heavens and on the earth?" Glorified and Exalted be He above all that which they associate as partners (with Him)!

Chapter 10: Yunus (Jonah), Verses 001-109

﴿ وَمَا كَانَ ٱلنَّاسُ إِلَّآ أُمَّةً وَٰحِدَةً فَٱخْتَلَفُوا۟ وَلَوْلَا كَلِمَةٌ سَبَقَتْ مِن رَّبِّكَ لَقُضِىَ بَيْنَهُمْ فِيمَا فِيهِ يَخْتَلِفُونَ ﴾ ۝

19. Mankind were but one community (i.e. on one religion - Islâmic Monotheism), then they differed (later), and had not it been for a Word that went forth before from your Lord, it would have been settled between them regarding what they differed.

Transliteration

18. WayaAAbudoona min dooni Allahi ma la yadurruhum wala yanfaAAuhum wayaqooloona haola-i shufaAAaona AAinda Allahi qul atunabbi-oona Allaha bima la yaAAlamu fee alssamawati wala fee alardi subhanahu wataAAala AAamma yushrikoona 19. Wama kana alnnasu illa ommatan wahidatan faikhtalafoo walawla kalimatun sabaqat min rabbika laqudiya baynahum feema feehi yakhtalifoona
Translation

Tafsir Ibn Kathir

What do the Idolators believe about Their Gods

Allah reproaches the idolators that worshipped others beside Allah, thinking that those gods would intercede for them before Allah. Allah states that these gods do not harm or benefit. They don't have any authority over anything, nor do they own anything. These gods can never do what the idolators had claimed about them. That is why Allah said:

(Say: `Do you inform Allah of that which He knows not in the heavens and on the earth') Ibn Jarir said: "This means, `Are you telling Allah about what may not happen in the heavens and earth' Allah then announced that His Glorious Self is far above their Shirk and Kufr by saying:

(Glorified and Exalted is He above all that which they associate as partners (with Him))!

Shirk is New

Allah then tells us that Shirk was new among mankind. It was not in existence in the beginning. He tells us that people were believers in one religion and that religion was Islam. Ibn `Abbas said: "There were ten centuries between Adam and Nuh. They were all on Islam. Then differences among people took place. They worshipped idols and rivals. So Allah sent extensive evidence and irrefutable proof with His Messengers."

(So that those who were to be destroyed (for rejecting the faith) might be destroyed after a clear evidence, and those who were to live might live after a clear evidence.)(8:42) Allah's statement:

(And had not it been for a Word that went forth before from your Lord...) means that if Allah had not decreed He would not punish anyone until the evidence is established against them. And also that if He had not given creatures a respite until a defined term had passed, He would have judged among them in what they disputed. Then He would have caused the believers to be happy and delighted and the disbelievers to be miserable and wretched.

Surah: 10 Ayah: 20

﴿ وَيَقُولُونَ لَوْلَا أُنزِلَ عَلَيْهِ ءَايَةٌ مِّن رَّبِّهِ ۖ فَقُلْ إِنَّمَا ٱلْغَيْبُ لِلَّهِ فَٱنتَظِرُوٓاْ إِنِّى مَعَكُم مِّنَ ٱلْمُنتَظِرِينَ ﴾

20. And they say: "How is it that not a sign is sent down on him from his Lord?" Say: "The unseen belongs to Allâh Alone, so wait you, verily I am with you among those who wait (for Allâh's Judgement)."

Transliteration

20. Wayaqooloona lawla onzila AAalayhi ayatun min rabbihi faqul innama alghaybu lillahi faintathiroo innee maAAakum mina almuntathireena Translation

Tafsir Ibn Kathir

The Idolators requested a Miracle

These stubborn, lying disbelievers said, "Why would not a sign be revealed to Muhammad from his Lord." They meant a sign such as given to Salih. Allah sent the she-camel to Thamud. They wanted Allah to change the mount of As-Safa into gold or remove the mountains of Makkah and replace them with gardens and rivers. Allah is capable of doing all of that, but He is All-Wise in His actions and statements. Allah said:

(Blessed be He Who, if He wills, will assign you better than (all) that -- Gardens under which rivers flow (Paradise) and will assign you palaces (in Paradise). Nay, they deny the Hour, and for those who deny the Hour, We have prepared a flaming Fire.)(25:10-11) He also said:

(And nothing stops Us from sending the Ayat but that the people of old denied them.) (17:59) Allah's way of dealing with His creatures is that He would give to them if they asked things from Him. But if they then didn't believe He would expedite punishment for them. When Allah's Messenger was given the choice of Allah giving the people what they requested but if they didn't believe they would be punished, or that their request would not be answered immediately, Allah's Messenger chose the latter. Allah guided His Prophet to answer their question by saying:

(Say: "The Unseen belongs only to Allah...") This Ayah means that the matter in its entirety is for Allah. He is well aware of the outcome of all matters.

("...so wait you, verily, I am with you among those who wait.") If you would not believe unless you witness that which you asked for, then wait for Allah's judgement for me, as well as for yourselves. Nonetheless, they had witnessed some of the signs and miracles of the Prophet, which were even greater than what they had asked for. In their presence, the Prophet pointed to the moon when it was full and it split into two parts, one part behind the mountain and the other before them. If they were seeking the guidance and firm knowledge by asking for signs, Allah would have known that and would have granted them what had been requested. But Allah knew that it was their obstinacy that was behind their request. Therefore Allah left them to suffer in their suspicion and doubt. Allah knew that none of them would believe. This is similar to Allah's statements:

(Truly, those, against whom the Word (Wrath) of your Lord has been justified, will not believe. Even if every sign should come to them.)(10:96-97) and;

(And even if We had sent down unto them angels, and the dead had spoken unto them, and We had gathered together all things before their very eyes, they would not have believed, unless Allah willed.)(6:111) This was in addition to their arrogance. As Allah said in another Ayah:

(And even if We opened to them a gate from the heaven.) (15:14) And He said:

(And if they were to see a piece of the heaven falling down.)(52:44) He also said:

(And even if We had sent down unto you (O Muhammad) a Message written on paper so that they could touch it with their hands, the disbelievers would have said: `This is nothing but obvious magic!')(6:7) Such people don't deserve to have their requests answered, for there is no benefit in answering them. These people are obstinate and stubborn as a result of their corruption and immorality. Therefore Allah told His Messenger to say:

(So wait you, verily, I am with you among those who wait.)

Surah: 10 Ayah: 21, Ayah: 22 & Ayah: 23

﴿ وَإِذَآ أَذَقْنَا ٱلنَّاسَ رَحْمَةً مِّنْ بَعْدِ ضَرَّآءَ مَسَّتْهُمْ إِذَا لَهُم مَّكْرٌ فِىٓ ءَايَاتِنَا ۚ قُلِ ٱللَّهُ أَسْرَعُ مَكْرًا ۚ إِنَّ رُسُلَنَا يَكْتُبُونَ مَا تَمْكُرُونَ ۝ ﴾

21. And when We let mankind taste mercy after some adversity has afflicted them, behold! they take to plotting against Our Ayât (proofs, evidences, verses, lessons, signs, revelations, etc.)! Say: "Allâh is more Swift in planning!" Certainly, Our Messengers (angels) record all of that which you plot.

﴿ هُوَ ٱلَّذِى يُسَيِّرُكُمْ فِى ٱلْبَرِّ وَٱلْبَحْرِ ۖ حَتَّىٰٓ إِذَا كُنتُمْ فِى ٱلْفُلْكِ وَجَرَيْنَ بِهِم بِرِيحٍ طَيِّبَةٍ وَفَرِحُوا۟ بِهَا جَآءَتْهَا رِيحٌ عَاصِفٌ وَجَآءَهُمُ ٱلْمَوْجُ مِن كُلِّ مَكَانٍ وَظَنُّوٓا۟ أَنَّهُمْ

﴿ أُحِيطَ بِهِمْ دَعَوُا۟ ٱللَّهَ مُخْلِصِينَ لَهُ ٱلدِّينَ لَئِنْ أَنجَيْتَنَا مِنْ هَـٰذِهِۦ لَنَكُونَنَّ مِنَ ٱلشَّـٰكِرِينَ ﴿٢٢﴾

22. He it is Who enables you to travel through land and sea, till when you are in the ships, and they sail with them with a favorable wind, and they are glad therein, then comes a stormy wind and the waves come to them from all sides, and they think that they are encircled therein. Then they invoke Allâh, making their Faith pure for Him Alone, (saying): "If You (Allâh) deliver us from this, we shall truly be of the grateful."

﴿ فَلَمَّآ أَنجَىٰهُمْ إِذَا هُمْ يَبْغُونَ فِى ٱلْأَرْضِ بِغَيْرِ ٱلْحَقِّ ۗ يَـٰٓأَيُّهَا ٱلنَّاسُ إِنَّمَا بَغْيُكُمْ عَلَىٰٓ أَنفُسِكُم ۖ مَّتَـٰعَ ٱلْحَيَوٰةِ ٱلدُّنْيَا ۖ ثُمَّ إِلَيْنَا مَرْجِعُكُمْ فَنُنَبِّئُكُم بِمَا كُنتُمْ تَعْمَلُونَ ﴿٢٣﴾

23. But when He delivered them, behold! They rebel (disobey Allâh) in the earth wrongfully. O mankind! Your rebellion (disobedience to Allâh) is only against your own selves, - a brief enjoyment of this worldly life, then (in the end) unto Us is your return, and We shall inform you that which you used to do.

Transliteration

21. Wa-itha athaqna alnnasa rahmatan min baAAdi darraa massat-hum itha lahum makrun fee ayatina quli Allahu asraAAu makran inna rusulana yaktuboona ma tamkuroona   22. Huwa allathee yusayyirukum fee albarri waalbahri hatta itha kuntum fee alfulki wajarayna bihim bireehin tayyibatin wafarihoo biha jaat-ha reehun AAasifun wajaahumu almawju min kulli makanin wathannoo annahum oheeta bihim daAAawoo Allaha mukhliseena lahu alddeena la-in anjaytana min hathihi lanakoonanna mina alshshakireena Translation   23. Falamma anjahum itha hum yabghoona fee al-ardi bighayri alhaqqi ya ayyuha alnnasu innama baghyukum AAala anfusikum mataAAa alhayati alddunya thumma ilayna marjiAAukum fanunabbiokum bima kuntum taAAmaloona Translation

Tafsir Ibn Kathir

Man changes when He receives Mercy after Times of Distress

Allah tells us that when He makes men feel His mercy after being afflicted with distress,

(They take to plotting against Our Ayat.) The coming of mercy after distress is like the coming of ease after hardship, fertility after aridity, and rain after drought. Mujahid said that man's attitude indicates a mockery and belying of blessings. The meaning here is similar to Allah's statement:

(And when harm touches man, he invokes Us, lying on his side, or sitting or standing.)(10:12) Al-Bukhari recorded that Allah's Messenger led the Subh (Dawn) prayer after it had rained during the night, then he said:

«هَلْ تَدْرُونَ مَاذَا قَالَ رَبُّكُمُ اللَّيْلَةَ؟»

(Do you know what your Lord has said last night) They replied, "Allah and His Messenger know better." He said:

«قَالَ: أَصْبَحَ مِنْ عِبَادِي مُؤْمِنٌ بِي وَكَافِرٌ، فَأَمَّا مَنْ قَالَ: مُطِرْنَا بِفَضْلِ اللهِ وَرَحْمَتِهِ فَذَاكَ مُؤْمِنٌ بِي كَافِرٌ بِالْكَوْكَبِ، وَأَمَّا مَنْ قَالَ: مُطِرْنَا بِنَوْءِ كَذَا وَكَذَا فَذَاكَ كَافِرٌ بِي مُؤْمِنٌ بِالْكَوْكَبِ»

(Allah said; "This morning, some of My servants have become believers and some disbelievers in Me. He who said: `We have had this rainfall due to the grace and mercy of Allah' is a believer in Me and a disbeliever in the stars. And he who said `we have had this rainfall due to the rising of such and such star' is a disbeliever in Me and a believer in the stars.) The Ayah:

(Say: "Allah is more swift in planning!") means that Allah is more capable of gradually seizing them with punishment, while granting them concession of a delay until the criminals think that they would not be punished. But in reality they are in periods of respite, then they will be taken suddenly. The noble writers (meaning the angels who write the deeds) will write everything that they do and keep count of their deeds. Then they will present it before the All-Knowing of the seen and unseen worlds. The Lord will then reward them for the significant deeds and even the seemingly insignificant that may be as tiny as a spot on a date pit. Allah further states:

(He it is Who enables you to travel through land and sea...) which means that He preserves you and maintains you with His care and watching.

(Till when you are in the ships, and they sail with them with a favorable wind, and they are glad therein...) meaning smoothly and calmly;

(then comes (these ships))

(a stormy wind)

o(and the waves come to them from all sides,)

(and they think that they are encircled therein) meaning that are going to be destroyed.

(Then they invoke Allah, making their faith pure for Him (alone)) meaning that in this situation they would not invoke an idol or statue besides Allah. They would single Him out alone for their supplications and prayers. This is similar to Allah's statement:

(And when harm touches you upon the sea, those that you call upon vanish from you except Him (Allah alone). But when He brings you safe to land, you turn away (from Him). And man is ever ungrateful.) (17:67) And in this Surah, He says:

(They invoke Allah, making their faith pure for Him (saying): "If You (Allah) deliver us from this (situation).")

("We shall truly, be of the grateful.") This means that we will not ascribe others as partners with You. We will later worship You alone as we are praying to You here and now. Allah states;

(But when He delivers them) from that distress,

(behold! They rebel (disobey Allah) in the earth wrongfully...) meaning: they returned as if they had never experienced any difficulties and had never promised Him anything. So Allah said:

(He passes on as if he had never invoked Us for a harm that touched him!)(10:12) Allah then said:

(O mankind! Your rebellion (disobedience to Allah) is only against yourselves,) it is you yourselves that will taste the evil consequence of this transgression. You will not harm anyone else with it, as comes in the Hadith,

«مَا مِنْ ذَنْبٍ أَجْدَرَ أَنْ يُعَجِّلَ اللهُ عُقُوبَتَهُ فِي الدُّنْيَا مَعَ مَا يَدَّخِرُ اللهُ لِصَاحِبِهِ فِي الْآخِرَةِ مِنَ الْبَغْيِ وَقَطِيعَةِ الرَّحِمِ»

(There is no sin that is more worthy that Allah hasten punishment for in this world -- on top of the punishment that Allah has in store for it in the Hereafter -- than oppression and cutting the ties of the womb.) Allah's statement:

(a brief enjoyment of this worldly life...) means that you only have a short enjoyment in this low and abased worldly life.

(then (in the end) unto Us is your return...) meaning your goal and final destination.

(and We shall inform you) of all your deeds. Then we shall recompense you for them. So let him who finds good (in his record) praise Allah, and let him who finds other than that blame no one but himself.

Surah: 10 Ayah: 24 & Ayah: 25

﴿ إِنَّمَا مَثَلُ ٱلْحَيَوٰةِ ٱلدُّنْيَا كَمَآءٍ أَنزَلْنَٰهُ مِنَ ٱلسَّمَآءِ فَٱخْتَلَطَ بِهِۦ نَبَاتُ ٱلْأَرْضِ مِمَّا يَأْكُلُ ٱلنَّاسُ وَٱلْأَنْعَٰمُ حَتَّىٰٓ إِذَآ أَخَذَتِ ٱلْأَرْضُ زُخْرُفَهَا وَٱزَّيَّنَتْ وَظَنَّ أَهْلُهَآ أَنَّهُمْ قَٰدِرُونَ عَلَيْهَآ أَتَىٰهَآ أَمْرُنَا لَيْلًا أَوْ نَهَارًا فَجَعَلْنَٰهَا حَصِيدًا كَأَن لَّمْ تَغْنَ بِٱلْأَمْسِ ۚ كَذَٰلِكَ نُفَصِّلُ ٱلْءَايَٰتِ لِقَوْمٍ يَتَفَكَّرُونَ ﴿٢٤﴾

24. Verily the likeness of (this) worldly life is as the water (rain) which We send down from the sky; so by it arises the intermingled produce of the earth of which men and cattle eat: until when the earth is clad with its adornments and is beautified, and its people think that they have all the powers of disposal over it, Our Command reaches it by night or by day and We make it like a clean-mown harvest, as if it had not flourished yesterday! Thus do We explain the Ayât (proofs, evidences, verses, lessons, signs, revelations, laws, etc.) in detail for the people who reflect.

﴿ وَٱللَّهُ يَدْعُوٓاْ إِلَىٰ دَارِ ٱلسَّلَٰمِ وَيَهْدِى مَن يَشَآءُ إِلَىٰ صِرَٰطٍ مُّسْتَقِيمٍ ﴿٢٥﴾

25. Allâh calls to the home of peace (i.e. Paradise, by accepting Allâh's religion of Islâmic Monotheism and by doing righteous good deeds and abstaining from polytheism and evil deeds) and guides whom He wills to the Straight Path.

Transliteration

24. Innama mathalu alhayati alddunya kama-in anzalnahu mina alssama-i faikhtalata bihi nabatu alardi mimma ya/kulu alnnasu waal-anAAamu hatta itha akhathati al-ardu zukhrufaha waizzayyanat wathanna ahluha annahum qadiroona AAalayha ataha amruna laylan aw naharan fajaAAalnaha haseedan kaan lam taghna bial-amsi kathalika nufassilu al-ayati liqawmin yatafakkaroona 25. WaAllahu yadAAoo ila dari alssalami wayahdee man yashao ila siratin mustaqeemin

Tafsir Ibn Kathir

The Parable of this Life

Allah the Almighty has set an example of the similitude of the life of this world, its glitter and the swiftness of its passage, likening it to the plant and vegetation that Allah brings out from the earth. This plant grows from the water that comes down from the sky. These plants are food for people, such as fruits and other different types and kinds of foods. Some other kinds are food for cattle such as clover plants (i.e. green fodder for the cattle) and herbage etc.

(until when the earth is clad in its adornments ,)

(and is beautified) meaning, it became good by what grows on its hills such as blooming flowers of different shapes and colors.

(and its people think...) those who planted it and put it in the ground,

(that they have all the powers of disposal over it) to cultivate it and harvest it. But while they were in that frame of mind, a thunderbolt or a severe, cold storm came to it. It dried its leaves and spoiled its fruits. Allah said:

(Our command reaches it by night or by day and We make it like a clean-mown harvest,) it became dry after it was green and flourishing.

(as if it had not flourished yesterday!) as if nothing existed there before. Qatadah said: "As if it had not flourished; as if it was never blessed." Such are things after they perish, they are as if they had never existed. Similarly, the Hadith,

«يُؤْتَى بِأَنْعَمِ أَهْلِ الدُّنْيَا، فَيُغْمَسُ فِي النَّارِ غَمْسَةً، فَيُقَالُ لَهُ: هَلْ رَأَيْتَ خَيْرًا قَطُّ؟ هَلْ مَرَّ بِكَ نَعِيمٌ قَطُّ؟ فَيَقُولُ: لَا، وَيُؤْتَى بِأَشَدِّ النَّاسِ عَذَابًا فِي الدُّنْيَا، فَيُغْمَسُ فِي النَّعِيمِ غَمْسَةً، ثُمَّ يُقَالُ لَهُ: هَلْ رَأَيْتَ بُؤْسًا قَطُّ؟ فَيَقُولُ لَا»

(A person who led the most prosperous life in this world will be brought up and dipped once in the Fire. He will then be asked: `Have you ever found any good or comfort' He will reply: `No.' And a person who had experienced extreme adversity in this world will be brought up and dipped once in the bliss (of Paradise). Then he will be asked: 'Did you ever face any hardship or misery' He will reply: `No.') Allah said about those who were destroyed:

(So they lay (dead), prostrate in their homes; as if they had never lived there.)(11:67-68) Allah then said:

(Thus do We explain the Ayat. ..) We do explain the proofs, and evidences, in detail

(for the people who reflect.) so they may take a lesson from this example in the swift vanishing of this world from its people while they are deceived by it. They would trust this world and its promises, and then it unexpectedly turns away from them. This world, in its nature, runs away from those who seek it but seeks those who run away from it. Allah mentioned the parable of this world and the plants of the earth in several Ayat in His Noble Book. He said in Surat Al-Kahf:

(And put forward to them the example of the life of this world: it is like the water (rain) which We send down from the sky, and the vegetation of the earth mingles with it, and becomes fresh and green. But (later) it becomes dry and broken pieces, which the winds scatter. And Allah is able to do everything.) (18:45) He also gave similar examples in both Surat Az-Zumar (39:21) and Surat Al-Hadid (57:20).

Invitation to the Everlasting Gifts that do not vanish

Allah said:

Chapter 10: Yunus (Jonah), Verses 001-109

(And Allah calls to the Abode of Peace) When Allah mentioned the swiftness of this world and its termination, He invited people to Paradise and encouraged them to seek it. He called it the Abode of Peace. It is the Abode of Peace because it is free from defects and miseries. So Allah said:

(Allah calls to the Home of Peace and guides whom He wills to the straight path.) It was narrated that Jabir bin `Abdullah said: "Allah's Messenger came out one day and said to us:

«إِنِّي رَأَيْتُ فِي الْمَنَامِ كَأَنَّ جِبْرِيلَ عِنْدَ رَأْسِي، وَمِيكَائِيلَ عِنْدَ رِجْلَيَّ، يَقُولُ أَحَدُهُمَا لِصَاحِبِهِ: اضْرِبْ لَهُ مَثَلًا، فَقَالَ: اسْمَعْ، سَمِعَتْ أُذُنُكَ، وَاعْقِلْ، عَقَلَ قَلْبُكَ، إِنَّمَا مَثَلُكَ وَمَثَلُ أُمَّتِكَ كَمَثَلِ مَلِكٍ اتَّخَذَ دَارًا، ثُمَّ بَنَى فِيهَا بَيْتًا، ثُمَّ جَعَلَ فِيهَا مَأْدُبَةً، ثُمَّ بَعَثَ رَسُولًا يَدْعُو النَّاسَ إِلَى طَعَامِهِ، فَمِنْهُمْ مَنْ أَجَابَ الرَّسُولَ، وَمِنْهُمْ مَنْ تَرَكَهُ، فَاللهُ الْمَلِكُ، وَالدَّارُ الْإِسْلَامُ، وَالْبَيْتُ الْجَنَّةُ، وَأَنْتَ يَا مُحَمَّدُ رَسُولٌ، فَمَنْ أَجَابَكَ دَخَلَ الْإِسْلَامَ، وَمَنْ دَخَلَ الْإِسْلَامَ دَخَلَ الْجَنَّةَ، وَمَنْ دَخَلَ الْجَنَّةَ أَكَلَ مِنْهَا»

(I have seen in my sleep that it was as if Jibril was at my head and Mika'il at my leg. They were saying to each other: `Give an example for him.' He said: `Listen, your ear may listen. And fathom, your heart may fathom. The parable of you and your Ummah is that of a king who has built a house on his land. He arranged a banquet in it. Then he sent a messenger to invite the people to his food. Some accepted the invitation and others did not. Allah is the King and the land is Islam, the house is Paradise and you Muhammad are the Messenger. Whosoever responds to your call enters Islam. And whosoever enters Islam enters Paradise. And whosoever enters Paradise eats from it.) Ibn Jarir recorded this Hadith. It was also reported that Abu Ad-Darda' said that Allah's Messenger said:

«مَا مِنْ يَوْمٍ طَلَعَتْ فِيهِ الشَّمْسُ إِلَّا وَبِجَنْبَيْهَا مَلَكَانِ يُنَادِيَانِ يَسْمَعُهُ خَلْقُ اللهِ كُلُّهُمْ إِلَّا الثَّقَلَيْنِ: يَا أَيُّهَا النَّاسُ هَلُمُّوا إِلَى رَبِّكُمْ، إِنَّ مَا قَلَّ وَكَفَى خَيْرٌ مِمَّا كَثُرَ وَأَلْهَى»

(Two angels descend every day in which the sun rises and say that which all Allah's creatures would hear except Jinn and humans: `O people! Come to your Lord!

Anything little and sufficient is better than a lot but distractive.') And He sent this down in the Qur'an when He said:

("Allah calls to the Abode of Peace".) Ibn Abi Hatim and Ibn Jarir recorded this.

Surah: 10 Ayah: 26

﴿ۚ لِّلَّذِينَ أَحْسَنُواْ ٱلْحُسْنَىٰ وَزِيَادَةٌۖ وَلَا يَرْهَقُ وُجُوهَهُمْ قَتَرٌ وَلَا ذِلَّةٌۚ أُوْلَـٰٓئِكَ أَصْحَـٰبُ ٱلْجَنَّةِۖ هُمْ فِيهَا خَـٰلِدُونَ ﴾

26. For those who have done good is the best (reward, i.e. Paradise) and even more (i.e. having the honor of glancing at the Countenance of Allâh (glorified and exalted be He). Neither darkness nor dust nor any humiliating disgrace shall cover their faces. They are the dwellers of Paradise, they will abide therein forever.

Transliteration

26. Lillatheena ahsanoo alhusna waziyadatun wala yarhaqu wujoohahum qatarun wala thillatun olaika as-habu aljannati hum feeha khalidoona

Tafsir Ibn Kathir

The Reward of the Good-Doers

Allah states that those who do good in this world -- by having faith and performing righteous deeds -- will be rewarded with a good reward in the Hereafter. Allah said:

(Is there any reward for good other than good)(55:60) Then Allah said:

(and even more.) the reward on the good deeds multiplied ten times to seven hundred times and even more on top of that. This reward includes what Allah will give them in Paradise, such as the palaces, Al-Hur (virgins of Paradise), and His pleasure upon them. He will give them what He has hidden for them of the delight of the eye. He will grant them on top of all of that and even better, the honor of looking at His Noble Face. This is the increase that is greater than anything that had been given. They will not deserve that because of their deeds, but rather, they will receive it by the grace of Allah and His mercy. The explanation that this refers to looking at Allah's Noble Face was narrated from Abu Bakr, Hudhayfah bin Al-Yaman, `Abdullah bin `Abbas, Sa`id bin Al-Musayyib, `Abdur-Rahman bin Abu Layla, `Abdur-Rahman bin Sabit, Mujahid, `Ikrimah, `Amir bin Sa`ad, `Ata', Ad-Dahhak, Al-Hasan, Qatadah, As-Suddi, Muhammad bin Ishaq, and others from the earlier and later scholars. There are many Hadiths that contain the same interpretation. Among these Hadiths is what Imam Ahmad recorded from Suhayb that Allah's Messenger recited this Ayah,

(For those who have done good is the best and even more.) And then he said:

Chapter 10: Yunus (Jonah), Verses 001-109

«إِذَا دَخَلَ أَهْلُ الْجَنَّةِ الْجَنَّةَ وَأَهْلُ النَّارِ النَّارَ نَادَى مُنَادٍ: يَا أَهْلَ الْجَنَّةِ إِنَّ لَكُمْ عِنْدَ اللهِ مَوْعِدًا يُرِيدُ أَنْ يُنْجِزَكُمُوهُ فَيَقُولُونَ: وَمَا هُوَ؟ أَلَمْ يُثَقِّلْ مَوَازِيَنَنَا؟ أَلَمْ يُبَيِّضْ وُجُوهَنَا وَيُدْخِلْنَا الْجَنَّةَ وَيُجِرْنَا مِنَ النَّارِ؟ قَالَ فَيَكْشِفُ لَهُمُ الْحِجَابَ، فَيَنْظُرُونَ إِلَيْهِ، فَوَاللهِ مَا أَعْطَاهُمُ اللهُ شَيْئًا أَحَبَّ إِلَيْهِمْ مِنَ النَّظَرِ إِلَيْهِ، وَلَا أَقَرَّ لِأَعْيُنِهِم»

(When the people of Paradise enter Paradise, a caller will say: `O people of Paradise, Allah has promised you something that He wishes to fulfill.' They will reply: `What is it Has He not made our Scale heavy Has He not made our faces white and delivered us from Fire' Allah will then remove the veil and they will see Him. By Allah, they have not been given anything dearer to them and more delightful than looking at Him.) Muslim and a group of Imams also related this Hadith. Allah then said:

(Neither darkness nor dust shall cover their faces. ..) meaning, no blackness or darkness will be on their faces during the different events of the Day of Judgment. But the faces of the rebellious disbelievers will be stained with dust and darkness.

(nor any humiliating disgrace) meaning, they will be covered with degradation and disgrace. The believers, however will not be humiliated internally or externally, on the contrary, they will be protected and honored. For as Allah has said:

l(So Allah saved them from the evil of that Day, and gave them Nadrah (brightness) and joy.) (76:11) meaning, light in their faces and delight in their hearts. May Allah make us among those by His grace and mercy.

Surah: 10 Ayah: 27

﴿ وَٱلَّذِينَ كَسَبُواْ ٱلسَّيِّـَٔاتِ جَزَآءُ سَيِّئَةٍ بِمِثْلِهَا وَتَرْهَقُهُمْ ذِلَّةٌ ۖ مَّا لَهُم مِّنَ ٱللَّهِ مِنْ عَاصِمٍ ۖ كَأَنَّمَآ أُغْشِيَتْ وُجُوهُهُمْ قِطَعًا مِّنَ ٱلَّيْلِ مُظْلِمًا ۚ أُوْلَٰٓئِكَ أَصْحَٰبُ ٱلنَّارِ ۖ هُمْ فِيهَا خَٰلِدُونَ ۝ ﴾

27. And those who have earned evil deeds, the recompense of an evil deed is the like thereof, and humiliating disgrace will cover them (their faces). No defender will they have from Allâh. Their faces will be covered as it were with pieces from the darkness of night. They are dwellers of the Fire, they will abide therein forever.

Transliteration

27. Waallatheena kasaboo alssayyi-ati jazao sayyi-atin bimithliha watarhaquhum thillatun ma lahum mina Allahi min AAasimin kaannama oghshiyat wujoohuhum qitaAAan mina allayli muthliman ola-ika as-habu alnnari hum feeha khalidoona

Tafsir Ibn Kathir

The Reward of the Wicked Criminals

After Allah told us about the state of those happy people who have done right and He promised increase in reward, He continued to tell us about the unlucky, miserable ones. He told us about His justice with them. He will reward them with similar evil, without any increase

(and will cover them) meaning that their faces will be covered and overtaken by humiliation because of their sins and their fear from these sins. Similarly Allah said:

(And you will see them brought forward to it, (Hell) made humble by disgrace.)(42:45) He also said:

(Consider not that Allah is unaware of that which the wrongdoers do, but He gives them respite up to a Day when the eyes will stare in horror. (They will be) hastening forward with necks outstretched, their heads raised up (towards the sky).)(14:42 - 43) Allah then said:

(No defender will they have from Allah.) meaning, there will be no protectors to prevent them from punishment as Allah said:

(On that Day man will say: "Where (is the refuge) to flee" No! There is no refuge! Unto your Lord (alone) will be the place of rest that Day.)(75:10-12) Allah's statement:

(Their faces will be covered as it were...) means that their faces will be dark in the Hereafter. This is similar to His statement:

(On the Day (the Day of Resurrection) when some faces will become white and some faces will become black; as for those whose faces will become black (to them will be said): "Did you reject faith after accepting it Then taste the torment (in Hell) for rejecting faith." And for those whose faces will become white, they will be in Allah's mercy (Paradise), therein they shall dwell forever.)(3:106-107) He also said:

(Some faces that Day will be bright, laughing, rejoicing at good news (of Paradise). And other faces that Day will be dust-stained.)(80:38-40)

Surah: 10 Ayah: 28, Ayah: 29 & Ayah: 30

﴿ وَيَوْمَ نَحْشُرُهُمْ جَمِيعًا ثُمَّ نَقُولُ لِلَّذِينَ أَشْرَكُوا مَكَانَكُمْ أَنتُمْ وَشُرَكَآؤُكُمْ فَزَيَّلْنَا بَيْنَهُمْ وَقَالَ شُرَكَآؤُهُم مَّا كُنتُمْ إِيَّانَا تَعْبُدُونَ ۝ ﴾

28. And the Day whereon We shall gather them all together, then We shall say to those who did set partners in worship with Us: "Stop at your place! You and your partners (whom you had worshipped in the worldly life)." then We shall separate them, and their (Allâh's so-called) partners shall say: "It was not us that you used to worship."

﴿ فَكَفَىٰ بِٱللَّهِ شَهِيدًۢا بَيْنَنَا وَبَيْنَكُمْ إِن كُنَّا عَنْ عِبَادَتِكُمْ لَغَٰفِلِينَ ۝ ﴾

29. "So sufficient is Allâh for a witness between us and you, that We indeed knew nothing of your worship of us."

﴿ هُنَالِكَ تَبْلُوا۟ كُلُّ نَفْسٍ مَّآ أَسْلَفَتْ ۚ وَرُدُّوٓا۟ إِلَى ٱللَّهِ مَوْلَىٰهُمُ ٱلْحَقِّ ۖ وَضَلَّ عَنْهُم مَّا كَانُوا۟ يَفْتَرُونَ ۝ ﴾

30. There! Every person will know (exactly) what he had earned before and they will be brought back to Allâh, their rightful Maula (Lord), and their invented false deities will vanish from them.

Transliteration

28. Wayawma nahshuruhum jameeAAan thumma naqoolu lillatheena ashrakoo makanakum antum washurakaokum fazayyalna baynahum waqala shurakaohum ma kuntum iyyana taAAbudoona 29. Fakafa biAllahi shaheedan baynana wabaynakum in kunna AAan AAibadatikum laghafileena 30. Hunalika tabloo kullu nafsin ma aslafat waruddoo ila Allahi mawlahumu alhaqqi wadalla AAanhum ma kanoo yaftaroona

Tafsir Ibn Kathir

The gods of the Idolators will claim Innocence from them on the Day of Resurrection

Allah said:

(And the Day whereon We shall gather them) Allah will gather together all the creatures of earth, human and Jinn, righteous and rebellious. He said in another Ayah:

(and We shall gather them all together so as to leave not one of them behind.)(18:47)

(then We shall say to those who did associate partners: "Stop at your place! You and your partners.") He then will command the idolators to stay where they are and not to move from their destined places so they would be separated from the place of the believers. Similarly, Allah said:

((It will be said): "And O you the criminals! Get you apart this Day (from the believers).)(36:59) Allah also said:

(And on the Day when the Hour will be established - that Day shall (all men) be separated (the believers will be separated from the disbelievers).)(30:14) In the same Surah, (Ar-Rum), Allah said:

(On that Day men shall be divided.) (30:43) means, they shall be divided in two. This is what will take place when Allah Almighty will come for Final Judgement. The believers intercede to Allah so the Final Judgement may come and they get rid of that state. The Prophet said,

»نَحْنُ يَوْمَ الْقِيَامَةِ عَلَى كُومٍ فَوْقَ النَّاسِ«

(On the Day of Resurrection, we will be in a visible place above the (other) people.) Allah tells us here what He is going to command the idolators and their idols to do on the Day of Resurrection

("Stop at your place! You and your partners." Then We shall separate them,) and that they would deny their worship and claim their innocence from them. Similarly, Allah said: `

(Nay, but they will deny their worship of them.)(19:82),

(When those who were followed declare themselves innocent of those who followed (them).)(2:166), and;

(And who is more astray than one who calls on (invokes) besides Allah, such as will not answer him till the Day of Resurrection, and who are (even) unaware of their calls (invocations) to them And when mankind are gathered (on the Day of Resurrection), they (false deities) will become their enemies)(46:5-6). This refers to the partners responding to those who worshipped them, Then Allah said:

(So sufficient is Allah as a witness between us and you.) They say that we did not know or think that you were worshipping us. Allah is a Witness between us and you that we never called upon you to worship us. We never ordered you to worship us; neither did we accept your worship of us. Allah said:

(There! Every person will know (exactly) what he had earned before) This will be the state of accounting on the Day of Resurrection. Every soul shall know all that it had sent forth, both good and evil. Similarly, Allah said:

(The Day when all the secrets will be examined.)(86:9),

(On that Day man will be informed of what he sent forward (of deeds), and what he left behind.)(75:13), and

(. ..and on the Day of Resurrection, We shall bring out for him a book which he will find wide open. (It will be said to him): "Read your book. You yourself are sufficient as a reckoner against you this Day.") (17:13-14) Then Allah said,

Chapter 10: Yunus (Jonah), Verses 001-109

(and they will be brought back to Allah, their rightful Mawla.) All affairs and matters will be brought back to Allah, the Judge, the All-Just. He will judge everyone, and then admit the people of Paradise in Paradise and the people of Hell to Hell.

(and will vanish from them) meaning what the idolators worshipped,

(what they invented) what they worshipped besides Allah that they invented.

Surah: 10 Ayah: 31, Ayah: 32 & Ayah: 33

﴿ قُلْ مَن يَرْزُقُكُم مِّنَ ٱلسَّمَآءِ وَٱلْأَرْضِ أَمَّن يَمْلِكُ ٱلسَّمْعَ وَٱلْأَبْصَـٰرَ وَمَن يُخْرِجُ ٱلْحَىَّ مِنَ ٱلْمَيِّتِ وَيُخْرِجُ ٱلْمَيِّتَ مِنَ ٱلْحَىِّ وَمَن يُدَبِّرُ ٱلْأَمْرَ ۚ فَسَيَقُولُونَ ٱللَّهُ ۚ فَقُلْ أَفَلَا تَتَّقُونَ ۝ ﴾

31. Say (O Muhammad (peace be upon him): "Who provides for you from the sky and the earth? Or who owns hearing and sight? And who brings out the living from the dead and brings out the dead from the living? And who disposes the affairs?" They will say: "Allâh." Say: "Will you not then be afraid of Allâh's punishment (for setting up rivals in worship with Allâh)?"

﴿ فَذَٰلِكُمُ ٱللَّهُ رَبُّكُمُ ٱلْحَقُّ ۖ فَمَاذَا بَعْدَ ٱلْحَقِّ إِلَّا ٱلضَّلَـٰلُ ۖ فَأَنَّىٰ تُصْرَفُونَ ۝ ﴾

32. Such is Allâh, your Lord in truth. So after the truth, what else can there be, save error? How then are you turned away?

﴿ كَذَٰلِكَ حَقَّتْ كَلِمَتُ رَبِّكَ عَلَى ٱلَّذِينَ فَسَقُوٓا۟ أَنَّهُمْ لَا يُؤْمِنُونَ ۝ ﴾

33. Thus is the Word of your Lord justified against those who rebel (disobey Allâh) that they will not believe (in the Oneness of Allâh and in Muhammad (peace be upon him) as the Messenger of Allâh).

Transliteration

31. Qul man yarzuqukum mina alssama-i waal-ardi amman yamliku alssamAAa waal-absara waman yukhriju alhayya mina almayyiti wayukhriju almayyita mina alhayyi waman yudabbiru al-amra fasayaqooloona Allahu faqul afala tattaqoona   32. Fathalikumu Allahu rabbukumu alhaqqu famatha baAAda alhaqqi illa alddalalu faanna tusrafoona   33. Thus is the Word of your Lord justified against those who rebel (disobey Allâh) that they will not believe (in the Oneness of Allâh and in Muhammad SAW as the Messenger of Allâh).

Tafsir Ibn Kathir

The Idolators recognize Allah's Tawhid in Lordship and the Evidence is established against Them through this Recognition.

Allah argues that the idolators' recognition of Allah's Oneness in Lordship is an evidence against them, for which they should admit and recognize the Oneness in divinity and worship. So Allah said:

(Say: "Who provides for you from the sky and the earth") meaning, who is He Who sends down water from the sky and splits the earth with His power and will and allows things to grow from it,

(Is there a god, besides Allah) (27:62) (Who provides;)

(Grains. And grapes and clover plants. And olives and date palms. And gardens dense with many trees. And fruits and herbage.)"(80:27-31)

(They will say: "Allah.")

("Who is he that can provide for you if He should withhold His provision) (67:21) Allah's statement,

(Or who owns hearing and sight) means that Allah is the One who granted you the power of sight and hearing. If He willed otherwise, He would remove these gifts and deprive you of them. Similarly, Allah said:

(Say it is He Who has created you, and endowed you with hearing and seeing.) (67:23) Allah also said:

(Say: "Tell me, if Allah took away your hearing and your sight.)(6:46) Then Allah said:

(And who brings out the living from the dead and brings out the dead from the living) by His great power and grace.

(And who disposes of the affairs) In Whose Hand is the dominion of everything Who protects all, while against Whom there is no protector Who is the One who judges with none reversing His judgement Who is the One that is not questioned about what He does while they will be questioned

(Whosoever is in the heavens and on earth begs of Him. Every day He is (engaged) in some affair!)(55:29) The upper and lower kingdoms and what is in them both, including the angels, humans, and Jinn are in desperate need of Him. They are His servants and are under His control.

(They will say: "Allah.") they say this knowingly and they admit it.

(Say: `Will you not then be afraid (of Allah's punishment)") meaning, don't you fear Him when you worship others because of your ignorance and false opinions Allah then said:

Chapter 10: Yunus (Jonah), Verses 001-109

(Such is Allah, your Lord in truth.) This Lord that you admitted is the One Who does all this, is your Lord and the True Deity that deserves to be worshipped alone.

(So after the truth, what else can there be, save error) any one worshipped other than Him is false, for there is no God but Allah, He Has no partners.

(How then are you turned away) How then can you turn away from His worship to worship others while you know that He is the Lord that has created everything, the One who controls and governs everything Allah then said:

(Thus is the Word of your Lord justified against those who rebel,) These idolators disbelieved and continued to practice their Shirk, and worship others beside Allah. But they knew that He is the Creator, the Sustainer and the only One of authority and control in this universe, the One Who sent His Messengers to single Him out for all worship. As they disbelieved and were persistent in their Shirk, Allah's Word proved true and was justified that they would be miserable inhabitants of the Fire. Allah said:

(They will say: "Yes," but the Word of torment has been justified against the disbelievers!) (39:71)

Surah: 10 Ayah: 34, Ayah: 35 & Ayah: 36

﴿ قُلْ هَلْ مِن شُرَكَآئِكُم مَّن يَبْدَؤُاْ ٱلْخَلْقَ ثُمَّ يُعِيدُهُۥ ۚ قُلِ ٱللَّهُ يَبْدَؤُاْ ٱلْخَلْقَ ثُمَّ يُعِيدُهُۥ ۖ فَأَنَّىٰ تُؤْفَكُونَ ﴿٣٤﴾ ﴾

34. Say: "Is there of your (Allâh's so-called) partners one that originates the creation and then repeats it?" Say: "Allâh originates the creation and then He repeats it. Then how are you deluded away (from the truth)?"

﴿ قُلْ هَلْ مِن شُرَكَآئِكُم مَّن يَهْدِىٓ إِلَى ٱلْحَقِّ ۚ قُلِ ٱللَّهُ يَهْدِى لِلْحَقِّ ۗ أَفَمَن يَهْدِىٓ إِلَى ٱلْحَقِّ أَحَقُّ أَن يُتَّبَعَ أَمَّن لَّا يَهِدِّىٓ إِلَّآ أَن يُهْدَىٰ ۖ فَمَا لَكُمْ كَيْفَ تَحْكُمُونَ ﴿٣٥﴾ ﴾

35. Say: "Is there of your (Allâh's so-called) partners one that guides to the truth?" Say: "It is Allâh Who guides to the truth. Is then He, Who gives guidance to the truth more worthy to be followed, or he who finds not guidance (himself) unless he is guided? Then, what is the matter with you? How judge you?"

﴿ وَمَا يَتَّبِعُ أَكْثَرُهُمْ إِلَّا ظَنًّا ۚ إِنَّ ٱلظَّنَّ لَا يُغْنِى مِنَ ٱلْحَقِّ شَيْـًٔا ۚ إِنَّ ٱللَّهَ عَلِيمٌۢ بِمَا يَفْعَلُونَ ﴿٣٦﴾ ﴾

36. And most of them follow nothing but conjecture. Certainly, conjecture can be of no avail against the truth. Surely, Allâh is All-Aware of what they do.

Transliteration

34. Qul hal min shuraka-ikum man yabdao alkhalqa thumma yuAAeeduhu quli Allahu yabdao alkhalqa thumma yuAAeeduhu faanna tu/fakoona   35. Qul hal min shuraka-ikum man yahdee ila alhaqqi quli Allahu yahdee lilhaqqi afaman yahdee ila alhaqqi ahaqqu an yuttabaAAa amman la yahiddee illa an yuhda fama lakum kayfa tahkumoona   36. Wama yattabiAAu aktharuhum illa thannan inna alththanna la yughnee mina alhaqqi shay-an inna Allaha AAaleemun bima yafAAaloona

Tafsir Ibn Kathir

This invalidates and falsifies their claims for committing Shirk with Allah and worshipping different idols and rivals.

(Say: "Is there of your partners one that originates the creation and then repeats it") meaning, who is the one who started the creation of these heavens and earth and created all the creatures in them Who can place the planets and the stars in their positions Who can then repeat the process of the creation

(Say: "Allah") It is He Who does this. He does it by Himself, alone without partners.

("Then how are you deluded away (from the truth)") How is it that you are so misled from the right path to falsehood

(Say: "Is there of your partners one that guides to the truth" Say: " It is Allah who guides to the truth. .".) You know that your deities are incapable of guiding those who are astray. It is Allah alone Who guides the misled and confused ones and turns the hearts from the wrong path to the right path. It is Allah, none has the right to be worshipped but He.

(Is then He Who guides to the truth more worthy to be followed, or he who finds not guidance (himself) unless he is guided) Will the servant then follow the one who guides to the truth so that he may see after he was blind, or follow one who doesn't guide to anything except towards blindness and muteness Allah said that Ibrahim said:

(O my father! Why do you worship that which hears not, sees not and cannot avail you in anything) (19:42) And said to his people

(Worship you that which you (yourselves) carve While Allah has created you and what you make!) (37: 95-96) Also, there are many Ayat in this regard. Allah then said:

(Then, what is the matter with you How judge you) What is the matter with you What has happened to your mind How did you make Allah's creatures equal to Him What kind of judgement did you make to turn away from Allah and worship this or that Why did you not worship the Lord -- Glorified be He, the True King, the Judge and the One Who guides to the truth Why didn't you call upon Him alone and turn towards Him Allah then explained that they did not follow their own religion out of evidence and proof. The fact is that they were following mere conjecture and imagination. But conjecture is in no way a substitute for the truth. At the end of this Ayah. He said,

(Allah is All-Aware of what they do.) This is both a threat and a promise of severe punishment. Allah said that He would reward them for their actions with a complete reward.

Surah: 10 Ayah: 37, Ayah: 38, Ayah: 39 & Ayah: 40

﴿ وَمَا كَانَ هَـٰذَا ٱلْقُرْءَانُ أَن يُفْتَرَىٰ مِن دُونِ ٱللَّهِ وَلَـٰكِن تَصْدِيقَ ٱلَّذِى بَيْنَ يَدَيْهِ وَتَفْصِيلَ ٱلْكِتَـٰبِ لَا رَيْبَ فِيهِ مِن رَّبِّ ٱلْعَـٰلَمِينَ ۝ ﴾

37. And this Qur'ân is not such as could ever be produced by other than Allâh (Lord of the heavens and the earth), but it is a confirmation of (the revelation) which was before it (i.e. the Taurât (Torah), and the Injeel (Gospel)) and a full explanation of the Book (i.e. laws, decreed for mankind) - wherein there is no doubt - from the Lord of the 'Alamîn (mankind, jinn, and all that exists).

﴿ أَمْ يَقُولُونَ ٱفْتَرَىٰهُ قُلْ فَأْتُوا۟ بِسُورَةٍ مِّثْلِهِ وَٱدْعُوا۟ مَنِ ٱسْتَطَعْتُم مِّن دُونِ ٱللَّهِ إِن كُنتُمْ صَـٰدِقِينَ ۝ ﴾

38. Or do they say: "He (Muhammad (peace be upon him)) has forged it?" Say: "Bring then a Sûrah (chapter) like unto it, and call upon whomsoever you can besides Allâh, if you are truthful!"

﴿ بَلْ كَذَّبُوا۟ بِمَا لَمْ يُحِيطُوا۟ بِعِلْمِهِ وَلَمَّا يَأْتِهِمْ تَأْوِيلُهُ كَذَٰلِكَ كَذَّبَ ٱلَّذِينَ مِن قَبْلِهِمْ فَٱنظُرْ كَيْفَ كَانَ عَـٰقِبَةُ ٱلظَّـٰلِمِينَ ۝ ﴾

39. Nay, they have belied the knowledge whereof they could not comprehend and what has not yet been fulfilled (i.e. their punishment). Thus those before them did belie. Then see what was the end of the Zâlimûn (polytheists and wrong-doers)!

﴿ وَمِنْهُم مَّن يُؤْمِنُ بِهِ وَمِنْهُم مَّن لَّا يُؤْمِنُ بِهِ وَرَبُّكَ أَعْلَمُ بِٱلْمُفْسِدِينَ ۝ ﴾

40. And of them there are some who believe therein; and of them there are some who believe not therein, and your Lord is All-Aware of the Mufsidûn (evil-doers, liars).

Transliteration

37. Wama kana hatha alqur-anu an yuftara min dooni Allahi walakin tasdeeqa allathee bayna yadayhi watafseela alkitabi la rayba feehi min rabbi alAAalameena   38. Am yaqooloona iftarahu qul fa/too bisooratin mithlihi waodAAoo mani istataAAtum min dooni Allahi in kuntum sadiqeena   39. Bal kaththaboo bima lam yuheetoo biAAilmihi walamma ya/tihim ta/weeluhu kathalika kaththaba allatheena min qablihim faonthur kayfa kana AAaqibatu aththalimeena   40. Waminhum man yu/minu bihi waminhum man la yu/minu bihi warabbuka aAAlamu bialmufsideena

Tafsir Ibn Kathir

The Qur'an is the True, Inimitable Word of Allah and It is a Miracle

The Qur'an has a miraculous nature that cannot be imitated. No one can produce anything similar to the Qur'an, nor ten Surahs or even one Surah like it. The eloquence, clarity, precision and grace of the Qur'an cannot be but from Allah. The great and abundant principles and meanings within the Qur'an -- which are of great benefit in this world and for the Hereafter -- cannot be but from Allah. There is nothing like His High Self and Attributes or like His sayings and actions. Therefore His Words are not like the words of His creatures. This is why Allah said:

(And this Qur'an is not such as could ever be produced by other than Allah) meaning, a book like this cannot be but from Allah. This is not similar to the speech uttered by humans.

(but it is a confirmation of (the revelation) which was before it,) Such as previous revelations and Books. The Qur'an confirms these books and is a witness to them. It shows the changes, perversions and corruption that have taken place within these Books. Then Allah said,

(and a full explanation of the Book -- wherein there is no doubt -- from the Lord of all that exists.) That is, fully and truly explaining and detailing the rules and the lawful and the unlawful. With this complete and more than sufficient explanation, the Qur'an leaves no doubt that it is from Allah, the Lord of all that exists. Allah says,

(Or do they say: "He has forged it" Say: "Bring then a Surah like unto it, and call upon whomsoever you can besides Allah, if you are truthful!") If you argue, claim and doubt whether this is from Allah then you uttered a lie and blasphemy, and you say it is from Muhammad -- Muhammad , however is a man like you, and since he came as you claim with this Qur'an -- then you produce a Surah like one of its Surahs. Produce something of the same nature and seek help and support with all the power you have from humans and Jinns. This is the third stage, Allah challenged them and called them to produce a counterpart of the Qur'an if they were truthful in their claim that it was simply from Muhammad . Allah even suggested that they seek help from anyone they chose. But He told them that they would not be able to do it. They would have no way of doing so. Allah said:

(Say: "If the mankind and the Jinn were together to produce the like of this Qur'an, they could not produce the like thereof, even if they helped one another.") (17:88) Then He reduced the number for them to ten Surahs similar to it, in the beginning of Surah Hud, Allah said:

(Or they say, "He forged it." Say: "Bring you then ten forged Surah like unto it, and call whomsoever you can, other than Allah, if you speak the truth!")(11:13) In this Surah He went even further to challenge them to produce only one Surah like unto the Qur'an. So He said:

(Or do they say: "He has forged it" Say: "Bring then a Surah like unto it, and call upon whomsoever you can besides Allah, if you are truthful!") (10:38) He also challenged

Chapter 10: Yunus (Jonah), Verses 001-109

them in Surat Al-Baqarah, a Madinite Surah, to produce one Surah similar to it. He stated in that Surah that they would never be capable of doing so, saying:

(But if you do it not, and you can never do it, then fear the Fire (Hell).)(2:24) It should be noted here that eloquence was a part of the nature and character of the Arabs. Arabic poetry including Al-Mu`allaqat -- the oldest complete collection of the most eloquent ancient Arabic poems -- was considered to be the best in the literary arts. However Allah sent down to them something whose style none were familiar with, and no one is equal in stature to imitate. So those who believed among them, believed because of what they knew and felt in the Book, including its beauty, elegance, benefit, and fluency. They became the most knowledgeable of the Qur'an and its best in adhering to it. The same thing happened to the magicians during Fir`awn's time. They were knowledgeable of the arts of sorcery, however, when Musa performed his miracles, they knew that it must have come through someone that was supported and guided by Allah. They knew that no human could perform such acts without the permission of Allah. Similarly, `Isa was sent at the time of scholarly medicine and during the advancement in the treatment of patients. He healed the blind, lepers and raised the dead to life by Allah's leave. What `Isa was able to do was such that no form of treatment or medicine could reproduce. As a result, those who believed in him knew that he was Allah's servant and His Messenger. Similarly, in the Sahih, Allah's Messenger said,

«مَا مِنْ نَبِيَ مِنَ الْأَنْبِيَاءِ إِلَّا وَقَدْ أُوتِيَ مِنَ الْآيَاتِ مَا آمَنَ عَلَى مِثْلِهِ الْبَشَرُ، وَإِنَّمَا كَانَ الَّذِي أُوتِيتُهُ وَحْيًا أَوْحَاهُ اللهُ إِلَيَّ فَأَرْجُو أَنْ أَكُونَ أَكْثَرَهُمْ تَابِعًا»

(There was never a Prophet but he was given signs by which the people would recognize him, and that which I was given is revelation that Allah revealed, so I hope that I will have the most followers among them.) Allah then said:

(Nay, they have belied the knowledge whereof they could not comprehend and what has not yet been fulfilled.) They did not believe in the Qur'an and they have not yet grasped it or comprehended it.

(And what has not yet been fulfilled.) They have not attained the guidance and the true religion. So they belied it out of ignorance and foolishness.

(Those before them did belie.) meaning, the past nations,

(Then see what was the end of the wrongdoers!) Look at how we Destroyed them because they denied Our Messengers in their wickedness, pride, stubbornness and ignorance. So beware you who deny the message that the same end will befall you. Allah's statement,

(And of them there are some who believe therein;) means that among those you were sent to, O Muhammad, are people who will believe in this Qur'an, follow you and benefit from what has been sent to you.

(and of them there are some who believe not therein,) but dies as a disbeliever and will be resurrected as such.

(And your Lord is All-Aware of the mischief makers.) He best knows those who deserve guidance, so He guides them, and those who deserve to go astray, He allows to go astray. Allah is, however, the Just who is never unjust. He gives everyone what they deserve. All Glory is His, the Exalted. There is no God but He.

Surah: 10 Ayah: 41, Ayah: 42, Ayah: 43 & Ayah: 44

﴿ وَإِن كَذَّبُوكَ فَقُل لِّى عَمَلِى وَلَكُمْ عَمَلُكُمْ أَنتُم بَرِيئُونَ مِمَّآ أَعْمَلُ وَأَنَاْ بَرِىءٌ مِّمَّا تَعْمَلُونَ ﴾

41. And if they belie you, say: "For me are my deeds and for you are your deeds! You are innocent of what I do, and I am innocent of what you do!"

﴿ وَمِنْهُم مَّن يَسْتَمِعُونَ إِلَيْكَ أَفَأَنتَ تُسْمِعُ ٱلصُّمَّ وَلَوْ كَانُواْ لَا يَعْقِلُونَ ﴾

42. And among them are some who listen to you, but can you make the deaf to hear - even though they apprehend not?

﴿ وَمِنْهُم مَّن يَنظُرُ إِلَيْكَ أَفَأَنتَ تَهْدِى ٱلْعُمْىَ وَلَوْ كَانُواْ لَا يُبْصِرُونَ ﴾

43. And among them are some who look at you, but can you guide the blind - even though they see not?

﴿ إِنَّ ٱللَّهَ لَا يَظْلِمُ ٱلنَّاسَ شَيْئًا وَلَكِنَّ ٱلنَّاسَ أَنفُسَهُمْ يَظْلِمُونَ ﴾

44. Truly! Allâh wrongs not mankind in aught; but mankind wrong themselves.

Transliteration

41. Wa-in kaththabooka faqul lee AAamalee walakum AAamalukum antum baree-oona mimma aAAmalu waana baree-on mimma taAAmaloona 42. Waminhum man yastamiAAoona ilayka afaanta tusmiAAu alssumma walaw kanoo la yaAAqiloona 43. Waminhum man yanthuru ilayka afaanta tahdee alAAumya walaw kanoo la yubsiroona 44. Inna Allaha la yathlimu alnnasa shay-an walakinna alnnasa anfusahum yathlimoona

Tafsir Ibn Kathir

The Command to be Free and Clear from the Idolators

Allah said to His Prophet : `If these idolators belie you, then be clear from them and their deeds.'

(Say: "For me are my deeds and for you are your deeds!") Similarly, Allah said:

(Say: "O you disbelievers! I worship not that which you worship.")(109:1-2) to the end of the Surah. Ibrahim Al-Khalil (the Friend) and his followers said to the idolators among their people:

(Verily, we are free from you and whatever you worship besides Allah) (60:4) Allah then said:

(And among them are some who listen to you,) They listen to your beautiful talk and to the Glorious Qur'an. They listen to your truthful, eloquent and authentic Hadiths that are useful to the hearts, the bodies and their faith. This is indeed a great benefit and is sufficient. But guiding the people to the truth is not up to you or to them. You cannot make the deaf hear. Therefore you cannot guide these people except if Allah wishes. Y

(And among them are some who look at you,) They look at you and at what Allah has given you in terms of dignity, noble personality and great conduct. There is in all of this clear evidence of your prophethood to those who have reason and insight. Other people also look but they do not receive guidance like them. Believers look at you with respect and dignity while disbelievers regard you with contempt.

(And when they see you, they treat you only in mockery.)(25:41) Then Allah announces that He is never unjust with anyone. He guides whomever He wills and opens the eyes of the blind, makes the deaf hear and removes neglect from the hearts. At the same time He lets others go astray, moving away from faith. He does all of that yet He is always Just, for He is the Ruler and has full authority over His kingdom. He does whatever He wills without any restrictions. No one can question Him as to what He does while he will question everyone else. He is Omniscient, All-Wise, and All-Just. So Allah said:

(Truly, Allah wrongs not mankind in aught; but mankind wrong themselves.) In the Hadith narrated by Abu Dharr, he states that the Prophet related that His Lord, Exalted and High is He, said:

(O My servants! It is but your deeds that I reckon for you and then recompense you for. So let him who finds good (in the Hereafter) praise Allah. And let him who finds other than that blame no one but himself.) The complete version was recorded by Muslim.

Surah: 10 Ayah: 45

﴿ وَيَوْمَ يَحْشُرُهُمْ كَأَن لَّمْ يَلْبَثُوٓاْ إِلَّا سَاعَةً مِّنَ ٱلنَّهَارِ يَتَعَارَفُونَ بَيْنَهُمْ ۚ قَدْ خَسِرَ ٱلَّذِينَ كَذَّبُواْ بِلِقَآءِ ٱللَّهِ وَمَا كَانُواْ مُهْتَدِينَ ﴾

45. And on the Day when He shall gather (resurrect) them together, (it will be) as if they had not stayed (in the life of this world and graves) but an hour of a day. They will recognize each other. Ruined indeed will be those who denied the meeting with Allâh, and were not guided.

Transliteration

45. Wayawma yahshuruhum kaan lam yalbathoo illa saAAatan mina alnnahari yataAAarafoona baynahum qad khasira allatheena kaththaboo biliqa-i Allahi wama kanoo muhtadeena

Tafsir Ibn Kathir

The Feeling of Brevity toward the Worldly Life at the Gathering on the Day of Resurrection

To remind people of the establishment of the Hour and their resurrection from their graves to the gathering for the Day of Judgment, Allah says:

(And on the Day when He shall gather (resurrect) them.) Similarly Allah said:

(On the Day when they will see that (torment) with which they are promised (threatened, it will be) as if they had not stayed more than an hour in a single day.)(46:35) Allah also said:

(The Day they see it, (it will be) as if they had not tarried (in this world) except an afternoon or a morning.) (79:46)

(The Day when the Trumpet will be blown (the second blowing): that Day, We shall gather the criminals, blue eyed. They will speak in a very low voice to each other (saying): "You stayed not longer than ten (days)." We know very well what they will say, when the best among them in knowledge and wisdom will say: "You stayed no longer than a day!") (20:102-104) and,

(And on the Day that the Hour will be established, the criminals will swear that they stayed not but an hour.)(30:55) These all are evidence of the brevity of the worldly life compared to the Hereafter. Allah said:

(He (Allah) will say: "What number of years did you stay on earth" They will say: "We stayed a day or part of a day. Ask of those who keep account." He (Allah) will say: "You stayed not but a little, if you had only known!") (23:112-124) Allah then said:

(They will recognize each other) The children will know their parents and relatives will recognize one another. They will know them just like they used to know them during the life in this world. However, on that Day everyone will be busy with himself. Allah then said:

(Then, when the Trumpet is blown, there will be no kinship among them.)(23:101) Allah also said:

(And no friend will ask a friend (about his condition).)(70:10) Allah then said:

(Ruined indeed will be those who denied the meeting with Allah and were not guided.) This is similar to the Ayah:

(Woe that Day to the deniers.)(77:15) Woe to them because they will lose themselves and their families on the Day of Resurrection. That is indeed the great loss. There is no loss greater than the loss of one who will be taken away from his dear ones on the Day of Grief and Regret.

Surah: 10 Ayah: 46 & Ayah: 47

﴿ وَإِمَّا نُرِيَنَّكَ بَعْضَ ٱلَّذِى نَعِدُهُمْ أَوْ نَتَوَفَّيَنَّكَ فَإِلَيْنَا مَرْجِعُهُمْ ثُمَّ ٱللَّهُ شَهِيدٌ عَلَىٰ مَا يَفْعَلُونَ ﴾

46. Whether We show you (in your lifetime, O Muhammad (peace be upon him)) some of what We promise them (the torment), or We cause you to die - still unto Us is their return, and moreover, Allâh is Witness over what they used to do.

﴿ وَلِكُلِّ أُمَّةٍ رَّسُولٌ فَإِذَا جَآءَ رَسُولُهُمْ قُضِىَ بَيْنَهُم بِٱلْقِسْطِ وَهُمْ لَا يُظْلَمُونَ ﴾

47. And for every Ummah (a community or a nation), there is a Messenger; when their Messenger comes, the matter will be judged between them with justice, and they will not be wronged.

Transliteration

46. Wa-imma nuriyannaka baAAda allathee naAAiduhum aw natawaffayannaka fa-ilayna marjiAAuhum thumma Allahu shaheedun AAala ma yafAAaloona 47. Walikulli ommatin rasoolun fa-itha jaa rasooluhum qudiya baynahum bialqisti wahum la yuthlamoona

Tafsir Ibn Kathir

The Criminals will certainly be avenged -- whether in This World or in the Hereafter

Allah said to His Messenger :

(Whether We show you some of what We promise them (the torment),) We shall avenge them in your lifetime so your eye will be delighted.

(Or We cause you to die -- still unto Us is their return,) Allah will then be the Witness watching over their actions for you. Allah then said,

(And for every Ummah there is a Messenger; when their Messenger comes,) Mujahid said: "This will be on the Day of Resurrection.

(the matter will be judged between them with justice,) is similar to the Ayah:

(And the earth will shine with the light of its Lord (Allah),) (39:69) So every nation will be presented before Allah in the presence of its Messenger and the Book of its deeds.

All good and evil deeds will be witnessed upon them. Their guardian angels will be witnesses too. The nations will be brought forth, one by one. Our noble Ummah, while it is the last of the nations, is the first one on the Day of Resurrection to be questioned and judged. This was stated by Allah's Messenger in a Hadith recorded by both Al-Bukhari and Muslim. Allah's Messenger said:

«نَحْنُ الْآخِرُونَ السَّابِقُونَ يَوْمَ الْقِيَامَةِ، الْمَقْضِيُّ لَهُمْ قَبْلَ الْخَلَائِقِ»

(We are the last, the first on the Day of Resurrection. We will be judged before the rest of the creatures.) His Ummah attains the honor of precedence only by the honor of its Messenger , may Allah's peace and blesings be upon him forever, until the Day of Judgement.

Surah: 10 Ayah: 48, Ayah: 49, Ayah: 50, Ayah: 51 & Ayah: 52

﴿وَيَقُولُونَ مَتَىٰ هَـٰذَا ٱلْوَعْدُ إِن كُنتُمْ صَـٰدِقِينَ ۝﴾

48. And they say: "When will be this promise (the torment or the Day of Resurrection), if you speak the truth?"

﴿قُل لَّآ أَمْلِكُ لِنَفْسِى ضَرًّا وَلَا نَفْعًا إِلَّا مَا شَآءَ ٱللَّهُ ۗ لِكُلِّ أُمَّةٍ أَجَلٌ ۚ إِذَا جَآءَ أَجَلُهُمْ فَلَا يَسْتَـْٔخِرُونَ سَاعَةً وَلَا يَسْتَقْدِمُونَ ۝﴾

49. Say (O Muhammad (peace be upon him)) "I have no power over any harm or profit to myself except what Allâh may will. For every Ummah (a community or a nation), there is a term appointed; when their term comes, neither can they delay it nor can they advance it an hour (or a moment)." (Tafsir Al-Qurtubî).

﴿قُلْ أَرَءَيْتُمْ إِنْ أَتَىٰكُمْ عَذَابُهُۥ بَيَـٰتًا أَوْ نَهَارًا مَّاذَا يَسْتَعْجِلُ مِنْهُ ٱلْمُجْرِمُونَ ۝﴾

50. Say: "Tell me, if His torment should come to you by night or by day, which portion thereof would the Mujrimûn (disbelievers, polytheists, sinners, criminals) hasten on ?"

﴿أَثُمَّ إِذَا مَا وَقَعَ ءَامَنتُم بِهِۦٓ ۚ ءَآلْـَٰٔنَ وَقَدْ كُنتُم بِهِۦ تَسْتَعْجِلُونَ ۝﴾

51. Is it then that when it has actually befallen, you will believe in it? What! Now (you believe)? And you used (aforetime) to hasten it on!"

﴿ثُمَّ قِيلَ لِلَّذِينَ ظَلَمُوا۟ ذُوقُوا۟ عَذَابَ ٱلْخُلْدِ هَلْ تُجْزَوْنَ إِلَّا بِمَا كُنتُمْ تَكْسِبُونَ ۝﴾

52. Then it will be said to them who wronged themselves: "Taste you the everlasting torment! Are you recompensed (aught) save what you used to earn?"

Transliteration

48. Wayaqooloona mata hatha alwaAAdu in kuntum sadiqeena 49. Qul la amliku linafsee darran wala nafAAan illa ma shaa Allahu likulli ommatin ajalun itha jaa ajaluhum fala yasta/khiroona saAAatan wala yastaqdimoona 50. Qul araaytum in atakum AAathabuhu bayatan aw naharan matha yastaAAjilu minhu almujrimoona 51. Athumma itha ma waqaAAa amantum bihi al-ana waqad kuntum bihi tastaAAjiloona 52. Thumma qeela lillatheena thalamoo thooqoo AAathaba alkhuldi hal tujzawna illa bima kuntum taksiboona

Tafsir Ibn Kathir

The Deniers of the Day of Resurrection wish to hasten its Coming and their Response

Allah told us about the idolators who reject faith through their demand that the punishment be hastened, inquiring about the time of punishment. The response to such question is not inherently beneficial, yet they inquired anyway. Allah said:

(Those who believe not therein seek to hasten it, while those who believe are fearful of it, and know that it is the very truth.) (42:18) They know that it is the truth for it is definitely going to happen. It is going to take place even if they have no idea when it will occur. This is why Allah instructed His Messenger to answer them saying:

(Say: "I have no power over any harm or profit to myself.") (10:49, 7:188) I will not say except what He has taught me. I also have no authority over anything that Allah has not shown to me. I am Allah's servant and His Messenger to you. I was told that the Hour is going to come, but He has not told me when it will occur. But,

(For every Ummah, there is a term appointed;) meaning that for every generation or community there is a set term appointed for them. When the end of that term approaches,

(neither can they delay it nor can they advance it an hour (or a moment).) This is similar to what Allah said in another Ayah:

(And Allah grants respite to none when his appointed time (death) comes.) (63:11) Allah instructed His Messenger to tell the people that His punishment would come suddenly. He said:

(Say: "Tell me, if His torment should come to you by night or by day, which portion thereof would the criminals hasten on Is it then that when it has actually befallen, you will believe in it What! Now (you believe) And you used (aforetime) to hasten it on!") When the punishment befalls them, they will say:

("Our Lord! We have now seen and heard.") (32:12) Allah also said:

(So when they saw Our punishment, they said: "We believe in Allah alone and reject (all) that we used to associate with Him as (His) partners. Then their faith could not avail them when they saw Our punishment. (Like) this has been the way of Allah in dealing with His servants. And there the disbelievers lost utterly (when Our torment covered them).")(40:84-85)

(Then it will be said to them who wronged themselves: "Taste you the everlasting torment!") This will be said to them on the Day of Resurrection, blaming and rebuking them. As Allah said in another Ayah:

(The Day when they will be pushed down by force to the fire of Hell, with a horrible, forceful pushing. This is the Fire that you used to belie. Is this magic or do you not see Taste you therein its heat and whether you are patient of it or impatient of it, it is all the same. You are only being requited for what you used to do.) (52:13-16)

Surah: 10 Ayah: 53 & Ayah: 54

﴿۞ وَيَسْتَنْبِئُونَكَ أَحَقٌّ هُوَ قُلْ إِى وَرَبِّى إِنَّهُ لَحَقٌّ وَمَا أَنتُم بِمُعْجِزِينَ ۞﴾

53. And they ask you (O Muhammad (peace be upon him)) to inform them (saying): "Is it true (i.e. the torment and the establishment of the Hour - the Day of Resurrection)?" Say: "Yes! By my Lord! It is the very truth! and you cannot escape from it!"

﴿ وَلَوْ أَنَّ لِكُلِّ نَفْسٍ ظَلَمَتْ مَا فِى ٱلْأَرْضِ لَٱفْتَدَتْ بِهِۦ ۗ وَأَسَرُّواْ ٱلنَّدَامَةَ لَمَّا رَأَوُاْ ٱلْعَذَابَ ۖ وَقُضِىَ بَيْنَهُم بِٱلْقِسْطِ وَهُمْ لَا يُظْلَمُونَ ۞﴾

54. And if every person who had wronged (by disbelieving in Allâh and by worshipping others besides Allâh) possessed all that is on earth and sought to ransom himself therewith (it will not be accepted), and they would feel in their hearts regret when they see the torment, and they will be judged with justice, and no wrong will be done unto them.

Transliteration

53. Wayastanbi-oonaka ahaqqun huwa qul ee warabbee innahu lahaqqun wama antum bimuAAjizeena 54. Walaw anna likulli nafsin thalamat ma fee al-ardi laiftadat bihi waasarroo alnnadamata lamma raawoo alAAathaba waqudiya baynahum bialqisti wahum la yuthlamoona

Tafsir Ibn Kathir

The Resurrection is Real

Allah said that they ask you to inform them (saying):

Chapter 10: Yunus (Jonah), Verses 001-109   99

("Is it true") asking about the return and the Resurrection from the graves, after the bodies become sand.

(Say: "Yes! By my Lord! It is the very truth! And you cannot escape it!") meaning that becoming sand does not make Allah incapable of bringing you back, since He originated you from nothing.

(Verily, His command, when He intends a thing, is only that He says to it, `Be!' - and it is!)(36:82) There are only two other Ayat in the Qur'an similar to this. Allah commands His Messenger to give an oath by Him to answer those who deny the return. He said in Surah Saba',

(Those who disbelieve say: "The Hour will not come to us." Say: "Yes, by my Lord!, it will come to you.") (34:3) The second is in Surat At-Taghabun, He said:

(The disbelievers claimed that they will never be resurrected. Say: "Yes! By my Lord! you will certainly be resurrected, then you will be informed of (and recompensed for) what you did; and that is easy for Allah.") (64:7) Then Allah informed us that when the Resurrection is established the disbelievers will wish that they could ransom themselves from Allah's punishment with the equivalent of the weight of the earth in gold.

(And they would feel in their hearts regret when they see the torment, and they will be judged with justice, and no wrong will be done unto them.)

Surah: 10 Ayah: 55 & Ayah: 56

﴿ أَلَا إِنَّ لِلَّهِ مَا فِي السَّمَاوَاتِ وَالْأَرْضِ أَلَا إِنَّ وَعْدَ اللَّهِ حَقٌّ وَلَكِنَّ أَكْثَرَهُمْ لَا يَعْلَمُونَ ۝ ﴾

55. No doubt, surely, all that is in the heavens and the earth belongs to Allâh. No doubt, surely, Allâh's Promise is true. But most of them know not.

﴿ هُوَ يُحْيِي وَيُمِيتُ وَإِلَيْهِ تُرْجَعُونَ ۝ ﴾

56. It is He Who gives life, and causes death, and to Him you (all) shall return.

Transliteration

55. Ala inna lillahi ma fee alssamawati waal-ardi ala inna waAAda Allahi haqqun walakinna aktharahum la yaAAlamoona   56. Huwa yuhyee wayumeetu wa-ilayhi turjaAAoona

Tafsir Ibn Kathir

Allah is the Owner of the heavens and earth. His promise is true and is indeed going to be fulfilled. He is the One Who gives life and causes death. To Him is the return of everyone, and He is the One who has the power over that, and the One Who knows everything about every creature; its deterioration, and where every speck of it has gone, be it land, oceans or otherwise.

Surah: 10 Ayah: 57 & Ayah: 58

﴿ يَـٰٓأَيُّهَا ٱلنَّاسُ قَدْ جَآءَتْكُم مَّوْعِظَةٌ مِّن رَّبِّكُمْ وَشِفَآءٌ لِّمَا فِى ٱلصُّدُورِ وَهُدًى وَرَحْمَةٌ لِّلْمُؤْمِنِينَ ﴾ ۝

57. O mankind! There has come to you a good advice from your Lord (i.e. the Qur'an, enjoining all that is good and forbidding all that is evil), and a healing for that (disease of ignorance, doubt, hypocrisy and differences) in your breasts, - a guidance and a mercy (explaining lawful and unlawful things) for the believers.

﴿ قُلْ بِفَضْلِ ٱللَّهِ وَبِرَحْمَتِهِ فَبِذَٰلِكَ فَلْيَفْرَحُوا۟ هُوَ خَيْرٌ مِّمَّا يَجْمَعُونَ ﴾ ۝

58. Say: "In the Bounty of Allâh, and in His Mercy (i.e. Islâm and the Qur'ân); - therein let them rejoice." That is better than what (the wealth) they amass.

Transliteration

57. Ya ayyuha alnnasu qad jaatkum mawAAithatun min rabbikum washifaon lima fee alssudoori wahudan warahmatun lilmu/mineena 58. Qul bifadli Allahi wabirahmatihi fabithalika falyafrahoo huwa khayrun mimma yajmaAAoona

Tafsir Ibn Kathir

The Qur'an is an Admonition, Cure, Mercy and Guidance

Allah confers a great favor on His creatures in what He has sent down of the Gracious Qur'an to His Noble Messenger . He said:

(O mankind! There has come to you good advice from your Lord.) A warning and a shield from shameful deeds.

(and a cure for that which is in your breasts,) A cure from suspicion and doubts. The Qur'an removes all the filth and Shirk from the hearts.

(a guidance and a mercy) The guidance and the mercy from Allah are attained through it. This is only for those who believe in it and have firm faith in what it contains. As Allah said:

(And We send down of the Qur'an that which is a cure and a mercy to those who believe, and it increases the wrongdoers nothing but loss.) (17:82) and;

(Say: "It is for those who believe, a guide and a cure.") (41: 44) Allah then said:

(Say: "In the bounty of Allah, and in His mercy; therein let them rejoice.") rejoice in what has come from Allah. Let them rejoice in the guidance and the religion of the truth. It is better than anything they might rejoice in,

That is better than what (the wealth) they amass. from the ruins of the world and its vanishing bloom undoubtedly.

Surah: 10 Ayah: 59 & Ayah: 60

﴿ قُلْ أَرَءَيْتُم مَّآ أَنزَلَ ٱللَّهُ لَكُم مِّن رِّزْقٍ فَجَعَلْتُم مِّنْهُ حَرَامًا وَحَلَـٰلًا قُلْ ءَآللَّهُ أَذِنَ لَكُمْ ۖ أَمْ عَلَى ٱللَّهِ تَفْتَرُونَ ﴿٥٩﴾ ﴾

59. Say (O Muhammad (peace be upon him) to these polytheists): "Tell me, what provision Allâh has sent down to you! And you have made of it lawful and unlawful." Say (O Muhammad (peace be upon him)) "Has Allâh permitted you (to do so), or do you invent a lie against Allâh?"

﴿ وَمَا ظَنُّ ٱلَّذِينَ يَفْتَرُونَ عَلَى ٱللَّهِ ٱلْكَذِبَ يَوْمَ ٱلْقِيَـٰمَةِ ۗ إِنَّ ٱللَّهَ لَذُو فَضْلٍ عَلَى ٱلنَّاسِ وَلَـٰكِنَّ أَكْثَرَهُمْ لَا يَشْكُرُونَ ﴿٦٠﴾ ﴾

60. And what think those who invent lies against Allâh, on the Day of Resurrection? (i.e. Do they think that they will be forgiven and excused! Nay, they will have an eternal punishment in the Fire of Hell). Truly, Allâh is full of Bounty to mankind, but most of them are ungrateful.

Transliteration

59. Qularaaytum ma anzala Allahu lakum min rizqin fajaAAaltum minhu haraman wahalalan qul allahu athina lakum am AAala Allahi taftaroona   60. Wama thannu allatheena yaftaroona AAala Allahi alkathiba yawma alqiyamati inna Allaha lathoo fadlin AAala alnnasi walakinna aktharahum la yashkuroona

Tafsir Ibn Kathir

None can make Anything Lawful or Unlawful except Allah or Those Whom Allah has allowed to do so

Ibn `Abbas, Mujahid, Ad-Dahhak, Qatadah, `Abdur-Rahman bin Zayd bin Aslam and others said: "This Ayah was revealed to criticize the idolators for what they used to make lawful and unlawful. Like the Bahirah, Sa'ibah and Wasilah." As Allah said:

(And they assign to Allah a share of the tilth and cattle which He has created.)(6:136) Imam Ahmad recorded a narration from Malik bin Nadlah who said, "I came to Allah's Messenger while in filthy clothes. He said,

«هَلْ لَكَ مَالٌ؟»

(Do you have wealth) I answered, `Yes.' He said,

$$\langle\!\langle\text{مِنْ أَيِّ الْمَالِ؟}\rangle\!\rangle$$

(what kind of wealth) I answered, `All kinds; camels, slaves, horses, sheep.' So he said,

$$\langle\!\langle\text{إِذَا آتَاكَ اللَّهُ مَالًا فَلْيُرَ عَلَيْك}\rangle\!\rangle$$

(If Allah gives you wealth, then let it be seen on you.) Then he said,

$$\langle\!\langle\text{هَلْ تُنْتَجُ إِبْلُكَ صِحَاحًا آذَانُهَا، فَتَعْمِدَ إِلَى مُوسَى فَتَقْطَعَ آذَانَهَا، فَتَقُولُ: هَذِهِ بُحْرٌ، وَتَشُقُّ جُلُودَهَا وَتَقُولُ: هَذِهِ صُرُمٌ، وَتُحَرِّمُهَا عَلَيْكَ وَعَلَى أَهْلِك}\rangle\!\rangle$$

؟ (It is not that your camels are born with healthy ears, you take a knife and cut them, then say, "This is a Bahr," tear its skin, then say, `This is a Sarm," and prohibit them for yourself and your family) I replied, `Yes.' He said,

$$\langle\!\langle\text{فَإِنَّ مَا آتَاكَ اللَّهُ لَكَ حِلٌّ، سَاعِدُ اللهِ أَشَدُّ مِنْ سَاعِدِكَ، وَمُوسَى اللهِ أَحَدُّ مِنْ مُوسَاك}\rangle\!\rangle$$

(What Allah has given you is lawful. Allah's Forearm is stronger than your forearm, and Allah's knife is sharper than your knife.)" And he mentioned the Hadith in its complete form, and the chain for this Hadith is a strong, good chain. Allah criticized those who make lawful what Allah has made unlawful or vice verse. This is because they are based on mere desires and false opinions that are not supported with evidence or proof. Allah then warned them with a promise of the Day of Resurrection. He asked:

(And what think those who invent a lie against Allah, on the Day of Resurrection) What do they think will happen to them when they return to Us on the Day of Resurrection Ibn Jarir said that Allah's statement:

(Truly, Allah is full of bounty to mankind,) indicated that the bounty is in postponing their punishment in this world. I (Ibn Kathir) say, the meaning could be that the Grace for people is in the good benefits that He made permissible for them in this world or in their religion. He also has not prohibited them except what is harmful to them in their world and the Hereafter.

(but most of them are ungrateful.) So they prohibited what Allah has bestowed upon them and made it hard and narrow upon themselves. They made some things lawful and others unlawful. The idolators committed these actions when they set laws for themselves. And so did the People of the Book when they invented innovations in their religion.

Surah: 10 Ayah: 61

﴿ وَمَا تَكُونُ فِى شَأْنٍ وَمَا تَتْلُواْ مِنْهُ مِن قُرْءَانٍ وَلَا تَعْمَلُونَ مِنْ عَمَلٍ إِلَّا كُنَّا عَلَيْكُمْ شُهُودًا إِذْ تُفِيضُونَ فِيهِ ۚ وَمَا يَعْزُبُ عَن رَّبِّكَ مِن مِّثْقَالِ ذَرَّةٍ فِى ٱلْأَرْضِ وَلَا فِى ٱلسَّمَآءِ وَلَآ أَصْغَرَ مِن ذَٰلِكَ وَلَآ أَكْبَرَ إِلَّا فِى كِتَٰبٍ مُّبِينٍ ﴾

61. Neither you (O Muhammad (peace be upon him)) do any deed nor recite any portion of the Qur'ân, - nor you (mankind) do any deed (good or evil) but We are Witness thereof, when you are doing it. And nothing is hidden from your Lord (so much as) the weight of an atom (or small ant) on the earth or in the heaven. Not what is less than that or what is greater than that but is (written) in a Clear Record. (Tafsir At-Tabarî).

Transliteration

61. Wama takoonu fee sha/nin wama tatloo minhu min qur-anin wala taAAmaloona min AAamalin illa __Intro Page27 of 46 kunna AAalaykum shuhoodan ith tufeedoona feehi wama yaAAzubu AAan rabbika min mithqali tharratin fee al-ardi wala fee alssama-i wala asghara min thalika wala akbara illa fee kitabin mubeenun

Tafsir Ibn Kathir

Everything Small or Large is within the Knowledge of Allah

Allah informed His Prophet that He knows and is well acquainted with all of the affairs and conditions of him and his Ummah and all of creation and its creatures at all times -- during every hour and second. Nothing slips or escapes from His knowledge and observation, not even anything the weight of a speck of dust within the heavens or earth, or anything that is smaller or larger than that. Everything is in a manifest Book, as Allah said:

(And with Him are the keys of the Ghayb (all that is hidden and unseen), none knows them but He. And He knows whatever there is in the land and in the sea; not a leaf falls, but He knows it. There is not a grain in the darkness of the earth nor anything fresh or dry, but is written in a Clear Record.)(6:59) He stated that He is Well-Aware of the movement of the trees and other inanimate objects. He is also Well-Aware of all grazing beasts. He said:

(There is not a moving creature on earth, nor a bird that flies with its two wings, but are communities like you.) (6:38) He also said:

(And no moving creature is there on earth but its provision is due from Allah.)(11:6) If this is His knowledge of the movement of these things, then what about His knowledge of the movement of the creatures that are commanded to worship Him Allah said:

(And put your trust in the Almighty, the Most Merciful, Who sees you when you stand up, and your movements among those who fall prostrate.)(26:217-219) That is why Allah said:

(Neither you do any deed nor recite any portion of the Qur'an, nor you do any deed, but We are Witness thereof when you are doing it.) meaning, `We are watching and hearing you when you engage in that thing.' When Jibril asked the Prophet about Ihsan, he said:

«أَنْ تَعْبُدَ اللهَ كَأَنَّكَ تَرَاهُ، فَإِنْ لَمْ تَكُنْ تَرَاهُ فَإِنَّهُ يَرَاكَ»

(It is that you worship Allah as if you are seeing Him. But since you do not see Him, be certain that He is watching you.)

Surah: 10 Ayah: 62, Ayah: 63 & Ayah: 64

﴿ أَلَا إِنَّ أَوْلِيَاءَ ٱللَّهِ لَا خَوْفٌ عَلَيْهِمْ وَلَا هُمْ يَحْزَنُونَ ۝ ﴾

62. No doubt! Verily, the Auliyâ' of Allâh (i.e. those who believe in the Oneness of Allâh and fear Allâh much (abstain from all kinds of sins and evil deeds which he has forbidden), and love Allâh much (perform all kinds of good deeds which He has ordained)) no fear shall come upon them nor shall they grieve.

﴿ ٱلَّذِينَ ءَامَنُوا۟ وَكَانُوا۟ يَتَّقُونَ ۝ ﴾

63. Those who believed (in the Oneness of Allâh - Islâmic Monotheism), and used to fear Allâh much (by abstaining from evil deeds and sins and by doing righteous deeds).

﴿ لَهُمُ ٱلْبُشْرَىٰ فِى ٱلْحَيَوٰةِ ٱلدُّنْيَا وَفِى ٱلْءَاخِرَةِ لَا تَبْدِيلَ لِكَلِمَٰتِ ٱللَّهِ ذَٰلِكَ هُوَ ٱلْفَوْزُ ٱلْعَظِيمُ ۝ ﴾

64. For them are glad tidings, in the life of the present world (i.e. through a righteous dream seen by the person himself or shown to others), and in the Hereafter. No change can there be in the Words of Allâh, this is indeed the supreme success.

Transliteration

62. Ala inna awliyaa Allahi la khawfun AAalayhim wala hum yahzanoona   63. Allatheena amanoo wakanoo yattaqoona   64. Lahumu albushra fee alhayati alddunya wafee al-akhirati la tabdeela likalimati Allahi thalika huwa alfawzu alAAatheemu

Chapter 10: Yunus (Jonah), Verses 001-109

Tafsir Ibn Kathir

Identifying the Awliya' of Allah

Allah tells us that His Awliya' (friends and allies) are those who believe and have Taqwa of Allah as He defined them. Every pious, God-fearing person is a friend of Allah, therefore,

(no fear shall come upon them) from the future horrors they will face in the Hereafter.

(nor shall they grieve.) over anything left behind in this world. Ibn Jarir recorded that Abu Hurayrah said that Allah's Messenger said:

«إِنَّ مِنْ عِبَادِ اللهِ عِبَادًا يَغْبِطُهُمُ الْأَنْبِيَاءُ وَالشُّهَدَاءُ»

(Among the servants of Allah there will be those whom the Prophets and the martyrs will consider fortunate). It was said: "Who are these, O Messenger of Allah, so we may love them" He said:

«هُمْ قَوْمٌ تَحَابُّوا فِي اللهِ مِنْ غَيْرِ أَمْوَالٍ وَلَا أَنْسَابٍ، وُجُوهُهُمْ نُورٌ عَلَى مَنَابِرَ مِنْ نُورٍ، لَا يَخَافُونَ إِذَا خَافَ النَّاسُ، وَلَا يَحْزَنُونَ إِذَا حَزِنَ النَّاسُ»

(These are people who loved one another for the sake of Allah without any other interest like money or kinship. Their faces will be light, upon platforms of light. They shall have no fear (on that Day) when fear shall come upon people. Nor shall they grieve when others grieve.) Then he recited:

(Behold!! Verily, the Awliya' (friends and allies) of Allah, no fear shall come upon them nor shall they grieve.)

The True Dream is a Form of Good News

Ibn Jarir narrated from `Ubadah bin As-Samit that he (recited) to Allah's Messenger :

(For them is good news, in the life of the present world, and in the Hereafter.) (and said,) "We know the good news of the Hereafter, it is Paradise. But what is the good news in this world" He said:

«الرُّؤْيَا الصَّالِحَةُ يَرَاهَا الْعَبْدُ أَوْ تُرَى لَهُ. وَهِيَ جُزْءٌ مِنْ أَرْبَعَةٍ وَأَرْبَعِينَ جُزْءًا أَوْ سَبْعِينَ جُزْءًا مِنَ النُّبُوَّة»

(It is the good dream that a servant may see or it is seen about him. This dream is one part from forty-four or seventy parts of Prophethood.) Imam Ahmad recorded that Abu Dharr said, "O Messenger of Allah! What about a man who does deeds that the people commend him for" Allah's Messenger said,

〈«تِلْكَ عَاجِلُ بُشْرَى الْمُؤْمِنِ»〉

(That is the good news that has been expedited for the believer.) Imam Ahmad recorded that `Abdullah bin `Amr said that Allah's Messenger said:

(لَهُمُ الْبُشْرَى فِي الْحَيَوةِ الدُّنْيَا وَفِي الْآخِرَةِ)

(For them is good news, in the life of the present world) Then he said,

«الرُّؤْيَا الصَّالِحَةُ يُبَشِّرُهَا الْمُؤْمِنُ، جُزْءٌ مِنْ تِسْعَةٍ وَأَرْبَعِينَ جُزْءًا مِنَ النُّبُوَّةِ، فَمَنْ رَأَى ذَلِكَ فَلْيُخْبِرْ بِهَا، وَمَنْ رَأَى سِوَى ذَلِكَ فَإِنَّمَا هُوَ مِنَ الشَّيْطَانِ لِيُحْزِنَهُ، فَلْيَنْفُثْ عَنْ يَسَارِهِ ثَلَاثًا، وَلْيُكَبِّرْ، وَلَا يُخْبِرْ بِهَا أَحَدًا»

(The good dream that comes as a good news for the believer is a part of forty-nine parts of prophethood. So if anyone of you has a good dream, he should narrate it to others. But if he has a dream that he dislikes, then it is from Shaytan to make him sad. He should blow to his left three times, and say: "Allahu Akbar," and should not mention it to anyone.") And it was also said, "The good news here is the glad tidings the angels bring to the believer at the time of death. They bring him the good news of Paradise and forgiveness." Similarly, Allah said:

(Verily, those who say: "Our Lord is Allah (alone)," and then they stand straight and firm, on them the angels will descend (at the time of their death) (saying): "Fear not, nor grieve! But receive the glad tidings of Paradise which you have been promised! We have been your friends in the life of this world and are (so) in the Hereafter. Therein you shall have (all) that your souls desire, and therein you shall have (all) for which you ask. An entertainment from (Allah), the Oft-Forgiving, Most Merciful.") (41:30-32) In the Hadith narrated by Al-Bara', the Prophet said:

«إِنَّ الْمُؤْمِنَ إِذَا حَضَرَهُ الْمَوْتُ جَاءَهُ مَلَائِكَةٌ بِيضُ الْوُجُوهِ بِيضُ الثِّيَابِ فَقَالُوا: اخْرُجِي أَيَّتُهَا الرُّوحُ الطَّيِّبَةُ إِلَى رَوْحٍ وَرَيْحَانٍ وَرَبٍّ غَيْرِ غَضْبَانَ، فَتَخْرُجُ مِنْ فَمِهِ كَمَا تَسِيلُ الْقَطْرَةُ مِنْ فَمِ السِّقَاءِ»

(When death approaches the believer, angels with white faces and white clothes come to him and say: "O good soul! Come out to comfort and provision and a Lord who is not angry." The soul then comes out of his mouth like a drop of water pouring out of a water skin.) Their good news in the Hereafter is as Allah said:

(The greatest terror (on the Day of Resurrection) will not grieve them, and the angels will meet them, (with the greeting:) "This is your Day which you were promised.") (21:103), and,

(On the Day you shall see the believing men and the believing women -- their light running forward before them and by their right hands. Glad tidings for you this Day! Gardens under which rivers flow (Paradise), to dwell therein forever! Truly, this is the great success!)(57:12) Allah then said:

(No change can there be in the Words of Allah.) meaning, this promise doesn't change or breach or fall short. It is decreed and firm, and going to happen undoubtedly.

(This is indeed the supreme success.)

Surah: 10 Ayah: 65, Ayah: 66 & Ayah: 67

﴿ وَلَا يَحْزُنكَ قَوْلُهُمْ إِنَّ ٱلْعِزَّةَ لِلَّهِ جَمِيعًا هُوَ ٱلسَّمِيعُ ٱلْعَلِيمُ ﴾

65. And let not their speech grieve you (O Muhammad (peace be upon him)) for all power and honor belong to Allâh. He is the All-Hearer, the All-Knower.

﴿ أَلَا إِنَّ لِلَّهِ مَن فِى ٱلسَّمَـٰوَٰتِ وَمَن فِى ٱلْأَرْضِ وَمَا يَتَّبِعُ ٱلَّذِينَ يَدْعُونَ مِن دُونِ ٱللَّهِ شُرَكَآءَ إِن يَتَّبِعُونَ إِلَّا ٱلظَّنَّ وَإِنْ هُمْ إِلَّا يَخْرُصُونَ ﴾

66. No doubt! Verily, to Allâh belongs whosoever is in the heavens and whosoever is in the earth. And those who worship and invoke others besides Allâh, in fact they follow not the (Allâh's so-called) partners, they follow only a conjecture and they only invent lies.

﴿ هُوَ ٱلَّذِى جَعَلَ لَكُمُ ٱلَّيْلَ لِتَسْكُنُوا۟ فِيهِ وَٱلنَّهَارَ مُبْصِرًا إِنَّ فِى ذَٰلِكَ لَـَٔايَـٰتٍ لِّقَوْمٍ يَسْمَعُونَ ﴾

67. He it is Who has appointed for you the night that you may rest therein, and the day to make things visible (to you). Verily, in this are Ayât (proofs, evidences, verses, lessons, signs, revelations, etc.) for a people who listen (i.e. those who think deeply).

Transliteration

65. Wala yahzunka qawluhum inna alAAizzata lillahi jameeAAan huwa alssameeAAu alAAaleemu   66. Ala inna lillahi man fee alssamawati waman fee al-ardi wama

yattabiAAu allatheena yadAAoona min dooni Allahi shurakaa in yattabiAAoona illa alththanna wa-in hum illa yakhrusoona 67. Huwa allathee jaAAala lakumu allayla litaskunoo feehi waalnnahara mubsiran inna fee thalika laayatin liqawmin yasmaAAoona

Tafsir Ibn Kathir

All Might and Honor is for Allah - He Alone has Full Authority within the Universe

Allah said to His Messenger,

(Do not greive) because of the remarks of these idolators, and depend on Allah and ask for His help. Put your trust in Him.

(For all power and honor belong to Allah.) All might and honor belong to Him, His Messenger and the believers.

(He is the All-Hearer, the All-Knower.) He hears the utterances of His servants and knows their affairs. Allah then stated that to Him is the dominion of the heavens and earth. But the idolators worship idols, that own nothing and can neither harm nor benefit anyone. They have no evidence to base their worship on them. They only follow their own conjecture, lies, and ultimately - falsehood. Allah then informed us that He is the One Who made the night for His servants to rest therein from weariness and exhaustion.

(And the day to make things visible (to you).) bright and clear for them to seek livelihood and to travel to fulfill their needs.

(Verily, in this are Ayat for a people who listen.) Those who hear these proofs and take a lesson from them, these Ayat can lead them to realize the greatness of their Creator and Sustainer.

Surah: 10 Ayah: 68, Ayah: 69 & Ayah: 70

﴿ قَالُوا۟ ٱتَّخَذَ ٱللَّهُ وَلَدًا ۗ سُبْحَٰنَهُۥ ۖ هُوَ ٱلْغَنِىُّ ۖ لَهُۥ مَا فِى ٱلسَّمَٰوَٰتِ وَمَا فِى ٱلْأَرْضِ ۚ إِنْ عِندَكُم مِّن سُلْطَٰنٍۭ بِهَٰذَآ ۚ أَتَقُولُونَ عَلَى ٱللَّهِ مَا لَا تَعْلَمُونَ ۝

68. They (Jews, Christians and pagans) say: "Allâh has begotten a son (children)." Glory is to Him! He is Rich (Free of all needs). His is all that is in the heavens and all that is in the earth. No warrant you have for this. Do you say against Allâh what you know not.

﴿ قُلْ إِنَّ ٱلَّذِينَ يَفْتَرُونَ عَلَى ٱللَّهِ ٱلْكَذِبَ لَا يُفْلِحُونَ ۝

69. Say: "Verily, those who invent a lie against Allâh will never be successful" -

﴿ مَتَٰعٌ فِى ٱلدُّنْيَا ثُمَّ إِلَيْنَا مَرْجِعُهُمْ ثُمَّ نُذِيقُهُمُ ٱلْعَذَابَ ٱلشَّدِيدَ بِمَا كَانُوا۟ يَكْفُرُونَ ۞ ﴾

70. (A brief) enjoyment in this world! - and then unto Us will be their return, then We shall make them taste the severest torment because they used to disbelieve (in Allâh, belie His Messengers, deny and challenge His Ayât (proofs, signs, verses, etc.))

Transliteration

68. Qaloo ittakhatha Allahu waladan subhanahu huwa alghaniyyu lahu ma fee alssamawati wama fee al-ardi in AAindakum min sultanin bihatha ataqooloona AAala Allahi ma la taAAlamoona 69. Qul inna allatheena yaftaroona AAala Allahi alkathiba la yuflihoona   70. MataAAun fee alddunya thumma ilayna marjiAAuhum thumma nutheequhumu alAAathaba alshshadeeda bima kanoo yakfuroona

Tafsir Ibn Kathir

Allah is Far Above taking a Wife or having Children

Allah criticizes those who claim that He has,

(...begotten a son. Glory is to Him! He is Rich (Free of all needs).) He is Greater than that and above it. He is Self-Sufficient, free of want or need of anything. Everything else is in desperate need of Him,

(His is all that is in the heavens and all that is in the earth.) So how can He have a son from what He has created Everything and everyone belongs to Him and is His servant.

(No warrant have you for this) Meaning, you have no proof for the lies and falsehood that you claim,

(Do you say against Allah what you know not.) This is a severe threat and a firm warning. Similarly, Allah threatened and said:

(And they say: "The Most Gracious has begotten a son." Indeed you have brought forth a terribly evil thing. Whereby the heavens are almost torn, and the earth is split asunder, and the mountains fall in ruins, that they ascribe a son to the Most Gracious. But it is not suitable for the Most Gracious that He should beget a son. There is none in the heavens and the earth but comes unto the Most Gracious as a servant. Verily, He knows each one of them, and has counted them a full counting. And everyone of them will come to Him alone on the Day of Resurrection.) (19:88-95) Then Allah warned the liars that fabricated the claim that He has begotten a son. He warned that they will not succeed, never prospering in this world or in the Hereafter. In this world Allah will lead them, step-by-step, to their ruin. He will give them respite and put up with them for a while. He will allow them to have little enjoyment, (then in the end We shall oblige them to (enter) a great torment.)(31:24) As Allah said here:

((A brief) enjoyment in this world!) meaning, only a short period,

(and then unto Us will be their return) on the Day of Resurrection;

(Then We shall make them taste the severest torment because they used to disbelieve.) meaning, `We shall make them taste the painful punishment because of their Kufr and lies about Allah.'

Surah: 10 Ayah: 71, Ayah: 72 & Ayah: 73

﴿ وَٱتْلُ عَلَيْهِمْ نَبَأَ نُوحٍ إِذْ قَالَ لِقَوْمِهِ يَـٰقَوْمِ إِن كَانَ كَبُرَ عَلَيْكُم مَّقَامِى وَتَذْكِيرِى بِـَٔايَـٰتِ ٱللَّهِ فَعَلَى ٱللَّهِ تَوَكَّلْتُ فَأَجْمِعُوٓاْ أَمْرَكُمْ وَشُرَكَآءَكُمْ ثُمَّ لَا يَكُنْ أَمْرُكُمْ عَلَيْكُمْ غُمَّةً ثُمَّ ٱقْضُوٓاْ إِلَىَّ وَلَا تُنظِرُونِ ۝ ﴾

71. And recite to them the news of Nûh (Noah). When he said to his people: "O my people, if my stay (with you), and my reminding (you) of the Ayât (proofs, evidences, verses, lessons, signs, revelations, etc.) of Allâh is hard on you, then I put my trust in Allâh. So devise your plot, you and your partners, and let not your plot be in doubt for you. Then pass your sentence on me and give me no respite.

﴿ فَإِن تَوَلَّيْتُمْ فَمَا سَأَلْتُكُم مِّنْ أَجْرٍ إِنْ أَجْرِىَ إِلَّا عَلَى ٱللَّهِ وَأُمِرْتُ أَنْ أَكُونَ مِنَ ٱلْمُسْلِمِينَ ۝ ﴾

72. "But if you turn away (from accepting my doctrine of Islâmic Monotheism, i.e. to worship none but Allâh), then no reward have I asked of you; my reward is only from Allâh, and I have been commanded to be one of the Muslims (i.e. those who submit to Allâh's Will)."

﴿ فَكَذَّبُوهُ فَنَجَّيْنَـٰهُ وَمَن مَّعَهُ فِى ٱلْفُلْكِ وَجَعَلْنَـٰهُمْ خَلَـٰٓئِفَ وَأَغْرَقْنَا ٱلَّذِينَ كَذَّبُواْ بِـَٔايَـٰتِنَا فَٱنظُرْ كَيْفَ كَانَ عَـٰقِبَةُ ٱلْمُنذَرِينَ ۝ ﴾

73. They denied him, but We delivered him, and those with him in the ship, and We made them generations replacing one after another, while We drowned those who belied Our Ayât (proofs, evidences, lessons, signs, revelations, etc.). Then see what was the end of those who were warned.

Transliteration

71. Waotlu AAalayhim nabaa noohin ith qala liqawmihi ya qawmi in kana kabura AAalaykum maqamee watathkeeree bi-ayati Allahi faAAala Allahi tawakkaltu faajmiAAoo amrakum washurakaakum thumma la yakun amrukum AAalaykum

ghummatan thumma iqdoo ilayya wala tunthirooni 72. Fa-in tawallaytum fama saaltukum min ajrin in ajriya illa AAala Allahi waomirtu an akoona mina almuslimeena 73. Fakaththaboohu fanajjaynahu waman maAAahu fee alfulki wajaAAalnahum khala-ifa waaghraqna allatheena kaththaboo bi-ayatina faonthur kayfa kana AAaqibatu almunthareena

Tafsir Ibn Kathir

The Story of Nuh and His People

Allah instructed His Prophet , saying:

(And recite to them) relate to the disbelievers of the Quraysh who belied you and rejected you,

(the news of Nuh) meaning, his story and news with his people who belied him. Tell them how Allah destroyed them and caused every last one of them all to drown. Let this be a lesson for your people, lest they will be destroyed like them.

(When he said to his people: "O my people, if my stay (with you), and my reminding (you) of the Ayat of Allah is hard on you, then I put my trust in Allah.") Meaning, `if you find that it is too much of an offense that I should live among you and preach to you the revelation of Allah and His signs and proofs, then I do not care what you think, and I will not stop inviting you.'

(So devise your plot, you and your partners), `get together with all of your deities (idols and statues) that you call upon beside Allah,'

(and let not your plot be in confusion for you) meaning, an`d do not be confused about this, rather come and let us settle this together if you claim that you are truthful,'

(and give me no respite.) `Do not give me respite even for one hour. Whatever you can do, go ahead and do it. I do not care, and I do not fear you, because you are not standing on anything.' This is similar to what Hud said to his people,

(I call Allah to witness, and you bear witness, that I am free from that which you ascribe as partners in worship with Him (Allah). So plot against me, all of you, and give me no respite. I put my trust in Allah, my Lord and your Lord!) (11:54-55)

Islam is the Religion of all of the Prophets

Nuh said,

(But if you turn away) if you belie the message and turn away from obedience.

(then no reward have I asked of you,) I have not asked you anything for my advice.

(My reward is only from Allah. And I have been commanded to be of the Muslims.) I submit to Islam. Islam is the religion of all of the Prophets from the first to the last.

Their laws and their rules may be of different types but the religion is the same. Allah said:

(To each among you, We have prescribed a law and a clear way.)(5:48) Ibn `Abbas said: "A way and a Sunnah." Here Nuh is saying:

(and I have been commanded to be of the Muslims.) Allah said about His friend, Ibrahim:

(When his Lord said to him, "Submit (be a Muslim)!" He said, "I have submitted myself (as a Muslim) to the Lord of all that exists." And this was enjoined by Ibrahim upon his sons and by Ya`qub (saying), "O my sons! Allah has chosen for you the (true) religion, then die not except as Muslims.")(2:131-132) Yusuf said:

(My Lord! You have indeed bestowed on me of the sovereignty, and taught me something of the interpretation of dreams -- the (Only) Creator of the heavens and the earth! You are my Guardian in this world and in the Hereafter. Cause me to die as a Muslim, and join me with the righteous.)(12:101) Musa said:

(O my people! If you have believed in Allah, then put your trust in Him if you are Muslims.)(10:84) The magicians said:

(Our Lord! pour out on us patience, and cause us to die as Muslims.)(7:126) Bilqis said:

(My Lord! Verily, I have wronged myself, and I submit (I have become Muslim) together with Sulayman to Allah, the Lord of all that exists.) (27:44) Allah said:

(Verily, We did send down the Tawrah, therein was guidance and light, by which the Prophets, judged for the Jews.)(5:44) He also said:

(And when I (Allah) inspired Al-Hawariyyin to believe in Me and My Messenger, they said: "We believe. And bear witness that we are Muslims.") (5:111) The last of the Messengers and the leader of mankind said:

(Verily, my Salah, my sacrifice, my living, and my dying are for Allah, the Lord of all that exists. He has no partner. And of this I have been commanded, and I am the first of the Muslims.) (6:162-163) meaning, from this Ummah. He said, in an authentic Hadith:

«نَحْنُ مَعْشَرَ الْأَنْبِيَاءِ أَوْلَادُ عَلَّاتٍ. وَدِينُنَا وَاحِدٌ»

(We, the Prophets are brothers with (the same father but) different mothers. Our religion is the same,) meaning, `we should worship Allah alone without partners while having different laws.'

The Evil Goal and End of Criminals

Allah said:

Chapter 10: Yunus (Jonah), Verses 001-109

(They denied him, but We delivered him, and those with him) meaning on his religion,

(in the (Fulk) ship) Fulk refers to the ark, and,

(We made them generations replacing one after another) on earth,

(while We drowned those who belied Our Ayat. Then see what was the end of those who were warned.) meaning `O Muhammad, see how We saved the believers and destroyed the deniers!'

Surah: 10 Ayah: 74

﴿ ثُمَّ بَعَثْنَا مِنْ بَعْدِهِ رُسُلاً إِلَىٰ قَوْمِهِمْ فَجَآءُوهُم بِٱلْبَيِّنَـٰتِ فَمَا كَانُواْ لِيُؤْمِنُواْ بِمَا كَذَّبُواْ بِهِ مِن قَبْلُ كَذَٰلِكَ نَطْبَعُ عَلَىٰ قُلُوبِ ٱلْمُعْتَدِينَ ۝ ﴾

74. Then after him We sent Messengers to their people. They brought them clear proofs, but they would not believe what they had already rejected beforehand. Thus We seal the hearts of the transgressors (those who disbelieve in the Oneness of Allâh and disobey Him).

Transliteration

74. Thumma baAAathna min baAAdihi rusulan ila qawmihim fajaoohum bialbayyinati fama kanoo liyu/minoo bima kaththaboo bihi min qablu kathalika natbaAAu AAala quloobi almuAAtadeena

Tafsir Ibn Kathir

Meaning; Then after Nuh We sent Messengers to their people.

They brought them clear proofs. and evidences of the truth that they came with.

(But they would not believe what they had already rejected beforehand) meaning the nations did not believe what their Messengers brought to them because they already rejected it from the beginning. Allah said:

(And We shall turn their hearts and their eyes away (from guidance).) (6:110) He then said here,

(Thus We seal the hearts of the transgressors.) This means that as Allah has set seals on the hearts of those people, such that they would not believe since they previously rejected faith, He would also set seals on the hearts of the people that are like them, who will come after them. They would not believe until they see the severe torment. This means that Allah destroyed the nations after Nuh. He destroyed the nations that rejected the Messengers and saved those who believed from among them. From the time of Adam to Nuh, people followed Islam. Then they invented the worship of idols. So Allah sent Nuh to them. That is why the believers will say to him on the Day of Resurrection, "You are the first Messenger Allah sent to the people of the earth." Ibn `Abbas said: "There were ten generations between Adam and Nuh, and all of them were following Islam." Allah also said:

(And how many generations have We destroyed after Nuh!) (17:17) This was a serious warning to the Arab pagans, who rejected the leader and last of the Messengers and Prophets. If the people before them who rejected their Messengers had received this much punishment, then what did they think will happen to them since they perpetrated even greater sins than others before them

Surah: 10 Ayah: 75, Ayah: 76, Ayah: 77 & Ayah: 78

﴿ ثُمَّ بَعَثْنَا مِنْ بَعْدِهِم مُّوسَىٰ وَهَـٰرُونَ إِلَىٰ فِرْعَوْنَ وَمَلَإِيْهِ بِـَٔايَـٰتِنَا فَٱسْتَكْبَرُوا۟ وَكَانُوا۟ قَوْمًا مُّجْرِمِينَ ۝ ﴾

75. Then after them We sent Mûsa (Moses) and Hârûn (Aaron) to Fir'aun (Pharaoh) and his chiefs with Our Ayât (proofs, evidences, verses, lessons, signs, revelations, etc.). But they behaved arrogantly and were Mujrimûn (disbelievers, sinners, polytheists, criminals) folk.

﴿ فَلَمَّا جَآءَهُمُ ٱلْحَقُّ مِنْ عِندِنَا قَالُوٓا۟ إِنَّ هَـٰذَا لَسِحْرٌ مُّبِينٌ ۝ ﴾

76. So when came to them the truth from Us, they said: "This is indeed clear magic."

﴿ قَالَ مُوسَىٰٓ أَتَقُولُونَ لِلْحَقِّ لَمَّا جَآءَكُمْ أَسِحْرٌ هَـٰذَا وَلَا يُفْلِحُ ٱلسَّـٰحِرُونَ ۝ ﴾

77. Mûsa (Moses) said: "Say you (this) about the truth when it has come to you? Is this magic? But the magicians will never be successful."

﴿ قَالُوٓا۟ أَجِئْتَنَا لِتَلْفِتَنَا عَمَّا وَجَدْنَا عَلَيْهِ ءَابَآءَنَا وَتَكُونَ لَكُمَا ٱلْكِبْرِيَآءُ فِى ٱلْأَرْضِ وَمَا نَحْنُ لَكُمَا بِمُؤْمِنِينَ ۝ ﴾

78. They said: "Have you come to us to turn us away from that (Faith) we found our fathers following, and that you two may have greatness in the land? We are not going to believe you two!"

Transliteration

75. Thumma baAAathna min baAAdihim moosa waharoona ila firAAawna wamala-ihi bi-ayatina faistakbaroo wakanoo qawman mujrimeena 76. Falamma jaahumu alhaqqu min AAindina qaloo inna hatha lasihrun mubeenun   77. Qala moosa ataqooloona lilhaqqi lamma jaakum asihrun hatha wala yuflihu alssahiroona   78. Qaloo aji/tana litalfitana AAamma wajadna AAalayhi abaana watakoona lakuma alkibriyao fee alardi wama nahnu lakuma bimu/mineena

Chapter 10: Yunus (Jonah), Verses 001-109

Tafsir Ibn Kathir

The Story of Musa and Fira`wn

Allah said:

(Then after them We sent) meaning ofter these Messengers,

(Musa and Harun to Fir`awn and his chiefs,) meaning his people

(with Our Ayat.) meaning; `Our proofs and evidences.'

(But they behaved arrogantly, and were a people who were criminals.) meaning they were too arrogant to follow the truth and submit to it, and they were criminals.

(So, when came to them the truth from us, they said: "This is indeed clear magic.") They were as if they gave an oath that what they had said was the truth. But they knew that what they were saying was a mere lie. As Allah said:

(And they belied them wrongfully and arrogantly, though they themselves were convinced thereof.)(27:14) Musa criticized them saying:

("Say you (this) about the truth when it has come to you Is this magic But the magicians will never be successful." They said: "Have you come to us to turn us away...)

(from that we found our fathers following) their religion.

(and that you two may have...)

(greatness) means grandeur and leadership

(...in the land, We are not going to believe you two!")

Surah: 10 Ayah: 79, Ayah: 80, Ayah: 81 & Ayah: 82

﴿ وَقَالَ فِرْعَوْنُ ٱئْتُونِى بِكُلِّ سَٰحِرٍ عَلِيمٍ ۝ ﴾

79. And Fir'aun (Pharaoh) said: "Bring me every well-versed sorcerer."

﴿ فَلَمَّا جَآءَ ٱلسَّحَرَةُ قَالَ لَهُم مُّوسَىٰٓ أَلْقُوا۟ مَآ أَنتُم مُّلْقُونَ ۝ ﴾

80. And when the sorcerers came, Mûsa (Moses) said to them: "Cast down what you want to cast!"

﴿ فَلَمَّآ أَلْقَوْا۟ قَالَ مُوسَىٰ مَا جِئْتُم بِهِ ٱلسِّحْرُ إِنَّ ٱللَّهَ سَيُبْطِلُهُۥٓ إِنَّ ٱللَّهَ لَا يُصْلِحُ عَمَلَ ٱلْمُفْسِدِينَ ۝ ﴾

81. Then when they had cast down, Mûsa (Moses) said: "What you have brought is sorcery, Allâh will surely make it of no effect. Verily, Allâh does not set right the work of Al-Mufsidûn (the evil-doers, corrupters).

﴿ وَيُحِقُّ ٱللَّهُ ٱلْحَقَّ بِكَلِمَـٰتِهِۦ وَلَوْ كَرِهَ ٱلْمُجْرِمُونَ ۝ ﴾

82. "And Allâh will establish and make apparent the truth by His Words, however much the Mujrimûn (criminals, disbelievers, polytheists, sinners) may hate it."

Transliteration

79. Waqala firAAawnu i/toonee bikulli sahirin AAaleemin   80. Falamma jaa alssaharatu qala lahum moosa alqoo ma antum mulqoona 81. Falamma alqaw qala moosa ma ji/tum bihi alssihru inna Allaha sayubtiluhu inna Allaha la yuslihu AAamala almufsideena 82. Wayuhiqqu Allahu alhaqqa bikalimatihi walaw kariha almujrimoona

Tafsir Ibn Kathir

Between Musa and the Magicians

Allah mentioned the story of the magicians and Musa in Surat Al-A`raf (there is a commentary on it in that Surah), this Surah, Surat Ta Ha, and in Surat Ash-Shu`ara'. Fir`awn, may Allah's curse be upon him, wanted to deceive the people and impress them with the tricks of the magicians in direct opposition to the plain truth that Musa brought. The result was the exact opposite and he therefore didn't attain his goal. The signs of the Lord prevailed in that public festival.

(And the sorcerers fell down prostrate. They said: "We believe in the Lord of all that exists -- the Lord of Musa and Harun.")(7:120-122) Fir`awn thought that he would achieve victory through the magicians over the Messenger sent by Allah, the All-Knower of all hidden things. But he failed, lost Paradise and was deserving of the Hellfire.

(And Fir`awn said: "Bring me every well-versed sorcerer." And when the sorcerers came, Musa said to them: "Cast down what you want to cast!") They stood in line after they received the promise of Fir`awn to become closer to him and obtain a generous reward. Musa wanted them to begin. He wanted the people to see what the magicians had made, then he would come with the truth after that to triumph over their falsehood.

(They said: "O Musa! Either you throw first or we be the first to throw" (Musa) said: "Nay, throw you (first)!") When the magicians cast their spells they bewitched the eyes of the people through their display of mighty sorcery. At that time,

(Musa conceived fear in himself. We (Allah) said: "Fear not! Surely, you will have the upper hand. And throw that which is in your right hand! It will swallow up that which they have made. That which they have made is only a magician's trick, and the magician will never be successful, to whatever amount (of skill) he may attain.") (20:67-69)

Chapter 10: Yunus (Jonah), Verses 001-109   117

Upon that, Musa said:

(What you have brought is sorcery, Allah will surely make it of no effect. Verily, Allah does not set right the work of the evildoers. And Allah will establish and make apparent the truth by His Words, however much the criminals may hate (it).)

Surah: 10 Ayah: 83

﴿ فَمَآ ءَامَنَ لِمُوسَىٰٓ إِلَّا ذُرِّيَّةٌ مِّن قَوْمِهِۦ عَلَىٰ خَوْفٍ مِّن فِرْعَوْنَ وَمَلَإِيْهِمْ أَن يَفْتِنَهُمْ ۚ وَإِنَّ فِرْعَوْنَ لَعَالٍ فِى ٱلْأَرْضِ وَإِنَّهُۥ لَمِنَ ٱلْمُسْرِفِينَ ﴾

83. But none believed in Mûsa (Moses) except the offspring of his people, because of the fear of Fir'aun (Pharaoh) and his chiefs, lest they should persecute them; and verily, Fir'aun (Pharaoh) was arrogant tyrant on the earth, he was indeed one of the Musrifûn (polytheists, sinners and transgressors, those who give up the truth and follow the evil, and commit all kinds of great sins).

Transliteration

83. Fama amana limoosa illa thurriyyatun min qawmihi AAala khawfin min firAAawna wamala-ihim an yaftinahum wa-inna firAAawna laAAalin fee al-ardi wa-innahu lamina almusrifeena

Tafsir Ibn Kathir

Only a Few Youth from Fir`awn's People believed in Musa

Allah tells us that despite all the clear signs and irrefutable evidence Musa came with, only a few offspring from Fir`awn's followers believed in him. They were even scared that Fir`awn and his followers would force them to return to Kufr (disbelief). Fir`awn was an evil tyrant and extremely arrogant. His people feared him and his power too much. Al-`Awfi reported that Ibn `Abbas said:

(But none believed in Musa except the offspring of his people because of the fear of Fir`awn and his chiefs, lest they should persecute them.) "The offspring that believed in Musa from Fir`awn's people, other than Banu Israel, were few. Among them were Fir`awn's wife, the believer who was hiding his faith, Fir`awn's treasurer, and his wife." The Children of Israel, however, themselves believed in Musa, all of them. They were glad to see him coming. They knew of his description and the news of his advent from their previous Books. They knew that Allah was going to save them through him from the capture of Fir`awn and give them power over him. So when this knowledge reached Fir`awn he was very wary. But his caution and weariness didn't help him one bit. When Musa arrived, Fir`awn subjected them to great harm, and

(They said: "We (Children of Israel) suffered troubles before you came to us, and since you have come to us." He said: "It may be that your Lord will destroy your enemy and make you successors on the earth, so that He may see how you act')(7:129) The fact that all of the Children of Israel became believers is evidenced by the following Ayat:

Surah: 10 Ayah: 84, Ayah: 85 & Ayah: 86

﴿ وَقَالَ مُوسَىٰ يَـٰقَوْمِ إِن كُنتُمْ ءَامَنتُم بِٱللَّهِ فَعَلَيْهِ تَوَكَّلُوٓا۟ إِن كُنتُم مُّسْلِمِينَ ۝ ﴾

84. And Mûsa (Moses) said: "O my people! If you have believed in Allâh, then put your trust in Him if you are Muslims (those who submit to Allâh's Will)."

﴿ فَقَالُوا۟ عَلَى ٱللَّهِ تَوَكَّلْنَا رَبَّنَا لَا تَجْعَلْنَا فِتْنَةً لِّلْقَوْمِ ٱلظَّـٰلِمِينَ ۝ ﴾

85. They said: "In Allâh we put our trust. Our Lord! Make us not a trial for the folk who are Zâlimûn (polytheists and wrong-doing) (i.e. do not make them overpower us).

﴿ وَنَجِّنَا بِرَحْمَتِكَ مِنَ ٱلْقَوْمِ ٱلْكَـٰفِرِينَ ۝ ﴾

86. "And save us by Your Mercy from the disbelieving folk."

Transliteration

84. Waqala moosa ya qawmi in kuntum amantum biAllahi faAAalayhi tawakkaloo in kuntum muslimeena   85. Faqaloo AAala Allahi tawakkalna rabbana la tajAAalna fitnatan lilqawmi aththalimeena   86. Wanajjina birahmatika mina alqawmi alkafireena

Tafsir Ibn Kathir

Musa encouraged His People to put Their Trust in Allah

Allah told us that Musa said to the Children of Israel:

(O my people! If you have believed in Allah, then put your trust in Him if you are Muslims.) Allah is sufficient for those who put their trust in Him.

(Is not Allah sufficient for His servant)(39:36)

(And whosoever puts his trust in Allah, then He will suffice him.)(65:3) Allah combines worship and reliance in many places. He said:

(So worship Him and put your trust in Him.)(11:123)

(Say: "He is the Most Gracious (Allah), in Him we believe, and in Him we put our trust..)(67:29) and

((He alone is) the Lord of the east and the west; none has the right to be worshipped but He. So take Him (alone) as a protector.)(73:9) And Allah commanded the believers to say many times in their Salah:

(You (Alone) we worship, and You (Alone) we ask for help (for each and everything).)(1:5) The Children of Israel complied with this command and said:

(In Allah we put our trust. Our Lord! Make us not a trial for the folk who are wrongdoers.) This means don't give them victory over us so that they rule us. So they might not think that they have authority over us because they were following the truth and we were falsehood. This might be a deceiving trial for them. This meaning was reported from Abu Mijliz and Abu Ad-Duha, `Abdur-Razzaq, in a narration from Mujahid, said,

(Our Lord! Make us not a trial for the folk who are wrongdoers) meaning, "Do not give them authority over us so they might make us fall into Fitnah." Allah's statement:

(And save us by Your mercy) means save us through Your mercy and beneficence

(from the disbelieving folk.) meaning, from those who denied the truth and covered it. We truly have believed in You and put our trust in You.

Surah: 10 Ayah: 87

﴿ وَأَوْحَيْنَا إِلَىٰ مُوسَىٰ وَأَخِيهِ أَن تَبَوَّءَا لِقَوْمِكُمَا بِمِصْرَ بُيُوتًا وَٱجْعَلُوا۟ بُيُوتَكُمْ قِبْلَةً وَأَقِيمُوا۟ ٱلصَّلَوٰةَ ۗ وَبَشِّرِ ٱلْمُؤْمِنِينَ ﴾

87. And We revealed to Mûsa (Moses) and his brother (saying): "Provide dwellings for your people in Egypt, and make your dwellings as places for your worship, and perform As-Salât (Iqâmat-as-Salât), and give glad tidings to the believers."

Transliteration

87. Waawhayna ila moosa waakheehi an tabawwaa liqawmikuma bimisra buyootan waijAAaloo buyootakum qiblatan waaqeemoo alssalata wabashshiri almu/mineena

Tafsir Ibn Kathir

They were commanded to pray inside Their Homes

Allah tells us why He saved the Children of Israel from Fir`awn and his people. He tells us how he saved them. Allah commanded Musa and his brother Harun to take houses for their people in Egypt,

(and make your dwellings as places for your worship,) Al-`Awfi reported that Ibn `Abbas said, while interpreting this Ayah: "The Children of Israel said to Musa, `We cannot offer our prayers in public in front of Fir`awn's people.' So Allah permitted them to pray in their houses. They were commanded to build their houses in the direction of the Qiblah." Mujahid commented,

(and make your dwellings as places for your worship,) When Banu Israel feared that Fir`awn might kill them in their gatherings at their temples, they were commanded to take their houses as places of worship. The houses should be facing the Qiblah and the prayer could be in secret." This was stated by Qatadah and Ad-Dahhak as well.

Surah: 10 Ayah: 88 & Ayah: 89

﴿ وَقَالَ مُوسَىٰ رَبَّنَآ إِنَّكَ ءَاتَيْتَ فِرْعَوْنَ وَمَلَأَهُۥ زِينَةً وَأَمْوَٰلاً فِى ٱلْحَيَوٰةِ ٱلدُّنْيَا رَبَّنَا لِيُضِلُّوا۟ عَن سَبِيلِكَ رَبَّنَا ٱطْمِسْ عَلَىٰٓ أَمْوَٰلِهِمْ وَٱشْدُدْ عَلَىٰ قُلُوبِهِمْ فَلَا يُؤْمِنُوا۟ حَتَّىٰ يَرَوُا۟ ٱلْعَذَابَ ٱلْأَلِيمَ ﴿٨٨﴾ ﴾

88. And Mûsa (Moses) said: "Our Lord! You have indeed bestowed on Fir'aun (Pharaoh) and his chiefs splendor and wealth in the life of this world, our Lord! that they may lead men astray from Your Path. Our Lord! Destroy their wealth, and harden their hearts, so that they will not believe until they see the painful torment."

﴿ قَالَ قَدْ أُجِيبَت دَّعْوَتُكُمَا فَٱسْتَقِيمَا وَلَا تَتَّبِعَآنِّ سَبِيلَ ٱلَّذِينَ لَا يَعْلَمُونَ ﴿٨٩﴾ ﴾

89. Allâh said: "Verily, the invocation of you both is accepted. So you both keep to the Straight Way (i.e. keep on doing good deeds and preaching Allâh's Message with patience), and follow not the path of those who know not (the truth i.e. to believe in the Oneness of Allâh, and also to believe in the Reward of Allâh: Paradise)."

Transliteration

88. Waqala moosa rabbana innaka atayta firAAawna wamalaahu zeenatan waamwalan fee alhayati alddunya rabbana liyudilloo AAan sabeelika rabbana itmis AAala amwalihim waoshdud AAala quloobihim fala yu/minoo hatta yarawoo alAAathaba al-aleema 89. Qala qad ojeebat daAAwatukuma faistaqeema wala tattabiAAanni sabeela allatheena la yaAAlamoona

Tafsir Ibn Kathir

Musa supplicated against Fir`awn and His Chiefs

Allah mentioned what Musa said when he prayed against Fir`awn and his chiefs after they refused to accept the truth. They continued to go astray and be haughty and arrogant. Musa said:

(Our Lord! You have indeed bestowed on Fir`awn and his chiefs splendor) and pleasure of this worldly life.

(and wealth) plentiful and abundant. Allah's statement,

(in the life of this world, Our Lord! That they may lead men astray from Your path.) was read with the word "Liyadillu" and "Liyudillu." The first is with a Fathah over the Ya, meaning that "You have given them that while You know they would not believe in what You have sent me with to them. You did that so they would gradually be drawn away from the truth." As Allah said:

(that We may test them thereby.)(20:131) and (72:17). Others read the word with a Dammah over the Ya. (i.e. Liyudillu) This makes the Ayah mean: You have given them that so whoever You willed from among Your creatures will be tried. Those whom You wish to misguide would think that You have given them that because You loved them and You cared about them."

("Our Lord! Destroy their wealth,") Ibn `Abbas and Mujahid said: "They asked Allah to destroy their wealth." Ad-Dahhak, Abu Al-`Aliyah and Ar-Rabi`a bin Anas said: "Allah made their wealth into engraved stones as it was before." About Allah's statement,

(and harden their hearts) Ibn `Abbas said, "Harden their hearts means put a seal on them."

(so that they will not believe until they see the painful torment.) This prayer was from Musa because he was angry for the sake of Allah and His religion. He prayed against Fir`awn and his chiefs when he was certain that there was no good in them. Similarly, Nuh prayed and said:

(My Lord! Leave not one of the disbelievers on the earth! If You leave them, they will mislead Your servants, and they will beget none but wicked disbelievers.) (71:26-27) Harun said "Amin" to his brother's prayer. And Allah answered Musa's prayer. Allah said:

(Verily, the invocation of you both is accepted.) `in destroying Fir`awn's people.

(Verily I have answered your prayers (both of you). So you both keep to the straight way) So as I have answered your prayer, you should remain steadfast on My command.' Ibn Jurayj narrated that Ibn `Abbas said about this Ayah: "Be steadfast and follow My command."

Surah: 10 Ayah: 90, Ayah: 91 & Ayah: 92

﴿ ۞ وَجَاوَزْنَا بِبَنِىٓ إِسْرَٰٓءِيلَ ٱلْبَحْرَ فَأَتْبَعَهُمْ فِرْعَوْنُ وَجُنُودُهُۥ بَغْيًا وَعَدْوًا ۖ حَتَّىٰٓ إِذَآ أَدْرَكَهُ ٱلْغَرَقُ قَالَ ءَامَنتُ أَنَّهُۥ لَآ إِلَٰهَ إِلَّا ٱلَّذِىٓ ءَامَنَتْ بِهِۦ بَنُوٓا۟ إِسْرَٰٓءِيلَ وَأَنَا۠ مِنَ ٱلْمُسْلِمِينَ ۝ ﴾

90. And We took the Children of Israel across the sea, and Fir'aun (Pharaoh) with his hosts followed them in oppression and enmity, till when drowning overtook him, he said: "I believe that none has the right to be worshipped but He (Allah) in Whom the Children of Israel believe, and I am one of the Muslims (those who submit to Allâh's Will)."

﴿ ءَآلْـَٰٔنَ وَقَدْ عَصَيْتَ قَبْلُ وَكُنتَ مِنَ ٱلْمُفْسِدِينَ ۝ ﴾

91. Now (you believe) while you refused to believe before and you were one of the Mufsidûn (evil-doers, the corrupters).

﴿ فَٱلْيَوْمَ نُنَجِّيكَ بِبَدَنِكَ لِتَكُونَ لِمَنْ خَلْفَكَ ءَايَةً وَإِنَّ كَثِيرًا مِّنَ ٱلنَّاسِ عَنْ ءَايَـٰتِنَا لَغَـٰفِلُونَ ﴾

92. So this day We shall deliver your (dead) body (out from the sea) that you may be a sign to those who come after you! And verily, many among mankind are heedless of Our Ayât (proofs, evidences, verses, lessons, signs, revelations, etc.).

Transliteration

90. Wajawazna bibanee isra-eela albahra faatbaAAahum firAAawnu wajunooduhu baghyan waAAadwan hatta itha adrakahu algharaqu qala amantu annahu la ilaha illa allathee amanat bihi banoo isra-eela waana mina almuslimeena 91. Al-ana waqad AAasayta qablu wakunta mina almufsideena

92. Faalyawma nunajjeeka bibadanika litakoona liman khalfaka ayatan wa-inna katheeran mina alnnasi AAan ayatina laghafiloona

Tafsir Ibn Kathir

The Children of Israel were saved and Fir`awn's People drowned

Allah tells us how He caused Fir`awn and his soldiers to drown. The Children of Israel left Egypt in the company of Musa. It was said that there were six hundred thousand soldiers, plus offspring. They borrowed a lot of ornaments from the Coptics and took that with them. Fir`awn became very angry with them. So he sent heralds to all the cities to send their soldiers. He embarked, following behind them, filled with great pride and with massive armies. Allah wanted this to happen for He had a plan for them. No one that had any authority or power remained behind in Fir`awn's kingdom. They were all together and caught the Children of Israel at sunrise.

(And when the two hosts met each other, the companions of Musa said: "We are sure to be overtaken.") (26:61) They said that because when they got to the seashore Fir`awn was behind them. The two groups met face to face. The people with Musa kept asking, "How can we be saved today" Musa replied, "I have been commanded to come this way." Musa said:

(Nay, verily, with me is my Lord. He will guide me.) (26:62) It had been so difficult, but it suddenly became easy. Allah commanded him to strike the ocean with his staff. He did and the sea was cleft asunder, each part stood like a mighty mountain. The sea was split into twelve paths, each route for each Israelite tribe. Allah then commanded the wind and the path was dry for them.

(And strike a dry path for them in the sea, fearing neither to be overtaken (by Fir`awn) nor being afraid (of drowning in the sea).)(20:77) The water in between the paths appeared as windows and every tribe was able to see the other so they would not think that others were destroyed. The Children of Israel crossed the sea. When the last one crossed, Fir`awn and his soldiers had arrived at the edge of the other shore. They were one hundred thousand black horses in addition to horsemen of other colors. When Fir`awn saw the sea he was frightened. He wanted to turn back, but it was too late. Allah's decree prevailed and the prayer of Musa was answered. Jibril came on a war stallion. He passed by Fir`awn's horse. Jibril's horse whinnied at Fir`awn's and then Jibril rushed into the sea, and Fir`awn did the same behind him. Fir`awn no longer had any control over matters. He wanted to sound strong before his chiefs, so he said: "The Children of Israel do not have more right in the sea." So they rushed into the sea. Mika'il was behind their army pushing them all to join. When they all were in the sea and the first of them was about to emerge on the other side, Allah, the All-Powerful, commanded the sea to strand them. The sea closed over them and none was saved. The waves took them up and down. The waves accumulated above Fir`awn and he was overwhelmed by the stupors of death. While in this state, he said:

(I believe that none has the right to be worshipped but He (Allah) in Whom the Children of Israel believe, and I am one of the Muslims.) He believed at a time when he couldn't benefit from his faith.

(So when they saw Our punishment, they said: "We believe in Allah Alone and reject (all) that we used to associate with Him as (His) partners." Then their faith could not avail them when they saw Our punishment. (Like) this has been the way of Allah in dealing with His servants. And there the disbelievers lost utterly (when Our torment covered them).)(40:84-85) Therefore Allah said, as a response to Fir`awn,

(Now (you believe) while you refused to believe before) do you say that just now when you have disobeyed Allah before that.

(And you were one of the mischief-makers.) You were among the makers of mischief on the earth who misled the people.

(and We made them leaders inviting to the Fire: and on the Day of Resurrection, they will not be helped.) (28:41) These facts about Fir`awn and his status at that time were among the secrets of the Unseen that Allah revealed to His Messenger, Muhammad . Similarly Abu Dawud At-Tayalisi recorded that Ibn `Abbas said that Allah's Messenger said;

«قَالَ لِي جِبْرِيلُ: لَوْ رَأَيْتَنِي وَأَنَا آخِذٌ مِنْ حَالِ الْبَحْرِ فَأَدُسُّهُ فِي فَمِ فِرْعَوْنَ مَخَافَةَ أَنْ تُدْرِكَهُ الرَّحْمَةُ»

(Jibril said to me, "If you could have seen me while I was taking black mud from the sea and placing into the mouth of Fir`awn out of fear that the mercy would reach him.") Abu `Isa At-Tirmidhi and Ibn Jarir also recorded it. At-Tirmidhi said, "Hasan Gharib Sahih." About Allah's statement,

(So this day We shall deliver your (dead) body (out from the sea) that you may be a sign to those who come after you!) Ibn `Abbas and others from among the Salaf have said: "Some of the Children of Israel doubted the death of Fir`awn so Allah commanded the sea to throw his body -- whole, without a soul -- with his known armor plate. The body was thrown to a high place on the land so that the Children of Israel could confirm his death and destruction." That is why Allah said,

("So this day We shall deliver your..") meaning that We will put your body on a high place on the earth. Mujahid said,

(your (dead) body) means, `your physical body."

(that you may be a sign to those who come after you!) meaning, so that might be a proof of your death and destruction for the Children of Israel. That also stood as a proof that Allah is All-Powerful, in Whose control are all the creatures. Nothing can bear His anger. Fir`awn and his people were destroyed on the day of `Ashura', as recorded by Al-Bukhari, Ibn `Abbas said, "When the Prophet arrived at Al-Madinah, the Jews fasted the day of `Ashura'. So he asked,

«مَا هَذَا الْيَوْمُ الَّذِي تَصُومُونَهُ؟»

(What is this day that you are fasting) They responded `This is the day in which Musa was victorious over Fir`awn.' So the Prophet said,

«أَنْتُمْ أَحَقُّ بِمُوسَى مِنْهُمْ فَصُومُوه»

(You have more right to Musa than they, so fast it.)

Surah: 10 Ayah: 93

﴿ وَلَقَدْ بَوَّأْنَا بَنِى إِسْرَءِيلَ مُبَوَّأَ صِدْقٍ وَرَزَقْنَـهُم مِّنَ الطَّيِّبَـتِ فَمَا اخْتَلَفُواْ حَتَّى جَآءَهُمُ الْعِلْمُ إِنَّ رَبَّكَ يَقْضِى بَيْنَهُمْ يَوْمَ الْقِيَـمَةِ فِيمَا كَانُواْ فِيهِ يَخْتَلِفُونَ ﴾

93. And indeed We settled the Children of Israel in an honorable dwelling place (Shâm and Misr), and provided them with good things, and they differed not until the knowledge came to them. Verily, Allâh will judge between them on the Day of Resurrection in that in which they used to differ.

Transliteration

93. Walaqad bawwa/na banee isra-eela mubawwaa sidqin warazaqnahum mina alttayyibati fama ikhtalafoo hatta jaahumu alAAilmu inna rabbaka yaqdee baynahum yawma alqiyamati feema kanoo feehi yakhtalifoona

Tafsir Ibn Kathir

The Establishment of the Children of Israel in the Land and Their Provision from the Good Things

In these Ayat, Allah tells us about all the worldly and religious gifts which He bestowed upon the Children of Israel. Allah's statement,

(honorable dwelling place) means in Egypt and Syria, around Jerusalem, as it was said by some. When Allah destroyed Fir`awn and his soldiers, the Mosaic State took control of all of Egypt as Allah said:

(And We made the people who were considered weak to inherit the eastern parts of the land and the western parts thereof which We have blessed. And the fair Word of your Lord was fulfilled for the Children of Israel, because of their endurance. And We destroyed completely all the great works and buildings which Fir`awn and his people erected.)(7:137) He said in other Ayat:

(So, We expelled them from gardens and springs. Treasures, and every kind of honorable place. Thus, and We caused the Children of Israel to inherit them.)(26:57 - 59) He also said:

(How many of gardens and springs that they left behind. ..) (44:25-27) They then continued with Musa, to seek Jerusalem -- the land of Ibrahim, the friend of Allah. There were giant people in Jerusalem. The Children of Israel refrained from fighting them. So Allah expelled them into the wilderness for forty years. During this time in the wilderness, first Harun died and then Musa. Yusha` bin Nun led after them. Allah supported them to conquer Jerusalem and rule it for a period of time. His statement,

(and provided them with good things) means from the lawful, pure and useful provision that is good in nature and in Law. Then Allah said:

(and they differed not until the knowledge came to them.) There should be no reason for them to have any disputes among them since Allah has sent them knowledge and explained different matters and issues to them. It has been mentioned in a Hadith,

«إِنَّ الْيَهُودَ اخْتَلَفُوا عَلَى إِحْدَى وَسَبْعِينَ فِرْقَةً، وَإِنَّ النَّصَارَى اخْتَلَفُوا عَلَى اثْنَتَيْنِ وَسَبْعِينَ فِرْقَةً، وَسَتَفْتَرِقُ هَذِهِ الْأُمَّةُ عَلَى ثَلَاثٍ وَسَبْعِينَ فِرْقَةً، مِنْهَا وَاحِدَةٌ فِي الْجَنَّةِ، وَاثْنَتَانِ وَسَبْعُونَ فِي النَّارِ»

(The Jews separated into seventy-one sects, and the Christians separated into seventy-two sects, and this Ummah will separate into seventy-three sects, one of which is in Paradise, seventy-two in the Fire.) They asked, "Who are they O Messenger of Allah!" He replied;

«مَا أَنَا عَلَيْهِ وَأَصْحَابِي»

(Those upon what I and my Companions are upon.) It was recorded by Al-Hakim in his Mustadrak with this wording. So here Allah said,

(Verily your Lord will judge between them) Here the meaning is, to distinguish between them

(the Day of Resurrection in that which they used to differ.)

Surah: 10 Ayah: 94, Ayah: 95, Ayah: 96 & Ayah: 97

﴿ فَإِن كُنتَ فِى شَكٍّ مِّمَّآ أَنزَلْنَآ إِلَيْكَ فَسْـَٔلِ ٱلَّذِينَ يَقْرَءُونَ ٱلْكِتَـٰبَ مِن قَبْلِكَ لَقَدْ جَآءَكَ ٱلْحَقُّ مِن رَّبِّكَ فَلَا تَكُونَنَّ مِنَ ٱلْمُمْتَرِينَ ۝ ﴾

94. So if you (O Muhammad (peace be upon him)) are in doubt concerning that which We have revealed unto you, (i.e. that your name is written in the Taurât (Torah) and the Injeel (Gospel)) then ask those who are reading the Book (the Taurât (Torah) and the Injeel (Gospel)) before you. Verily, the truth has come to you from your Lord. So be not of those who doubt (it).

﴿ وَلَا تَكُونَنَّ مِنَ ٱلَّذِينَ كَذَّبُوا۟ بِـَٔايَـٰتِ ٱللَّهِ فَتَكُونَ مِنَ ٱلْخَـٰسِرِينَ ۝ ﴾

95. And be not one of those who belie the Ayât (proofs, evidences, verses, lessons, signs, revelations, etc.) of Allâh, for then you shall be one of the losers.

﴿ إِنَّ ٱلَّذِينَ حَقَّتْ عَلَيْهِمْ كَلِمَتُ رَبِّكَ لَا يُؤْمِنُونَ ۝ ﴾

96. Truly! Those, against whom the Word (Wrath) of your Lord has been justified, will not believe.

﴿ وَلَوْ جَآءَتْهُمْ كُلُّ ءَايَةٍ حَتَّىٰ يَرَوُا۟ ٱلْعَذَابَ ٱلْأَلِيمَ ۝ ﴾

97. Even if every sign should come to them, until they see the painful torment.

Transliteration

94. Fa-in kunta fee shakkin mimma anzalnna ilayka fais-ali allatheena yaqraoona alkitaba min qablika laqad jaaka alhaqqu min rabbika fala takoonanna mina almumtareena 95. Wala takoonanna mina allatheena kaththaboo bi-ayati Allahi fatakoona mina alkhasireena 96. Inna allatheena haqqat AAalayhim kalimatu rabbika la yu/minoona 97. Walaw jaat-hum kullu ayatin hatta yarawoo alAAathaba al-aleema

Tafsir Ibn Kathir

Previous books Attest to the Truth of the Qur'an

Allah said:

Chapter 10: Yunus (Jonah), Verses 001-109

(Those who follow the Messenger, the Prophet who can neither read nor write whom they find written of with them in the Tawrah and the Injil.)(7:157) They are as certain of this as they are about who their children are, yet they hide it and distort it. They did not believe in it despite its clear evidence. Therefore Allah said:

(Truly, those, against whom the Word (wrath) of your Lord has been justified, will not believe. Even if every sign should come to them, until they see the painful torment.) meaning they would not believe in a way that they might benefit from that belief. This is when they believe at a time one may not be able to benefit from his belief. An example is when Musa prayed against Fir`awn and his chiefs, saying:

(Our Lord! Destroy their wealth, and harden their hearts, so that they will not believe until they see the painful torment.)(10:88) And Allah said:

(And even if We had sent down unto them angels, and the dead had spoken unto them, and We had gathered together all things before their very eyes, they would not have believed, unless Allah willed, but most of them behave ignorantly.) (6:111) Allah then said:

Surah: 10 Ayah: 98

﴿ فَلَوْلَا كَانَتْ قَرْيَةٌ ءَامَنَتْ فَنَفَعَهَا إِيمَٰنُهَآ إِلَّا قَوْمَ يُونُسَ لَمَّآ ءَامَنُواْ كَشَفْنَا عَنْهُمْ عَذَابَ ٱلْخِزْيِ فِى ٱلْحَيَوٰةِ ٱلدُّنْيَا وَمَتَّعْنَٰهُمْ إِلَىٰ حِينٍ ۝ ﴾

98. Was there any town (community) that believed (after seeing the punishment), and its Faith (at that moment) saved it (from the punishment)? (The answer is none) - except the people of Yûnus (Jonah); when they believed, We removed from them the torment of disgrace in the life of the (present) world, and permitted them to enjoy for a while.

Transliteration

98. Falawla kanat qaryatun amanat fanafaAAaha eemanuha illa qawma yoonusa lamma amanoo kashafna AAanhum AAathaba alkhizyi fee alhayati alddunya wamattaAAnahum ila heenin

Tafsir Ibn Kathir

Belief at the Time of Punishment did not help except with the People of Yunus

Allah asked, `did any town from the previous nations, believe in its entirety when they received the Messengers All of the Messengers That We sent before you, O Muhammad, were denied by their people or the majority of their people.' Allah said,

(Alas for mankind! There never came a Messenger to them but they used to mock at him.)(36:30)

(Likewise, no Messenger came to those before them but they said: "A sorcerer or a madman!")(51:52) and

(And similarly, We sent not a warner before you to any town (people) but the luxurious ones among them said: "We found our fathers following a certain way and religion, and we will indeed follow their footsteps.")(43:23) As found in the authentic Hadith,

《عُرِضَ عَلَيَّ الْأَنْبِيَاءُ فَجَعَلَ النَّبِيُّ يَمُرُّ وَمَعَهُ الْفِئَامُ مِنَ النَّاسِ، وَالنَّبِيُّ يَمُرُّ مَعَهُ الرَّجُلُ، وَالنَّبِيُّ مَعَهُ الرَّجُلَانِ، وَالنَّبِيُّ لَيْسَ مَعَهُ أَحَدٌ》

(The Prophets were displayed before me. There was a Prophet who passed with a group of people, and a Prophet who passed with only one man, a Prophet with two men, and a Prophet with no one.) Then he mentioned the mulititude of followers that Musa had, peace be upon him, then that he saw his nation of people filling from the west to the east. The point is that between Musa and Yunus, there was no nation, in its entirety, that believed except the people of Yunus, the people of Naynawa (Nineveh). And they only believed because they feared that the torment from which their Messenger warned them, might strike them. They actually witnessed its signs. So they cried to Allah and asked for help. They engaged in humility in invoking Him. They brought their children and cattle and asked Allah to lift the torment from which their Prophet had warned them. As a result, Allah sent His mercy and removed the scourge from them and gave them respite. Allah said: (Except the people of Yunus; when they believed, We removed from them the torment of disgrace in the life of the world, and permitted them to enjoy for a while.) In interpreting this Ayah, Qatadah said: "No town has denied the truth and then believed when they saw the scourge, and then their belief benefited them, with the exception of the people of Yunus. When they lost their Prophet and they thought that the scourge was close upon them, Allah sent through their hearts the desire to repent. So they wore woolen fabrics and they separated each animal from its offspring. They then cried out to Allah for forty nights. When Allah saw the truth in their hearts and that they were sincere in their repentance and regrets, He removed the scourge from them." Qatadah said: "It was mentioned that the people of Yunus were in Naynawa, the land of Mosul." This was also reported from Ibn Mas`ud, Mujahid, Sa`id bin Jubayr and others from the Salaf.

Surah: 10 Ayah: 99 & Ayah: 100

﴿ وَلَوْ شَاءَ رَبُّكَ لَآمَنَ مَن فِي ٱلْأَرْضِ كُلُّهُمْ جَمِيعًا ۚ أَفَأَنتَ تُكْرِهُ ٱلنَّاسَ حَتَّىٰ يَكُونُوا۟ مُؤْمِنِينَ ۝ ﴾

99. And had your Lord willed, those on earth would have believed, all of them together. So, will you (O Muhammad (peace be upon him)) then compel mankind, until they become believers.

﴿ وَمَا كَانَ لِنَفْسٍ أَن تُؤْمِنَ إِلَّا بِإِذْنِ ٱللَّهِ وَيَجْعَلُ ٱلرِّجْسَ عَلَى ٱلَّذِينَ لَا يَعْقِلُونَ ۝ ﴾

100. It is not for any person to believe, except by the Leave of Allâh, and He will put the wrath on those who are heedless.

Transliteration

99. Walaw shaa rabbuka laamana man fee al-ardi kulluhum jameeAAan afaanta tukrihu alnnasa hatta yakoonoo mu/mineena 100. Wama kana linafsin an tu/mina illa bi-ithni Allahi wayajAAalu alrrijsa AAala allatheena la yaAAqiloona

Tafsir Ibn Kathir

It is not Part of Allah's Decree to compel Belief

Allah said:

(And had your Lord willed) meaning `O Muhammad, if it had been the will of your Lord, He would make all the people of the earth believe in what you have brought to them. But Allah has wisdom in what He does.' Similarly, Allah said:

(And if your Lord had so willed, He could surely have made mankind one Ummah, but they will not cease to disagree. Except him on whom your Lord has bestowed His mercy and for that did He create them. And the Word of your Lord has been fulfilled (His saying): "Surely, I shall fill Hell with Jinn and men all together.") (11:118-119) He also said,

(Have not then those who believed yet known that had Allah willed, He could have guided all mankind) (13:31) Therefore, Allah said:

(So, will you then compel mankind) and force them to believe.

(until they become believers.) meaning, it is not for you to do that. You are not commanded to do that either. It is Allah Who

(sends astray whom He wills, and guides whom He wills.)(35:8).

(So do not destroy yourself in sorrow for them.)

(It is not up to you to guide them, but Allah guides whom He wills.)(2:272).

(It may be that you would kill yourself with grief because they are not believers.) (26:3)

(you guide not who you like..) (28:56)

(Your duty is only to convey, and it is up to Us to reckon.) (13:40)

(So remind, you are only one who reminds. You are not a dictator over them.) (88:21-22) There are other Ayat besides these which prove that Allah is the doer of what He wants, guiding whom He wills, leading whom He wills to stray, all out of His knowledge, wisdom, and justice. Similarly, He said,

(It is not for any person to believe, except by the leave of Allah, and He will put the Rijs) That is, disorder and misguidance

(upon those who do not reason) meaning, Allah's proofs and evidences, and He is the Just in all matters, guiding whom He wills to guide, and leading whom He wills astray.

Surah: 10 Ayah: 101, Ayah: 102 & Ayah: 103

﴿ قُلِ ٱنظُرُوا۟ مَاذَا فِى ٱلسَّمَـٰوَٰتِ وَٱلْأَرْضِ ۚ وَمَا تُغْنِى ٱلْـَٔايَـٰتُ وَٱلنُّذُرُ عَن قَوْمٍ لَّا يُؤْمِنُونَ ﴿١٠١﴾

101. Say: "Behold all that is in the heavens and the earth," but neither Ayât (proofs, evidences, verses, lessons, signs, revelations, etc.) nor warners benefit those who believe not.

﴿ فَهَلْ يَنتَظِرُونَ إِلَّا مِثْلَ أَيَّامِ ٱلَّذِينَ خَلَوْا۟ مِن قَبْلِهِمْ ۚ قُلْ فَٱنتَظِرُوٓا۟ إِنِّى مَعَكُم مِّنَ ٱلْمُنتَظِرِينَ ﴿١٠٢﴾

102. Then do they wait for (anything) save for (a destruction) like the days of the men who passed away before them? Say: "Wait then, I am (too) with you among those who wait."

﴿ ثُمَّ نُنَجِّى رُسُلَنَا وَٱلَّذِينَ ءَامَنُوا۟ ۚ كَذَٰلِكَ حَقًّا عَلَيْنَا نُنجِ ٱلْمُؤْمِنِينَ ﴿١٠٣﴾

103. Then (in the end) We save Our Messengers and those who believe! Thus it is incumbent upon Us to save the believers.

Transliteration

101. Quli onthuroo matha fee alssamawati waal-ardi wama tughnee al-ayatu waalnnuthuru AAan qawmin la yu/minoona   102. Fahal yantathiroona illa mithla ayyami allatheena khalaw min qablihim qul faintathiroo innee maAAakum mina almuntathireena   103. Thumma nunajjee rusulana waallatheena amanoo kathalika haqqan AAalayna nunjee almu/mineena

Tafsir Ibn Kathir

The Command to reflect upon the Creation of the Heavens and the Earth

Allah, the Exalted, guides His servants to reflect upon His blessings. What Allah has created in the heavens and the earth is part of the clear signs for those who possess correct understanding. From that which is in the heavens are the luminous stars, the firmaments, the moving planetary bodies, the sun and the moon. This also includes the night and day, their alternating, and their merging so that one is long and the other is short. Then they alternate (through the year) so that the long one becomes short and the short one becomes long. Likewise, from the signs in the heavens is the rising of the sun, its vastness, its beauty and its adornment. Also, whatever rain that Allah sends down from the heavens, thereby bringing the earth to life after its death, and causing various types of fruits, crops, flowers and plants to grow, is from its signs. Whatever Allah creates in the earth from the various species of beasts, with their differing colors and benefits (for man), are signs. The mountains, plains, deserts, civilizations, structures and barren lands of the earth are signs. Then there are the wonders of the sea and its waves. Yet, it still has been made subservient and submissive to those who travel upon its surface. It carries their ships, allowing them to traverse upon it with ease. This is all under the control of the Most Able; there is no God worthy of worship except Him and there is no true Lord other than Him. Concerning Allah's statement,

(But neither Ayat nor warners benefit those who do not believe.) This means, `What thing will benefit such disbelieving people besides the heavenly and earthly signs, and the Messengers with their miracles, proofs and evidences that clearly prove the truthfulness of their message' This is similar to Allah's statement,

(Truly! Those against whom the Word of your Lord has been justified, will not believe.) (10:96) Concerning Allah's statement,

(Then do they wait save for the likes of the days of men who passed away before them) This means, `Are these who reject you Muhammad, waiting for the vengeance and torment like the Days of Allah, when He punished those who came before them of the previous nations that rejected their Messengers'

(Say: "Wait then, I am waiting with you among those who wait." Then We save Our Messengers and those who believe!) This means, `Verily, We destroy those who reject the Messengers.'

(Thus it is incumbent upon Us to save the believers.) This means that this is a right that Allah, the Exalted, has obligated upon His Noble Self. This is similar to His statement,

(Your Lord has written (prescribed) mercy for Himself) (6:54)

Surah: 10 Ayah: 104, Ayah: 105, Ayah: 106 & Ayah: 107

﴿قُلْ يَٰٓأَيُّهَا ٱلنَّاسُ إِن كُنتُمْ فِى شَكٍّ مِّن دِينِى فَلَآ أَعْبُدُ ٱلَّذِينَ تَعْبُدُونَ مِن دُونِ ٱللَّهِ وَلَٰكِنْ أَعْبُدُ ٱللَّهَ ٱلَّذِى يَتَوَفَّىٰكُمْ ۖ وَأُمِرْتُ أَنْ أَكُونَ مِنَ ٱلْمُؤْمِنِينَ ۝﴾

104. Say (O Muhammad (peace be upon him)) "O you mankind! If you are in doubt as to my religion (Islâm), then (know that) I will never worship those whom you worship, besides Allâh. But I worship Allâh Who causes you to die, I am commanded to be one of the believers.

﴿ وَأَنْ أَقِمْ وَجْهَكَ لِلدِّينِ حَنِيفًا وَلَا تَكُونَنَّ مِنَ ٱلْمُشْرِكِينَ ۝ ﴾

105. "And (it is revealed to me): Direct your face (O Muhammad (peace be upon him)) entirely towards the religion Hanîf (Islâmic Monotheism, i.e. to worship none but Allâh Alone), and never be one of the Mushrikûn (those who ascribe partners to Allâh, polytheists, idolaters, disbelievers in the Oneness of Allâh, and those who worship others along with Allâh).

﴿ وَلَا تَدْعُ مِن دُونِ ٱللَّهِ مَا لَا يَنفَعُكَ وَلَا يَضُرُّكَ ۖ فَإِن فَعَلْتَ فَإِنَّكَ إِذًا مِّنَ ٱلظَّٰلِمِينَ ۝ ﴾

106. "And invoke not besides Allâh, any that will neither profit you nor hurt you, but if (in case) you did so, you shall certainly be one of the Zâlimûn (polytheists and wrong-doers).''

﴿ وَإِن يَمْسَسْكَ ٱللَّهُ بِضُرٍّ فَلَا كَاشِفَ لَهُ إِلَّا هُوَ ۖ وَإِن يُرِدْكَ بِخَيْرٍ فَلَا رَآدَّ لِفَضْلِهِ ۚ يُصِيبُ بِهِ مَن يَشَآءُ مِنْ عِبَادِهِ ۚ وَهُوَ ٱلْغَفُورُ ٱلرَّحِيمُ ۝ ﴾

107. And if Allâh touches you with hurt, there is none who can remove it but He, and if He intends any good for you, there is none who can repel His Favor which He causes it to reach whomsoever of His slaves He wills. And He is the Oft-Forgiving, the Most Merciful.

Transliteration

104. Qul ya ayyuha alnnasu in kuntum fee shakkin min deenee fala aAAbudu allatheena taAAbudoona min dooni Allahi walakin aAAbudu Allaha allathee yatawaffakum waomirtu an akoona mina almu/mineena 105. Waan aqim wajhaka lilddeeni haneefan wala takoonanna mina almushrikeena 106. Wala tadAAu min dooni Allahi ma la yanfaAAuka wala yadurruka fa-in faAAalta fa-innaka ithan mina aththalimeena 107. Wa-in yamsaska Allahu bidurrin fala kashifa lahu illa huwa wa-in yuridka bikhayrin fala radda lifadlihi yuseebu bihi man yashao min AAibadihi wahuwa alghafooru alrraheemu

Tafsir Ibn Kathir

The Command to worship Allah Alone and rely upon Him

Allah, the Exalted, says to His Messenger, Muhammad , `Say: O mankind! If you are in doubt about the correctness of that which I have been sent with the Hanif (monotheism) religion - the religion which Allah has revealed to me -- then know that I do not worship those whom you worship besides Allah. Rather, I worship Allah alone, ascribing no partners to Him. He is the One Who causes you to die just as He gives you life. Then, unto Him is your final return. If the gods that you call upon are real, I still refuse to worship them. So call upon them and ask them to harm me, and you will see that they can bring no harm or benefit. The only One Who holds the power of harm and benefit in His Hand is Allah alone, Who has no partners.'

(And I was commanded to be one of the believers.) (10:104) Concerning Allah's statement,

(And that you direct your face towards the Hanif religion) This means to make one's intention in worship solely for Allah alone, being a Hanif. Hanif means one who turns away from associating partners with Allah. For this reason Allah says,

(and not be one of the idolators.) This statement is directly connected with the previous statement,

(And I was commanded to be one of the believers.) Concerning His statement,

(And if Allah touches you with harm,) This verse contains the explanation that good, evil, benefit and harm only come from Allah alone and no one shares with His power over these things. Therefore, He is the One Who deserves to be worshipped alone, without ascription of partners. Concerning His statement,

(And He is the Pardoning, the Merciful.) This means that He is forgiving and merciful towards those who turn to Him in repentance, regardless of what sin the person has committed. Even if the person associated a partner with Allah, verily Allah would forgive him if he repented from it.

Surah: 10 Ayah: 108 & Ayah: 109

﴿ قُلْ يَٰٓأَيُّهَا ٱلنَّاسُ قَدْ جَآءَكُمُ ٱلْحَقُّ مِن رَّبِّكُمْ ۖ فَمَنِ ٱهْتَدَىٰ فَإِنَّمَا يَهْتَدِى لِنَفْسِهِۦ ۖ وَمَن ضَلَّ فَإِنَّمَا يَضِلُّ عَلَيْهَا ۖ وَمَآ أَنَا۠ عَلَيْكُم بِوَكِيلٍ ۞ ﴾

108. Say: "O you mankind! Now truth (i.e. the Qur'ân and Prophet Muhammad (peace be upon him)) has come to you from your Lord. So whosoever receives guidance, he does so for the good of his own self, and whosoever goes astray, he does so to his own loss, and I am not (set) over you as a Wakîl (disposer of affairs to oblige you for guidance)."

﴿ وَٱتَّبِعْ مَا يُوحَىٰٓ إِلَيْكَ وَٱصْبِرْ حَتَّىٰ يَحْكُمَ ٱللَّهُ ۚ وَهُوَ خَيْرُ ٱلْحَٰكِمِينَ ۞ ﴾

109. And (O Muhammad (peace be upon him)) follow the inspiration sent unto you, and be patient till Allâh gives judgement. And He is the Best of judges.

Transliteration

108. Qul ya ayyuha alnnasu qad jaakumu alhaqqu min rabbikum famani ihtada fa-innama yahtadee linafsihi waman dalla fa-innama yadillu AAalayha wama ana AAalaykum biwakeelin 109. WaittabiAA ma yooha ilayka waisbir hatta yahkuma Allahu wahuwa khayru alhakimeena

Tafsir Ibn Kathir

Allah, the Exalted, commands His Messenger to inform the people that that which he has brought them from Allah is the truth. It is a message concerning which there is no doubt or suspicion. Therefore, whoever is guided by it and follows it, then he only benefits himself by doing so. Likewise, whoever is misguided away from this message, then he will suffer the consequences against his own self.

(And I am not set over you as a guardian) This means, `I am not a guardian over you in order for you to become believers. I am only a warner to you and guidance belongs to Allah, the Exalted.' Concerning Allah's statement,

(And follow what has been revealed to you, and be patient) This means, `Adhere to that which Allah has revealed to you, and inspired you with, and be patient with the opposition that you meet from the people.'

(until Allah gives judgment) This means, `Until Allah judges between you and them.'

(And He is the best of judges.) This means that He is the best of those who pass judgment, due to His Justice and His wisdom.

INTRODUCTION TO CHAPTER (SURAH) 11: HUD

Ibn Kathir's Introduction

Surah Hud made the Prophet's Hair turn Gray

Abu `Isa At-Tirmidhi recorded from Ibn `Abbas that Abu Bakr said, "O Messenger of Allah, verily your hair has turned gray." The Prophet replied,

«شَيَّبَتْنِي هُودٌ وَالْوَاقِعَةُ وَالْمُرْسَلَاتُ وَعَمَّ يَتَسَاءَلُونَ وَإِذَا الشَّمْسُ كُوِّرَتْ»

(Surahs Hud, Al-Waqi`ah, Al-Mursalat, `Amma Yatasa'lun (An-Naba') and Idhash-Shamsu Kuwwirat (At-Takwir) have turned my hair gray.) In another narration he said,

«هُودٌ وَأَخَوَاتُهَا»

(Surah Hud and its sisters...)

CHAPTER (SURAH) 11: HUD, VERSES 001-005

﴿بِسْمِ اللَّهِ الرَّحْمَنِ الرَّحِيمِ﴾

In the Name of Allâh, the Most Gracious, the Most Merciful.

Surah: 11 Ayah: 1, Ayah: 2, Ayah: 3 & Ayah: 4

﴿الر كِتَابٌ أُحْكِمَتْ ءَايَتُهُ ثُمَّ فُصِّلَتْ مِن لَّدُنْ حَكِيمٍ خَبِيرٍ﴾

Chapter 11: Hud (Hud), Verses 001-005

1. Alif-Lâm-Râ. (These letters are one of the miracles of the Qur'ân and none but Allâh (Alone) knows their meanings). (This is) a Book, the Verses whereof are perfected (in every sphere of knowledge, etc.), and then explained in detail from One (Allâh), Who is All-Wise and Well-Acquainted (with all things).

﴿ أَلَّا تَعْبُدُوٓاْ إِلَّا ٱللَّهَ إِنَّنِى لَكُم مِّنْهُ نَذِيرٌ وَبَشِيرٌ ۝ ﴾

2. (Saying) worship none but Allâh. Verily, I (Muhammad (peace be upon him)) am unto you from Him a warner and a bringer of glad tidings.

﴿ وَأَنِ ٱسْتَغْفِرُوا۟ رَبَّكُمْ ثُمَّ تُوبُوٓا۟ إِلَيْهِ يُمَتِّعْكُم مَّتَـٰعًا حَسَنًا إِلَىٰٓ أَجَلٍ مُّسَمًّى وَيُؤْتِ كُلَّ ذِى فَضْلٍ فَضْلَهُۥ ۖ وَإِن تَوَلَّوْا۟ فَإِنِّىٓ أَخَافُ عَلَيْكُمْ عَذَابَ يَوْمٍ كَبِيرٍ ۝ ﴾

3. And (commanding you): "Seek the forgiveness of your Lord, and turn to Him in repentance, that He may grant you good enjoyment, for a term appointed, and bestow His abounding Grace to every owner of grace (i.e. the one who helps and serves the needy and deserving, physically and with his wealth, and even with good words). But if you turn away, then I fear for you the torment of a Great Day (i.e. the Day of Resurrection).

﴿ إِلَى ٱللَّهِ مَرْجِعُكُمْ ۖ وَهُوَ عَلَىٰ كُلِّ شَىْءٍ قَدِيرٌ ۝ ﴾

4. To Allâh is your return, and He is Able to do all things."

Transliteration

1. Alif-lam-ra kitabun ohkimat ayatuhu thumma fussilat min ladun hakeemin khabeerin 2. Alla taAAbudoo illa Allaha innanee lakum minhu natheerun wabasheerun 3. Waani istaghfiroo rabbakum thumma tooboo ilayhi yumattiAAkum mataAAan hasanan ila ajalin musamman wayu/ti kulla thee fadlin fadlahu wa-in tawallaw fa-inee akhafu AAalaykum AAathaba yawmin kabeerin 4. Ila Allahi marjiAAukum wahuwa AAala kulli shay-in qadeerun

Tafsir Ibn Kathir

The Qur'an and its Call to (worship) Allah Alone

A discussion concerning the letters of the alphabet (which appear at the beginning of some chapters of the Qur'an) has already preceded at the beginning of Surat Al-Baqarah. That discussion is sufficient without any need for repetition here. Concerning Allah's statement,

(The Ayat whereof are perfect and then explained in detail) This means perfect in its wording, detailed in its meaning. Thus, it is complete in its form and its meaning. This interpretation was reported from Mujahid and Qatadah, and Ibn Jarir (At-Tabari) preferred it. Concerning the meaning of Allah's statement, (from One (Allah), Who is All-Wise, Well-Acquainted.) This means that it (the Qur'an) is from Allah, Who is Most Wise in His statements and His Laws, and Most Aware of the final outcome of matters.

((Saying) worship none but Allah.) This means that this Qur'an descended, perfect and detailed, with the purpose of Allah's worship alone, without any partners. This is similar to the statement of Allah, the Exalted,

(And We did not send any Messenger before you but We revealed to him (saying): There is no God but I, so worship Me.) (21:25) It is similar to Allah's statement,

(And verily, We have sent among every Ummah a Messenger (proclaiming): `Worship Allah (Alone), and avoid Taghut (calling false deities.)')(16:36) In reference to Allah's statement,

(Verily, I am unto you from Him a warner and a bringer of glad tidings.) This means, "Verily, I am unto you a warner of the punishment if you oppose Him (Allah), and a bringer of the good news of reward if you obey Him." This meaning has been recorded in the authentic Hadith which states that the Messenger of Allah ascended mount As-Safa and called out to his near relatives of the Quraysh tribe. When they gathered around him, he said,

«يَا مَعْشَرَ قُرَيْشٍ أَرَأَيْتُمْ لَوْ أَخْبَرْتُكُمْ أَنَّ خَيْلًا تُصَبِّحُكُمْ أَلَسْتُمْ مُصَدِّقِيَّ؟»

(O people of Quraysh, if I informed you that a cavalry was going to attack you in the morning, would you not believe me) They replied, "We have not found you to be a liar." He said,

«فَإِنِّي نَذِيرٌ لَكُمْ بَيْنَ يَدَيْ عَذَابٍ شَدِيدٍ»

(Verily I am a warner unto you before a severe punishment.) Concerning His statement,

(And (commanding you): `Seek the forgiveness of your Lord, and turn to Him in repentance, that He may grant you good enjoyment, for a term appointed, and bestow His abounding grace to every owner of grace.) This means, "I am commanding you to seek forgiveness from previous sins and to turn to Allah from future sins, and thereafter you abide by that."

(that He may grant you good enjoyment,) This is in reference to this worldly life.

(for a term appointed, and bestow His abounding grace to every owner of grace.) This refers to the Hereafter, according to Qatadah. "This is like the statement of Allah,

(Whoever works righteousness -- whether male or female -- while a true believer, verily to him We will give a good life.)(16:97) Concerning Allah's statement,

Chapter 11: Hud (Hud), Verses 001-005

(But if you turn away, then I fear for you the torment of a Great Day.) This is a severe threat for whoever turns away from the commandments of Allah, the Exalted, and rejects His Messengers. Verily, the punishment will afflict such a person on the Day of Resurrection and there will be no escape from it.

(To Allah is your return,) This is means your return on the Day of Judgement.

(and He is able to do all things.) This means that He is capable of doing whatever He wishes, whether it be goodness towards His Awliya' (friends and allies), or vengeance upon His enemies. This also includes His ability to repeat the creation of His creatures on the Day of Resurrection. This section encourages fear, just as the previous section encourages hope.

Surah: 11 Ayah: 5

﴿ أَلَا إِنَّهُمْ يَثْنُونَ صُدُورَهُمْ لِيَسْتَخْفُوا مِنْهُ أَلَا حِينَ يَسْتَغْشُونَ ثِيَابَهُمْ يَعْلَمُ مَا يُسِرُّونَ وَمَا يُعْلِنُونَ إِنَّهُ عَلِيمٌ بِذَاتِ الصُّدُورِ ﴾

5. No doubt! They did fold up their breasts, that they may hide from Him. Surely, even when they cover themselves with their garments, He knows what they conceal and what they reveal. Verily, He is the All-Knower of the (innermost secrets) of the breasts.

Transliteration

5. Ala innahum yathnoona sudoorahum liyastakhfoo minhu ala heena yastaghshoona thiyabahum yaAAlamu ma yusirroona wama yuAAlinoona innahu AAaleemun bithati alssudoori

Tafsir Ibn Kathir

Allah is Aware of All Things

Ibn `Abbas said, "They used to dislike facing the sky with their private parts, particularly during sexual relations. Therefore, Allah revealed this verse." Al-Bukhari recorded by way of Ibn Jurayj, who reported from Muhammad bin `Abbad bin Ja`far who said, "Ibn `Abbas recited, "Behold their breasts did fold up." So I said: `O Abu Al-`Abbas! What does -their breasts did fold up- mean' He said, `The man used to have sex with his woman, but he would be shy, or he used to have answering the call of nature (in an open space) but, he would be shy. Therefore, this verse, (No doubt! They did fold up their breasts,) was revealed.'" In another wording of this narration, Ibn `Abbas said, "There were people who used to be shy to remove their clothes while answering the call of nature in an open space and thus be naked exposed to the sky. They were also ashamed of having sexual relations with their women due to fear of being exposed towards the sky. Thus, this was revealed concerning them." Al-Bukhari reported that Ibn `Abbas said that (they cover themselves) means that they cover their heads.

www.ingramcontent.com/pod-product-compliance
Lightning Source LLC
Chambersburg PA
CBHW081113080526
44587CB00021B/3573